An Anthropology of the Enlightenment

ASA Monographs ISSN 0066-9679

Locating the Field: Space, Place and Context in Anthropology, eds S. Coleman and P. Collins
Anthropology and Science: Epistemologies in Practice, eds J. Edwards, P. Harvey and P. Wade
Creativity and Cultural Improvisation, eds E. Hallam and T. Ingold
Anthropology and the New Cosmopolitanism: Rooted, Feminist and Vernacular Perspectives, ed. P. Werbner
Thinking Through Tourism, eds J. Scott and T. Selwyn
Ownership and Appropriation, eds V. Strang and M. Busse
Archaeology and Anthropology, eds D. Shankland
The Interview: An Ethnographic Approach, eds J. Skinner
Living Beings: Perspectives on Interspecies Engagements, ed. P. Dransart
Art and Aesthetics in a Globalizing World, eds R. Kaur and P. Dave-Mukherji
World Anthropologies in Practice, ed. J. Gledhill

ASA Series Editor

Andrew Irving (Manchester University, UK)
All chapters accepted for inclusion in ASA volumes are sent out for peer review to two or more reviewers in addition to the volume editor. The ASA draws on the expertise of its Editorial Board – appointed from the ASA membership – in selecting appropriate peer reviewers.

Editorial Board

An Anthropology of the Enlightenment

Moral Social Relations Then and Today

Edited by
Nigel Rapport and Huon Wardle

BLOOMSBURY ACADEMIC
LONDON • NEW YORK • OXFORD • NEW DELHI • SYDNEY

BLOOMSBURY ACADEMIC
Bloomsbury Publishing Plc
50 Bedford Square, London, WC1B 3DP, UK
1385 Broadway, New York, NY 10018, USA

BLOOMSBURY, BLOOMSBURY ACADEMIC and the Diana logo
are trademarks of Bloomsbury Publishing Plc

First published in Great Britain 2018

Copyright © The Association of Social Anthropologists, 2018

The Association of Social Anthropologists has asserted its right under
the Copyright, Designs and Patents Act, 1988, to be identified as Editors
of this work.

Cover illustration: *Japanese Spoon*, 2018, by Huon Wardle

Bloomsbury Publishing Plc does not have any control over, or responsibility
for, any third-party websites referred to or in this book. All internet addresses
given in this book were correct at the time of going to press. The author and
publisher regret any inconvenience caused if addresses have changed or sites
have ceased to exist, but can accept no responsibility for any such changes.

A catalogue record for this book is available from the British Library.

A catalog record for this book is available from the Library of Congress.

ISBN: HB: 978-1-3500-8660-9
        PB: 978-1-3500-8659-3
        ePDF: 978-1-3500-8662-3
        ePUB: 978-1-3500-8661-6

Typeset by Integra Software Services Pvt. Ltd.
Printed and bound in Great Britain

To find out more about our authors and books visit www.bloomsbury.com
and sign up for our newsletters.

Contents

Contributors

Arnar Árnason is a senior lecturer in social anthropology at the University of Aberdeen. His research focuses on death, trauma, emotion and subjectivity. He has done research in north east England, Japan, rural Scotland and Iceland.

Diane Austin-Broos is Professor Emerita of anthropology at the University of Sydney where she retired as Professor and Chair in 2008. She is an elected fellow of the Academy of Social Sciences in Australia and of the Royal Society of New South Wales. She has pursued extended field research in both Jamaica and central Australia. Her research is focused on religion, economy and the politics of moral order in society, especially as the latter affects subaltern women. Her recent publication is a co-edited collection (with Francesca Merlan), *People and Change in Indigenous Australia*. Her current research is biographical and concerns the life and times of a mid-twentieth-century Jamaican politician.

Jon Bialecki is a fellow in the School of Social and Political Science at the University of Edinburgh. His academic interests include the anthropology of religion, anthropology of the subject, ontology and temporality, religious language ideology, and religious transhumanist movements. His first monograph, *A Diagram for Fire: Miracles and Variation in an American Charismatic Movement*, was awarded the 2017 Sharon Stephans book prize by the American Ethnological Society. He is currently working on his second manuscript, *A Machine for Making Gods: Mormonism, Transhumanism, and Speculative Thought*.

Nigel Clark is Professor of social sustainability and human geography at Lancaster University, UK. He is the author of *Inhuman Nature: Sociable Life on a Dynamic Planet* (2011) and co-editor of *Material Geographies* (2008) and *Extending Hospitality* (2009), and recently co-edited (with Kathryn Yusoff) a *Theory, Culture & Society* special issue on 'Geosocial Formations and the Anthropocene' (2017). His current research interests include pyrotechnology, the politics of ancient climate change, speculative geology, and the intersection of social and geological rifting. He is working on a book (with Bronisław Szerszynski) entitled *The Anthropocene and Society* and a monograph called something like *Bare Life on Molten Rock: Magma, Fires, Futures*.

Anne Line Dalsgård is Associate Professor at the Department of Anthropology, Aarhus University. She is the author of the book *Matters of Life and Longing* (2004), which was translated and published in Brazil in 2006. Dalsgård has twenty years of research commitments in Brazil, where she has studied reproductive health, poverty, youth and futurities in the northeast region. Throughout her career as an anthropologist she has had a keen interest in experimental writing and text as a medium for reflection. Presently, she is engaged in research on the experience and use of literature in reading groups in Denmark.

Elisabeth Kirtsoglou is an associate professor in anthropology at Durham University. She has researched and published extensively on gender and politics in Greece. She is the author of *For the Love of Women: Gender, Identity and Same-Sex Relationships in a Greek Provincial Town* (2003) and co-editor of *United in Discontent: Local Responses to Cosmopolitanism and Globalisation* (2009). She is also the deputy director of Durham Global Security Institute, an interdisciplinary research institute for the study of securitization, conflict, international diplomacy and peace processes.

Nigel Rapport is Professor of anthropological and philosophical studies at the University of St. Andrews, Scotland. He is also Founding Director of the St Andrews Centre for Cosmopolitan Studies; he has held the Canada research chair in Globalization, Citizenship and Justice at Concordia University of Montreal. His research interests include social theory; phenomenology; identity and individuality; community; conversation analysis; and links between anthropology and literature and philosophy. His most recent books are *Distortion and Love: An Anthropological Reading of the Life and Art of Stanley Spencer* (2016); and, as editor, *Distortion: Social Processes beyond the Structured and Systemic* (2018). His current focus is on love as a civic virtue.

David Shankland is Director of the Royal Anthropological Institute and Honorary Professor of anthropology at University College London. A social anthropologist by training, he has conducted fieldwork mainly in Turkey and has made a special study of the Alevis, a heterodox religious minority. From early on in his career, he has been interested in when, and how, anthropology split into a number of sub-disciplines and is currently conducting long-term research into the period before Malinowski. His work on Westermarck is part of this project, which also includes examining other significant figures from this period such as F. W. Hasluck, J. L. Myres and R. Marett.

Ronald Stade is Professor of peace and conflict studies with specialization in anthropology at Malmö University, Sweden. Driven by curiosity and serendipity, he has conducted research on world culture and local politics in Guam, the social life of political keywords like 'global governance', 'political culture', 'cosmopolitanism' and 'political correctness', the politics of waste in Accra, Ghana and, most recently, the situation of Syrian refugees in Lebanon and Jordan. He is the founding editor of *Conflict & Society*, which serves as a platform for ethnographically informed research on violent conflicts. A project he keeps postponing is to write a plausible biography of Diogenes of Sinope.

Rupert Stasch is a lecturer in the Department of Social Anthropology at the University of Cambridge, and he previously taught for sixteen years at Reed College and the University of California-San Diego. He is the author of *Society of Others: Kinship and Mourning in a West Papuan Place* (2009), and is preparing a book about interactions between Korowai people of Indonesian Papua and international tourists and media professionals.

Marilyn Strathern is Emeritus Professor of social anthropology, and life fellow of Girton College, Cambridge University. She had the good fortune to receive initial – and indelible – research training in Papua New Guinea, which led to work among other things on kinship and gender relations. In the UK she subsequently became involved with anthropological approaches to the new reproductive technologies, intellectual property, audit cultures and interdisciplinarity. Now retired from the Cambridge Department of Social Anthropology, she is (honorary) life president of the ASA. Strathern is currently working on issues in the conceptualization of relations, some of which were sketched out in her 2005 book, *Kinship, Law and the Unexpected: Relatives Are Often a Surprise*.

Huon Wardle is Head of the Department of Social Anthropology at the University of St Andrews. He is author of *An Ethnography of Cosmopolitanism in Kingston, Jamaica* (2000). His fieldwork has centred on the Caribbean and his theoretical work has had a special focus on Kant's Anthropology. Recent edited volumes include (with Moises Lino e Silva) *Freedom in Practice* (2017) and (with Justin Shaffner) *Cosmopolitics* (2017). His essay, 'The Artist Carl Abrahams and the Cosmopolitan Work of Centring and Peripheralizing the Self' won the J. B. Donne Prize in 2014.

Preface:
The 'Star' Consortium and the ASA Decennial Conference

In the year that Scotland voted in the independence referendum, the Association for Social Anthropology (ASA) held its decennial conference in Edinburgh, its capital city. The theme for the conference, 'Anthropology and Enlightenment', took its inspiration from the Scottish Enlightenment, a time of intellectual enervation and excitement, when the broadest questions around what it is to be human were discussed and debated; a milieu rather than a school of thought, and an opening out of public argument and discussion. The spirit of the times gave birth to anthropology, and this conference was an attempt to rekindle that era of debate and discussion, appropriate for our times and to discuss anthropology's relationship with other disciplines within a context of historical and disciplinary reflection. Key themes from the Enlightenment were identified as thematic ideas around which the conference would hinge, with plenary sessions on Human Nature; Natural Religion; Time, Earth and the Cosmos; Beauty, Order, Harmony and Design; Do Wealthy Nations Make for Healthy Publics?; and Moral Sentiments.

While the conference was held in the capital city, the organizing of this conference was very much a Scottish affair, involving the broad cooperation of staff and students from all the universities where social anthropology is studied: Aberdeen, Edinburgh, Glasgow and St Andrews, under the Scottish Training in Anthropological Research (STAR) consortium.

Initially set up in 2006, and supported by the UK Economic and Social Research Council (ESRC), STAR was established to allow the universities in Scotland involved in teaching anthropology to coordinate and work together to train PhD students and early career researchers. Over the last decade STAR has been running vibrant annual residential workshops for pre- and post-fieldwork doctoral students. The pre-fieldwork workshops are designed for postgraduate students who are finishing their pre-fieldwork training: the themes and issues chosen and discussed are driven by the PhD students themselves, and linked to innovative methods of engagement. The post-fieldwork training events involve masterclasses with international scholars, and provide the opportunity to think further on writing, publishing, career training and the like.

In recent years STAR has expanded its remit to undertake other activities linking the departments. In 2013, STAR and National Museums Scotland together hosted the Royal Anthropological Institute (RAI) International Film Festival, which highlights the relationship between film, art and anthropology. That same year STAR hosted the Undergraduate RAI conference, in St Andrews, which was entirely organized by undergraduates; also the 3rd Annual Postgraduate Conference, in Aberdeen, which addressed the theme, 'Ideas in movement'.

The organizing of the ASA Decennial Conference was in the spirit of this broader cooperation that STAR has enabled and facilitated across the Scottish universities. Since then, further cooperative activities have included departmental members co-organizing panels at conferences, student organized workshops on human and animal relations, creative writing workshops and the co-organizing and running of a Scottish Anthropology Day for school students considering social anthropology as a university degree. Anthropology in Scotland, with the increased departmental cooperation facilitated through STAR, continues to go from strength to strength. This volume emerges from that vitality.

Ian Harper

Chair of the Organising Committee for the 2014 ASA Decennial Conference

Introduction:
Moral Social Relations as Methodology and as Everyday Practice

Nigel Rapport and Huon Wardle

I

We live in an era of far-reaching intellectual uncertainty, not just for social and cultural anthropology, but for social and philosophical inquiry in general. The question 'How do we know what we know about human lives?' has become both more pressing than ever and instigatory of ever more fragmented and divergent paradigms and methodological responses. There is probably less agreement about what it means to be human, or how even to phrase the question effectively, than there has ever been in academia. For its part, anthropology is used to acknowledging, exploring and interpreting divergence and ideological conflict over human meaning from within the lived pattern and concrete boundaries of its fieldsites, and it has a large conceptual toolkit for doing so. Indeed, anthropologists might say that their discipline has persisted quite successfully on a footing of epistemological 'crisis' for many decades – such that the perpetual 'reinvention'[1] of anthropology is a defining project. As long ago as the 1970s, Gerald Berreman was demanding answers from academic anthropology that may seem as unrealistic now as they did when he penned them:

> What so many yearn for in our profession as in academia generally – and some have virtually abandoned hope – is [...] a redefinition of our aims [...] That redefinition entails first of all a return to the Enlightenment vision of a social science whose aim is the enhancement of the freedom of the human spirit [...] a humane, responsible, and relevant science of man rather than [one] abandon[ed] to the social technicians who will surely replace us and may already outnumber us. (1972: 96–7)

So the current situation of 'malaise', if it has certain new features, is by no means new all told, even while the triumph of the 'social technicians' may seem ever more complete. Most recently, though, it has been collapse of confidence not in anthropology but in more techno-scientifically oriented social disciplines – laboratory psychology (failure to replicate findings[2]) and mainstream macro-economics (failure to predict economic events based on identified data[3]) – that has shaken the 'sciences' of the social, and opened up the foundational ideas in these disciplines to ever more intense and diverse kinds of critique and ethical challenge.

This current period of fundamental uncertainty cannot be detached from how the pluralization of information technology in recent decades has made possible unprecedented and unpredictable types of critical questioning and dispute around guiding assumptions and from multiple directions. Much academic social science has grown used to rejecting as naïve any claim to offer comprehensive answers to human problems. Ironically, at the same moment, the arrival of new digital media has instituted a novel kind of public sphere comparable in key respects to the theatre of ideas that emerged during the Enlightenment. As Chris Kelty (2016) shows, contemporary internet platforms contain – quite literally programmed into them – key Enlightenment principles of free open inquiry and knowledge construction. In this way, in a turbulent period of abrasively competing visions, fresh light is cast on the central ideas of the eighteenth century by way of the search for common human knowledge in today's world.

In this volume we centre our attention, in particular, on how 'moral sentiment' offered a guiding idea in Enlightenment thought. The idea of an 'Anthropology of the Enlightenment' set running many of the intellectual hares that still figure in twenty-first-century social science, central amongst which is a seemingly irreducible contrast between the breathing, imagining, free-acting moral human individual as against objective 'systems' that seem to envelop it at a larger scale. For philosophers of the Scottish Enlightenment, in particular, *the 'moral sentiment' of the individual human being had a crucial role in pre-figuring the making of society*. Enlightenment thinkers were fully aware that life could be led according to a plurality of customs (whether in a tree on the Oronoco River or in a French chateau), but *what was, nevertheless, universally shared was the urgency of the underlying human 'passions' involved in that life and the attempt to reconcile them rationally under different sociocultural and geophysical conditions*. Is it an attempt to grapple with this pre-figuring role of 'moral sentiment' that is now reappearing in the ethical anxieties of contemporary anthropology? This volume makes an initial survey towards an answer to this question, tracing historical connections and fissures, and focusing in particular on Adam Smith's attempts toward an understanding of what would later be called 'modernity' – where the realism that allows us to understand individual experience appears at odds with the realism which takes on the grand-scale social processes of, for example, 'globalization'.

In two books written in the second half of the eighteenth century, Adam Smith extrapolates the social consequences of contrasting features of human nature; what he says there continues to echo in contemporary social anthropology. In *The Theory of Moral Sentiments* (1759), Smith builds what we might now take to be a social psychology out of our natural sympathy for those nearest to us, showing how a moral community is built out of the common sense of ordinary people. In *The Wealth of Nations* (1776), Smith again extrapolates from a human universal – the tendency toward exchange – this time creating perhaps the first fully modern work of structural sociology. To experience sympathy is to sense the closeness of community – both its warmth and its coerciveness. Out of the activity of sympathizing emerge the conventions that guide our morality: the hierarchical and topographical habits of sympathy and antipathy that shape how we imagine the world as a morally charged totality. In contrast, the opportunity to exchange engages self-interested, in certain respects amoral, sentiments; exchange offers additional opportunities, though, for free action, self-differentiation. Writ large, exchange creates the structure of society as a sequence of acts of exchange, which in combination set in train the division of labour.

Philosopher Forman-Barzilai argues that it is helpful to read Smith's account of moral sentiments as a critical revision of the Stoic notion of 'circles of sympathy' or oikeiosis (2010). For the Stoics, in order to follow a self-willed moral life, each individual should begin to transfer affection from the closer toward the outer circles of their relationships – the aim being to arrive at a cosmopolitan love of the world and humanity at large. For Smith, this is unrealistic – human beings naturally sympathize with those closest to themselves. In contrast, as he argues in the *Wealth of Nations*, it is an equally natural desire for self-interested exchange with others that causes us to build relationships beyond our closer circles of sympathy. Society comes to have two faces – one concrete and immediate, thoroughly imbued with human sentiment and good sense, another abstract, impersonal and beyond individual sensory reach (though accessible scientifically), regarding which locally learnt sympathies are at best a poor guide. With regard to this latter domain a more abstract notion of justice becomes necessary as Smith elaborates in his *Lectures on Jurisprudence* (1763). Where at the level of the local community we can expect good common sense to orient us, at the level of the anonymous society at large laws and the state are needed to protect the person, property and reputation.

On top of his rule of thumb that sympathy and distance from self vary inversely, Smith is able to elaborate a sophisticated and abstract social psychology. Sympathy, he argues, becomes moral sentiment and then moral judgement because each *sees* and *judges* those nearby in the awareness that they are likewise *seen* and *judged*. How we judge follows from how we imagine ourselves to be positioned in some other person's gaze. Sympathy is in this way regulative and indeed *coercive* – the price of sympathy is the development of our own moral consciousness – another's eyes judging me from inside myself, rules and virtues that correspond to this. Echoes of Smith's optics in Freud, Sartre, Goffman or Foucault should be clear. From the experience of sympathetic reaction, the self makes a habit and pattern of moral approval and disapproval. Smith's method is empirical (phenomenological we might well say now) and centred on discrete observations; a method followed by Kant in his anthropology. Between the various editions of the *Theory* the significance of the view from outside – the 'impartial spectator' judging the moral sensibility of the individual – becomes increasingly significant, ultimately approaching Kant's notion of a guiding imperative that the self derives from, and with regard to, the conduct of its own life. To what extent the emergence of this inner sense of abstract impartiality depends on engagement in the wider society of anonymous relations Smith never fully clarifies.

Aspects of Stoic cosmopolitanism do re-emerge, though. Our sympathies may depend on closeness but we also transact in other ways. For Smith, the capacity for sympathy is something that humans have in common with other animals, but human beings are clearly distinguishable by their love of, and interest in, 'truck and barter', which he suggests is a correlate of the ability to speak or to engage in conversation. Greyhounds show sympathy when they run and sport together – animals can build complex communities and hierarchies of sympathy – but no animal except the human has elaborated a system of exchange. Exchange is the rational means of forming social connection, and communicating, with, people *outside our immediate circles of sympathy*. Disinterested exchange beyond the local circle offers the path to a kind of freedom through self-differentiation. In addition, while, for Smith, there may be no spooky 'sympathy at a distance' (to paraphrase Einstein), even so, when we have exchanged them, the goods we transact still retain a trace of the good will or good sense of the person who made them; morality extends beyond face-to-face relations insofar as each is paid the full value of the labour they have added to a commodity at the point of exchange. In turn, exchange maximizes the overall well-being of society as a collective body while extending sensibility as a concrete element of the commodity exchanged. Smith thus offers a recipe for free individual participation in a political economy where morality can otherwise only be accounted for impersonally. And so, to some extent, he squares the circle: the modern society coming into focus is defined by anonymous relations, in contrast sympathy is tied to the face-to-face level; nonetheless, individual moral sensibility remains embedded in the one activity people share despite their differences, labour, hence it exists in the ever-replaced fabric of a society created out of division of labour – a spooky, or perhaps ironic, kind of moral entanglement. This argument, crucial for Marx, was jettisoned by neo-classical economists, who nonetheless continue to trace their heritage to Smith's otherwise abstract view of the economy as an equilibrating system.

We can recover Smith's theory of moral sentiment, then, or a version thereof, in Malinowski's 'flesh and blood' convention-following Trobriander who is also a fame-seeking inter-island trader (whose valuable gifts leave a trace connecting different island communities); or in Raymond Firth's idea of 'propinquity' (sympathetic proximity) as a stabilizing moral force balancing principles of social structure (Malinowski 1922; Firth 1936). And, as noted, we can find Smith's theory of generative, unintended, patterns of exchange in the structuralism of Levi-Strauss and Leach. Something of Smith's duality persists too: the strength of local sentiment found in ethnographic description versus structural abstraction when it comes to understanding society writ large. Likewise, a still extant tendency to view society as achieving a natural equilibrium if left to itself. There are some features of Smith's account missing from social anthropology, though. Twentieth-century anthropology sacrificed its own interest in the development of human interiority or selfhood in order to build disciplinary boundaries with psychology – psychologists would deal with interiority, the self, the psyche; anthropology was left with the exteriority of moral relationships – role and personhood. But, in many respects this compromise represented a poor exchange; at worst, it led to the stance that human interiority and character are simply folds of public morality, which is very far from what Smith knew to be the case.

Similarly, Smith's (and the Enlightenment's) emphasis on free action was obscured too (Lino e Silva and Wardle 2016). In the 1760s the movement of Scottish villagers and their access to markets for their produce was still under the unquestioned control of local landowners. Certainly, the freedom to transact of the self-interested actor gained a special providentialist significance of its own in economics once divorced from Smith's account of how our sympathies are learnt: economies are self-regulated through the equilibration of supply and demand; as Hayek would have it, to interfere politically in this natural system is the dictatorial 'road to serfdom' (1944). However, the idea that moral sentiment might become entirely subordinated to the values and practices of the market was something never conceived by Smith, even while he gave the first delineation of a liberal society where individuals are free to transact as they wish (Polanyi 1957). Smith saw the potential in 'truck and barter' to achieve a measure of freedom for the individual from the constraints of local moralizing; but the dichotomy he sets up – closeness is to distance as moral constraint is to moral freedom – is one he never resolves. Human sympathies are always close at hand, learnt locally, in contrast society works at a distance according to a 'hidden', seemingly amoral but in fact providential, mechanism of equilibrium.

Far more profoundly cosmopolitanized and 'hyper-diverse' urban times than Smith's show up some of the fallacious concreteness in his view: the equation between sympathy and distance is not at all simple. Kant showed that it is not that space is concrete while morality is imagined as Smith presupposed – both space as place, and morality as a schema of moral relations, must be constituted subjectively. Arguably, the connections between sympathy and place that Smith took as self-evident were already being irrevocably transformed by the same practices of trade that he understood as a kind of freedom. Under modern conditions, as Simmel pointed out a century after Smith, human beings are capable of becoming indifferent to what is close at hand and profoundly emotionally engaged with what is far away. Smith himself shows sympathy for the child worker reducing his labour time so he can spend more time at play, antipathy to the absentee landlord who contributes nothing to the greater benefit of economy and society. Even so, society can no longer plausibly be understood as an equilibrium brought into being by the 'hidden' providence of individual acts of self-interest: it is possible to recognize now how the kind of 'order' Smith saw coming into being can 'float' in larger fields of stochastic 'disorder' (Rapport 2017). So the question returns in a new way; what part does moral sentiment play in the making of contemporary world structure? One thing we can be certain of is that Smith's concerns with space, sympathy, interiority, exchange and freedom will continue to acquire new analytical configurations for anthropologists in the twenty-first century. Indeed, opening up his ideas on moral sentiment to scrutiny and revision, thereby creating new types of connection to Enlightenment concerns, was a principle aim of this volume.

II

As mentioned, this volume of essays emerges from the 2014 Decennial Conference of the Association of Social Anthropologists', 'Anthropology and Enlightenment', organized and convened by social anthropologists based at St Andrews, Aberdeen, Edinburgh and Glasgow universities. The theme for the conference, 'Anthropology and

Enlightenment', took its inspiration from the tradition of the Scottish Enlightenment and an era when intellectual life in Scotland was at its most cosmopolitan and outward-facing. The choice of theme aimed to rekindle the spirit of both intellectual and moral enquiry that gave birth to the modern discipline of anthropology – first named by Immanuel Kant in the same period, and defined as the study of what human beings freely make of themselves ([1798] 2006). The aim was to rethink the terms of Enlightenment anthropology in a manner and an idiom appropriate to the contemporary era; the theme would combine historical reflection with an exploration of anthropology's current disciplinarity, including its relations with other disciplines (philosophy, psychology, literature, political economy, theology, history, architecture, medicine, law, geography, sociology). What kind of intellectual accommodation does anthropology currently make with what Smith termed 'the great system of the universe'?

The more specific focus of this emergent volume is on moral social relations and 'moral sentiments', a phrase central to the Enlightenment writings of Adam Smith, as we have seen, but also David Hume. In the light of the obsolescence of mid-twentieth-century notions of 'culture' and 'society' we address the challenge set to contemporary social science to write with a moral voice and vision. The volume explores moral social relations in two main ways: as these might be seen to concern anthropological methods, how anthropologists work with their research subjects and write their accounts; and as these might figure in conceptualizations of moral society, how an anthropologically inspired moral social vision might look. In different ways all the contributions to the volume explore the ways and extents to which 'Enlightenment' ideas impact on contemporary methodology, ontology and epistemology in anthropology. Singly and together the contributions interrogate how 'moral sympathy' might be situated in contemporary anthropological thinking on social relations and personhood, on identity and civil society.

III

As a method and a practice, and as an accumulation of knowledge, anthropology can reasonably lay claim to be the most cosmopolitan of the social science disciplines in its reach for universalism. Anthropologists are in many ways exemplary intellectual individualists; often discontented with the limited value-set presented to them as their 'own culture', they set out to seek alternatives. There is an irony, though, to how the culturally relativistic (or 'perspectivalist') phrasings anthropologists often deploy act to box the lives of others into hermetic worlds. Ulrich Beck, from a neo-Kantian perspective, captures frustration with the 'methodological nationalism' that anthropologists continue to deploy in favour of the discreteness and incommensurability of cultures:

> The global context is varied, mixed, and jumbled—in it, mutual interference and dialogue (however problematic, incongruous, and risky) are inevitable and ongoing. The fake joys of incommensurability are escape routes leading nowhere, certainly not away from our intercultural destiny. (Beck 2004: 436)

The stance of this volume is that such relativism denies the people who have hosted the anthropologist true moral and intellectual equality, autonomy and contemporaneity. A major work of this book has, therefore, been to interrogate this contradiction: the granting of moral recognition to otherness while not allowing difference to suggest moral incommensurability.

The philosopher Bernard Williams described cultural relativism (or 'perspectivism' as it might pass today [Viveiros de Castro 2012; Kohn 2015]) as 'the anthropologist's heresy' and 'possibly the most absurd view to have been advanced even in moral philosophy' (1978: 34). Relativism, as Clifford Geertz more approvingly described it, has been a major source of anthropology's ability to 'disturb the intellectual peace' in the Western academy; through its relativism, anthropology has asserted the illusionary nature of objective, 'pasteurized' knowledge and insisted that provincialism is a greater danger (epistemological as well as political) than spiritual entropy (2000: 42–6). Through the lens of culture one espied the 'set of control mechanisms – plans, recipes, rules, instructions (what computer engineers call "programs") – for the governing of behavior' (Geertz 1970: 57).

In other words, claiming culture as foundational, mid-twentieth-century anthropology approached mind and body alike not as the vehicle of a 'free-acting' being intent on developing its own 'character' as Kant had described, but as social constructions, and knowledge practices, epiphenomena of symbolic exchange. Culture represented a totality of symbol-systems (religion, ideology, economics, sport) in terms of which people made their worlds: made sense of themselves and their world, and represented themselves to themselves and to others. Human 'common sense' which had offered a foundation to the Enlightenment anthropology of ethical life was in particular taken to be contingently systematized via culture. The imposition of meaning on life was the major end and primary condition of human existence, and culture provided the patternings 'of' and 'for' social practice. Knowledge was a matter of an encompassing, collective, public and shared cultural context; hence anthropology's 'outdoor psychology' (Geertz 1983: 151). Considering 'the impact of the concept of Culture on the concept of Man', Geertz concluded that while 'becoming human is becoming individual', we nevertheless 'become individual under the guidance of cultural patterns, historically created systems of meaning in terms of which we give form, order, point and direction to our lives' (1970: 63). Representing a 'manipulation of cultural forms', of systems of symbols of collective possession, public authority and social exchange, human thought was 'out in the world' (Geertz 1983: 151). The symbolic logic of thought, and the formal conceptual structuring, may not be explicit, but they were socially established, sustained and legitimized. Affording meaning to the world was not something that happened in private, in insular individual heads, but something dependent on an exchange of common symbols whose 'natural habitat is the house yard, the market place, and the town square' (Geertz 1970: 57).

Meaning from this perspective was something publicly enacted, tied to concrete social events and occasions, and instantiating of a common social world. Hence, outdoor activities such as ploughing or peddling were as good examples of 'individual thought' as were closet experiences such as wishing or regretting: cognition, imagination, emotion, motivation, perception and memory were irrevocably social affairs. A cultural anthropology insisted on human life as a matter of *plein air* proceedings, public, organized and collective: all always live in worlds of 'group efforts, group clashes, and group commitments' (Geertz 2000: 44, 164). Culture, society, psyche and organism should not be considered separate levels of being, Geertz concluded: one did not adhere to a stratigraphic conception of human nature. The human brain may subsist in individual heads, but 'cabbages, kings and a number of things' – including mind – existed outside it (Geertz 2000: 204). Mid-twentieth-century anthropologists would have considered the Enlightenment providentialism of Adam Smith and his contemporaries as distinctly naïve, but their own methods had replaced it with a totalizing view which made of 'culture' something at least as reified and certainly more unanswerable morally.

Anthropology was not unique in its turn to the relativism of closed thought systems. Both Geertz and E. E. Evans-Pritchard drew heavily on the (revolutionary) ordinary-language philosophy of Ludwig Wittgenstein (1978). Geertz was happy to acknowledge Wittgenstein as his 'master' (2000: xi), for the way in which he turned human knowledge into a language-game: not something accumulative but a series of positionings with regard to an assortment of ends. Nor was Geertz's reference, above, to 'what computer engineers call "programs"' incidental. In *How Reason Almost Lost Its Mind* (2013), Erickson et al. chart how advances in computing during the Cold War encouraged social scientists to view culture as akin to computer code. In this analogy human practical reason was no longer a cause but an output: the passionate and fallible reasoning of human minds (Malinowski's Trobriand Islanders, for example) had been surpassed by the 'deeper' rationality of cultural 'programs'. For his part, Evans-Pritchard adverted to Wittgenstein's notion of a 'form of life' famously to argue that people could not but think within the rubrics of their own cultural logic and the limits this set; the Azande affirmed witchcraft beliefs and practices which challenged the limits of Western rationality because this was all they could know: the rest was silence, or chaos (1976). Cultural relativism brought anthropology to possess a new kind of claim on human nature: 'if one sees the behaviour of a living thing, one sees its soul' (Wittgenstein 1978: #357). To be human was to behave under the aegis of particular, cultural forms of life.

But this has never been the whole story. The universal processes of human social interaction and organization have remained an anthropological concern. Ernest Gellner (1995), then, was scathing concerning what he described as 'the carnival of cheap relativism' in intellectual circles that undermines criteria for rational critique and ultimately underwrites arbitrary dogmatism. More precisely, a world of reasonably identifiable, separable cultural islands, each carrying its own norms of validity and each equally valid, in no way describes our reality of 'overlapping cultural units, in rapid change, frequently undergoing fission or fusion' in the face of disputes concerning what that 'culture' actually is (Gellner 1995: 7). Surely any anthropological exploration of the social construction of reality must be balanced by an appreciation of the natural construction of society. To quote Gellner in full:

> Cognitive relativism is nonsense, moral relativism is tragic. You cannot understand the human condition if you ignore or deny its total transformation by the success of the scientific revolution.

The recognition of the inequality of cognitive claims in no way involves unequal treatment of people, quite the reverse. The accidental initiators of the scientific revolution have no monopoly on it, and are not necessarily its best practitioners. Valid knowledge ignores and does not engender frontiers. One simply cannot understand our shared social condition unless one starts from the indisputable fact that genuine knowledge of nature is possible and has occurred, and has totally transformed the terms of reference in which human societies operate.

To pretend that the scientific revolution of the seventeenth century, and its eventual application in the later stage of the industrial revolution, have not transformed the world, but are merely changes from one culture to another, is simply an irresponsible affectation.

At the same time, the great change which brought us understanding and control of nature has also deprived us of the possibility of underwriting our values, something to which large segments of humanity have become accustomed during the age of faith in doctrinal religion. Moral legitimation requires a firm data base, so to speak, for our world and its rigid linkage to moral assessment. Both kinds of rigidity are proscribed by the very form of knowledge which has also freed us from penury. So our moral crisis is also the fruit of our liberation from want and tyranny. Our predicament is to work out the social options of our affluent and disenchanted condition. We have no choice about this. To pretend otherwise, to claim that the problem does not even arise, but has been replaced by the 'Permanent Carnival', is absurd. (Gellner 1995: 8)

It is the case, Gellner recognized (1993: 3), that 'mobility, egalitarianism and free choice of identity' by individuals have better prospects in our contemporary world than they had in the past, but establishing this modern civilitude as a set of universal moral propositions, as opposed to a merely fortunate outcome of the rise of Western liberalism, raised enormous difficulties. The route from 'is' to 'ought', from scientific knowledge to global morality, has been a questionable one at least since the days of Hume, and a history of colonialism and post-colonialism makes the undertaking no easier. As Gellner indicated, the ironic result of the extension of scientific thought is that contemporary anthropologists can no longer ground their claims in the greater wisdom of providence or nature, as Enlightenment philosophers often did (1964). At the very least, however, a focus on anthropology's relationship to the Enlightenment means that the challenge that Gellner outlined is taken seriously: it returns the discipline to the Enlightenment roots of its project.

Immanuel Kant refigured the term 'anthropology' for a new purpose which he depicted as not only a modern scientific endeavour but also a cosmopolitan enterprise that all human beings could participate in. Anthropology should no longer be thought of as an inquiry into the human as a natural or physical being, but instead should study what humans make of themselves as 'free-acting' beings who progressively create the 'maxims' by which they lead their own lives. For Kant 'the first character of a human being is the capacity as a rational being to obtain a character as such for his person as well as for the society in which nature has placed him': rephrasing Kant's insight as a question, 'How is society possible?', Simmel would later follow and elaborate

Kant in arguing that it is the imaginative vocation of the individual to find a place for themselves in 'it' that endows society with its conditions of actuality (Kant 2006: 234; Simmel 1910). Anthropology is the form of inquiry that explores the complexity of this fact and its consequences. In turn, anthropology offers a hospitable space of thought for humans to discover and understand themselves better and, thus, come to express their inner character fully. As such, Kant, Smith and Hume all sought through their anthropological reflections to formulate modes of moral scientific inquiry with universal human reach. For Hume, impartial feeling was key: to treat all like cases in a like way. For Kant, reason was key: to act morally entailed seeking out universal maxims or 'regulative ideas' to help guide subjective experience, working out the uses and crucially the limits of moral, aesthetic and teleological thought. For both Hume and Kant, though, the need to eschew cultural specificities of caprice, arbitrariness, ignorance and partiality or special pleading was paramount.

Opening a new dialogue with the Enlightenment can allow us, then, to reappraise anthropology's puzzling, awkward and uncertain presence amongst the human sciences: anthropology's task should always have been to question the character and constitution of human experience, to alert minds to the open-ended possibilities of being human, not to allow them to close around a convenient but fundamentally nonsensical image of incommensurable cultures. Foundational questioning of human experience should surely be of the essence of anthropology in its fuller sense.

In *The Theory of Moral Sentiments* Adam Smith deployed Hume's 'experimental method' (the appeal to human experience) but sought to refine his thesis of impartial feeling. The psychological motives behind a moral sense were surely multiple and 'interested', and found their essence in a 'principle of sympathy'. 'Sympathy' was the core of moral sentiments: the feeling-with-the-passions-of-others, arising from an innate desire to identify with others' emotions. Sympathy operated through a logic of mirroring, in which a spectator imaginatively reconstructed the experience of the person being watched. Smith wrote:

> As we have no immediate experience of what other men feel, we can form no idea of the manner in which they are affected, but by conceiving what we ourselves should feel in the like situation [... Our senses will never] carry us beyond our own person [...] By the imagination, we place ourselves in his situation. (Smith 2004: 11)

Smith's emphasis on mirroring calls to mind the more recent theorizations of Rene Girard (1978); while the emphasis on imagining concurs with Jean-Paul Sartre's ([1948] 1963) description of the imaginative as that which effects a transcending of current life-worlds. Even more provocatively, the emphasis on an innate identification with the human other recalls Emmanuel Levinas's theorizations of 'face' (1989). For Levinas, to elaborate in brief, our moral consciousness is lodged in the experience of coming face to face with another individual human being; morality derives from experiencing this as an event free from preconceptions, free from the mythology of culture and its narrowing orthodoxies. Levinas understood the encounter with an individual other as a kind of 'passion', a 'surplus' and an 'anarchy': one's emotional sensibility is affected in spite of itself. 'When I really stare, with a straightforwardness devoid of trickery or evasion, into the unguarded, absolutely unprotected eyes' of another living individual, Levinas wrote, and if I am honest with my emotions, then I experience a mystery that is as absolute as death: the body that abuts against my own is 'a relationship with a singularity without the mediation of any principle, any ideality'. And what is one's duty relative to this event? How should it translate into an item of transferable knowledge and a life project? It is surely a relation with ignorance, Levinas concludes. One has absolutely no idea and no way of conceiving of what life is like beneath the surface of that distinct embodiment, beneath the skin of the other individual being: one encounters an otherness independent of any *a priori*, and incommensurable with any such. And yet that encountered body now summons one out of a conceited, solipsistic, merely cultural, world-view. There is a moral summons to recognize that body as distinctly individual, as a life unto itself. The human world is a universe of plural individualities about which one is ignorant – and must remain so (as, too, in regard to death) – but towards which one has a moral duty of recognition. When looking at a creature that looks back at you – and not just a human creature – no abstract principles are involved; there are only two individual lives, face to face, with the right to hope for the best from one another.

There is much here with which anthropology can interest itself: The paradox of an 'ethnographic' encounter with a particular other that is also universal and towards which one may have a categorical moral duty. One aim of this volume is to engage theoretically with such moral notions to which the Enlightenment gave birth as questions of rational engagement, in particular Adam Smith's of 'moral sentiments' and their roots in 'sympathy'. We consider the origins of moral human behaviour from a *theoretical* perspective, and how such issues might be formulated so as to address questions of universal – 'cosmopolitan', 'humane', 'civil' – practice. How might a universal morality of rights and recognitions be conceptualized and how might it be framed as practice? How could it be reconciled with the unlimited diversity of manners of self-making that we witness in human life both globally and locally?

IV

'Emotional bonds are the essence of the social structure', wrote novelist Amos Oz (1975: 115), in his ethnographic treatment of kibbutz life, *Touch the Water: Touch the Wind*. While interestingly attuned to some of the assessments, above, from Smith and Levinas, an anthropologist (whether 'Anglo-Saxon' or 'Continental') might be initially sceptical of Oz's assertion. Is not social structure essentially normative: the overt laws and customs by which social life is organized and policed? Is not social structure essentially cognitive: the unconscious organization of the mind by cultural classifications of the world? Nonetheless, all of the contributions to this volume can be said to refer to Oz in different ways.

The volume is divided into four main parts, concluding with an afterword. Part One contains chapters that address the morality of anthropological engagement (Dalsgård, Árnarson, Wardle): issues that arise out of the ethnographic situation of meeting otherness. Of 'After Sympathy, a Question', Anne Line Dalsgård explains:

Within a discussion of fieldwork, friendship and ethics, I describe how a piece of fictional writing worked as a sympathetic experiment that both changed my understanding of a young woman's situation and deepened my relationship to her. Subjectivity – the enjoying of a first-person access to one's own experiential life – is a basic condition of human life and, consequently, of anthropology; yet we have no direct access to the subjective world of others and can only inhabit their point of view by way of imagination. Writing literary-ethnographic texts is one way, I will argue, of experimenting with such sympathetic imagination.

I employ Adam Smith's concept of sympathy: the sentiment of an impartial and well-informed spectator by means of which one may imaginatively put oneself in the situation of another. Our senses alone, Smith writes, cannot tell us what another suffers, and sympathy does not arise so much from the view of the person as from that of the situation which excites it. The precondition for sympathy is thus a willingness to let oneself be moved by the situation of the other, which implies a thorough insight into all that this situation consists of.

Drawing upon a particular fieldwork focusing upon young people's perception of their future possibilities (undertaken in a low-income neighbourhood on the outskirts of the city of Recife, northeast Brazil), I describe how sympathy leads to a question about the proper response to the distress of another. The piece of fictional writing in question concerns a young mother who, by becoming pregnant without means to bring up the child, finds herself confirming all prejudices about teenage pregnancy and irresponsible youth. I describe the responses I receive from readers of the text, and focus in particular on one young woman's elaboration of a similarly fictional but romantic ending to my piece.

The argument developed in the chapter is particularly tied to the kind of fieldwork in which you live with the people you study over lengthy periods and return regularly, whereby relationships in the field may become more than simply instrumental. It leads to a definition of friendship based on the mutual recognition of difference. It also leads to a question of responsibility that transcends the framework of research: it shows us that fiction can be real (including the 'fiction' of anthropological field research as identified by Clifford Geertz) in that it has real consequences.

Of 'His Father Came to Him in His Sleep: An Essay on Enlightenment, Mortalities and Immortalities in Iceland', Arnar Árnason writes:

His father came to him in his sleep. They were at the time somewhere over the North Atlantic, on a flight to New York from Iceland. It was a journey he had made many times before, once in reverse as a permanent and triumphant return home having established his reputation in the United States. His father had come to relate to him a poem, a poem amounting to a reflection on the state of their 'nation', its health, its wealth, its language, its culture, its future. It was a poem he was to share, along with a description of its provenance, with their 'nation' a few days later in an opinion piece in one of its leading newspapers. On the poem and the authority of his father, he built arguments for his particular vision of the immediate and more long-term future of their nation.

Starting from the event described above and drawing on Michael Carrithers's work on culture and rhetoric, Marilyn Ivy's anthropological interpretation of Jacques Lacan and the 'thing', and de Certeau's work on the voice, in this chapter I examine discourses on enlightenment and mortality/immortality in Iceland. The discussion centres around two points of tension: between different forms of futurity and between the ways in which enlightenment might secure the immediate future of the nation while endangering its immortality. The analysis focuses on a coming together of enlightenment and the dead around the task of securing the future of the 'nation' and its immortality.

And of 'On "Bad Mind"': Orienting Sentiments in Jamaican Street Life' Huon Wardle writes:

'Bad mind' is a ubiquitous descriptor in Jamaican street life, so it can appear to offer only banal moral descriptions, in particular a banal summation of human motivation as either 'malice' or 'benevolence'. But this chapter argues that in its intensity 'bad mind' inevitably points to something beyond a superficial outline of someone's disposition of this kind – the more complex claim is about the psychic-spiritual powers of the person involved – and these can be multitudinous. 'Bad mind' is not simply a momentary disposition, it describes a toxic misuse of the plural spiritual gifts that the individual in question brings to the situation. In the shadow of the 'good life' is the pathology of unchecked individual 'bad mind', but for all its seeming positivity, 'bad mind' indexes a fundamental ambiguity or absence of knowledge. What the interior spiritual properties involved consist in, though, or where they came from is much less readily agreed; indeed they remain an enigma. What kind of precedent can there be for any given individual as a moral being and where do their individual powers come from?

Contemporary Kingston, Jamaica, is the site of plural and fluctuating theories of self-in-the-world. While Pentecostalists may argue that the self should better itself by modelling its life on the image of Christ, by way of contrast, Rastafarians have created a divinized 'I' that encompasses all around it in a collective immanent, 'I-n-I'. Meanwhile, for Zion Revivalists the self appears as a 'Me' surrounded, often beset, by many spiritual voices and actors. What do these divergent theories of 'mind' or models of moral personhood suggest about understandings of community and sympathy in the city? Undoubtedly, they are the inheritors of a complex history of ideas shaped by slavery, enlightenment and emancipation.

Vox populi, vox dei: the voice of people is the voice of god. If we compare the image of self that appears in the writings of Enlightenment thinkers – for example, Adam Smith in his *Theory*, Adam Ferguson in his *History of Civil Society*, or Immanuel Kant in his *Anthropology* – with the ideas of moral sentiment in Jamaican street life, there emerges a key similarity. The Enlightenment thinkers and Jamaicans on the 'corner' and in the 'yard' have a 'spirited' view of the self as a free-acting being – a *homo noumenon* endowed with faculties and gifts that it makes use of freely in the world and in time.

Part Two contains chapters that interrogate conceptualizations that derive from Enlightenment thought (Shankland; Austin-Broos; Clark, Stasch and Bialecki): 'nature and culture', 'sympathy' and 'exchange', 'the emotions'. David Shankland writes of 'Westermarck, Moral Behaviour and Ethical Relativity':

> This chapter takes as its starting point the now neglected work of Edward Westermarck. Westermarck was a pioneering field researcher in Morocco and Malinowski's teacher at the LSE. He helped to create modern kinship through his *History of Human Marriage*. He was also the author of two major works on ethics: *The Origin and Development of the Moral Ideas*, and *Ethical Relativity*. Drawing on the Enlightenment philosophers, Hume and Adam Smith – but not Kant, whom he disliked – he attempted to develop a universal understanding of moral behaviour by arguing that morals are rooted in human emotions. Writing at a time when theories of relativism were not widely accepted, he claimed that understanding human behaviour in this way was liberating and did have universal application. Westermarck's overall contribution has been greatly neglected; looking at his philosophical works provides one way in to a wider appreciation of his influence on the discipline, and whilst simultaneously permitting us to trace a further way that modern anthropology has been influenced by Enlightenment thinkers.

Of 'Saving Sympathy: Adam Smith, Morality, Law and Commerce', Diane Austin-Broos explains:

> Notwithstanding today's common view that Adam Smith's corpus is an integrated one, much discussion of his work remains one-sided. Political and neo-classical economists focus mainly on *The Wealth of Nations* while the concern of humanists, including anthropologists, tends to be Smith's earlier work, *The Theory of Moral Sentiment*. The latter has been especially relevant to those anthropologists interested in human emotion which seems some distance from his writing on eighteenth-century commercial society, the precursor of modern liberal capitalism. This divide echoes an earlier one described by German scholars as 'Das Adam Smith Problem': the supposed conflict between two different accounts of society, the one based on sympathy or in Smith's term 'fellow-feeling', and the other on interest or as Smith described it 'self-love'. This type of view also often suggests that, in Smith's corpus, interest wins out over sympathy. In the later work on economics there is barely an explicit reference to ethics. Just as striking, this interpretation makes no mention of his extensive lectures on law and jurisprudence that have substantial links both to *Moral Sentiments* and to *Wealth of Nations*.
>
> The central focus of this chapter is Smith's account of moral sentiment: his generative and pragmatic account of ethics as integral to human sociality. My discussion begins, however, with a brief overview of his idea of human nature. The latter involves both sympathy and the desire for 'betterment', not only for oneself but for kith and kin, through the pursuit of interest. My suggestion is that Smith's thought was focused on the perennial tension he saw between these two human propensities. He sought to understand how this tension might be held

productively in check. To this end he proposed that, as virtues, justice was more central to society than human beneficence. Though law well-formulated could hold selfishness in check, morality alone could not fulfil that task. (Beneficence in particular might be overwhelmed or prove inconstant.) Hence his lengthy studies of jurisprudence. In sum, Smith was interested in the 'good' society, or the 'civilized' society as he sometimes described it: one in which beneficence, justice and 'opulence' or modest prosperity for all prevailed. Indeed, for Smith, morality was integral to social being.

This chapter describes Smith's work on ethics and then, more briefly, some of his ideas on jurisprudence and on markets, trade and accumulation. It notes those points at which Smithian ideas about morality evoke not only Stoicism and Hume but also Aristotelian ethics, Kant and even Durkheim. Finally, it considers some critics of Smith, notably Karl Marx but also C. B. Macpherson, Louis Dumont and Andrea Muehlebach. It suggests that neither standard-left critique nor neo-liberal endorsement should be the final word on Adam Smith's thought which has much to offer anthropologists.

And Jon Bialecki introduces 'Can We Have Our Nature/Culture Dichotomy Back, Please?', a discussion between Nigel Clark and Rupert Stasch, as follows:

In 1788, the Edinburgh geologist James Hutton published *A Theory of the Earth*, a work that became one of the enduring classics of the Scottish Enlightenment. Hutton's radical thesis was that the Earth's form had not remained fixed since the seven days of Creation, but was in a constant process of change: 'The result of our present enquiry is that we find no vestige of a beginning, no prospect of an end'. The reconceptualization foreshadowed the shock-waves caused by Darwin's *On the Origin of Species* some decades later.

Beginning from such Enlightenment moments when the fabric of understandings of the nature of being unravels, this chapter, which takes the form of a collaborative engagement, returns to the question of how, conceptually, 'nature' should be seen to relate to 'culture'.

A nature/culture distinction has recently received sustained social critique, accused of being too dependent on Western assumptions, and of obscuring how deeply humans are imbricated in the environment. The chief 'imbrication' that is supposedly hidden by nature/culture is the set of forces referred to as the Anthropocene: a term for a new geological age marked by the environmental effects of human activity being expressed on a global scale. One of the most alarming aspects of the possibility of the Anthropocene is that this era may in turn unleash forces that could lead to human extinction.

In their debate, Nigel Clark and Rupert Stasch argue that the nature/culture division may have more utility to think through the Anthropocene than the critics of this divide have suggested. For Clark, critiques of the nature/culture distinction have the benefit of opening up for reflection upon, and political use of, already existing relations between the human and the inhuman to make the world anew. But what these critiques do not grasp is that the Enlightenment vision of a nature/culture divide was created not to isolate and control nature, but to protect the concept of the human from the 'geotraumas' of deep time and of the cosmological forces that have formed and assailed the earth during those long pre-human ages. Contemporary critiques of nature/culture may be working to the same effect, emphasizing social–nature interplay, but blinding us to the autonomy of 'inhuman' forces.

Rupert Stasch makes a similar claim, but focuses again on human autonomy by reimaging the nature/culture divide as a comparative infra-language for addressing cultural sensibilities regarding both spaces of perceived lack of human determination, and also of space controlled by human intention. This would not be a covert return to Enlightenment Humanism, but instead a study of comparative humanisms; this reformulated divide would also allow for renewed ethnographic inquiry into nature and culture that could operate without invoking Western metaphysical baggage. Finally, such a reformulation of the nature/culture divide would allow us to see moments where opacity regarding intention facilitates not freedom but, rather, brings about unintended limitations on what can be the object of human intention – the chief of these moments being the Anthropocene itself.

Part Three of the volume contains chapters that address the morality of open society, of individual belonging and recognition, and anthropology's duty in this regard (Stade; Kirtsoglou; Rapport). What may and ought social anthropology say concerning the lineaments of a global human society? Of 'Who Are We to Judge? Two Metalogues on Morality' Ronald Stade writes:

In this chapter I discuss the relationship between the anthropology of morality and the morality of anthropology (and anthropologists) in two 'metalogues'. A metalogue, according to Gregory Bateson, is a discussion that is its own example. Moral issues can be considered from three vantage points: descriptive, prescriptive (or normative) and ascriptive (or essentialist); the first metalogue, entitled 'Three perspectives on morality and the absurdity of their coexistence', is devoted to the differences and connections between these three. Jomo Kenyatta's diploma thesis serves as an example in this context. Another example is anthropologists studying perpetrators of cruelty and what this entails in terms of moral dilemmas. Can such dilemmas be solved with the help of contemporary ascriptive perspectives on morality? Two ascriptive perspectives, one statistical, the other biological, are vetted in search for an answer. The first metalogue concludes by suggesting that it might be best to accept the absurdity of reviewing three perspectives on morality simultaneously as defining the field and practice of anthropology.

The second metalogue, titled 'Wobbly universalism', extends the argument of the first by reviewing the debate on cultural relativism and arguing that cultural diversity cannot be reduced to what Arnold Gehlen called 'institutions', or José Ortega y Gasset as *creencias* or Pierre Bourdieu as *doxa*. Cultural diversity also manifests itself in the most thoroughly thought through, elaborate and critically examined codes, as exemplified by legal diversity. This would seem to lend support to the relativist argument. In the conclusion to the second metalogue, however, a case is made for relativism being useful to the extent that it serves as a space for shedding convictions and certainties but not if it is made to function as the final destination. It is possible to pass through relativism and come out on the other side.

But then life knows no reversal. Anyone who has surrendered to relativism cannot return to an enchanted, innocent kind of universalism. A disenchanted universalism, erected on the shaky ground of relativity, will therefore remain forever wobbly. This is why the conclusion to the second metalogue resembles the conclusion of the first metalogue: there are contradictions that might prove insoluble, which is why certain fundamental inconsistencies must be treated as aporia.

Of '"We Are All Human": Cosmopolitanism as a Radically Political, Moral Project', Elisabeth Kirtsoglou writes:

Based on an eclectic and ethnographically substantiated reading of Kant, Smith, Hume, Levinas, Castoriadis and Rapport, I claim in my chapter that the recognition of our common humanity is an explicitly political expression of the cosmopolitan project. At the heart of the conceptualization of humanity as a state of being we all share, lies empathy which compels us (as per Kant's idea of humanity) to treat humanity as 'an end in itself' and as an ultimate 'moral limit' to what we can and cannot do. Empathy is an affirmative political praxis, an affective ethical technology through which we subvert and deconstruct narratives of radical alterity – that are usually based on cultural, national, religious, racial, gender distinctiveness – while still respecting difference.

Empathy has been discussed by different philosophers (Smith's concept of sympathy for instance) but contemporary scholarship (heavily influenced by Nietzsche) confuses empathy with sympathy and dismisses it as an hierarchical and potentially anti-political form of 'pity' that leads to philanthropy (in the common sense of the term). In order to address this confusion my analysis borrows from Castoriadis's emphasis on human capacity to teach oneself (to be an autodidact). I claim that human subjects are creative and imaginary beings. In the face of the Other – in my case, refugees – the Other's joy, bereavement, happiness or pain, strength or vulnerability, abundance or need, we initiate a process of *autodidaxis*. Namely, a process of trying to imagine what the Other's world may feel like and simultaneously a process of teaching oneself how to respond to the presence (the positive or negative circumstances) of the Other. We can feel – and see, understand, experience – the world from the Other's point of view, not because the Self and the Other are the same, but because they are uniquely capable of becoming autodidacts in each other's experiences, as well as learn from one another. We employ our imagination in order to put oneself in the position of the Other. Empathy does not come as a result of knowledge already acquired but as an effect of knowledge gained. The empathetic subject is always in the process of becoming and exists in an intersubjective relation with others. The problem of other incommensurable minds is, therefore, an artificial one if those other minds are not regarded as self-bounded entities but as embedded in webs of relationships.

This process of creating (instituting) and sharing knowledge makes empathy an equally cognitive *and* affective process between embodied subjects capable of creating spaces of sociality through initiating relationships of responsibility and obligation.

Lastly, Nigel Rapport writes of 'Transference and Cosmopolitan Politesse: Coming to Terms with the Distorted, "Tragic" Quality of Social Relations between Individual Human Beings':

> Enormous weight is placed on the fieldworker in ethnographic research. What a datum, a piece of local information, is, and how that datum properly connects with another and another to form a stream of data – a text, a discourse, a practice – is dependent on the experiencing and the interpreting of the anthropologist. He or she invents a 'social' reality in which there are units of information beyond his or her body and those units conventionally, normally coalesce into patterned shapes of habitual 'cultural' life. But, then, does this distinctive methodology not mimic in an insightful way the mundane experience of social life as this is practised by the cultural 'members' that the anthropologist has set out to examine? Their existence as members who 'belong' to social relations within a life-world – a locale, a community, a movement – is equally dependent on the individual sense-making they make from their particular bodily perspectives, with no certainty of understanding. Social life may indeed be characterized as an arbitrary affair: an existential domain characterized by likely misapprehension. To borrow a Freudian term, social life concerns 'transference', an uneasy truce between individual's personal systems of interpretation that are likely to remain solitary and phantastical. We invent the world around us according to blueprints that derive from personal ontogenies of individual development, as Sigmund Freud concludes.
>
> This gives a 'tragic' dimension to all social life, according to Georg Simmel, asking himself the question, 'How is society possible?', and estimating 'The problem of society'. First, the chapter reprises the way in which 'transference', even if by other names, accords with the ethnographic record and how anthropology has already seen fit to recognize the routine distortions and miscommunications of social life and exchange; an account of the author's fieldwork as a porter in a Scottish hospital provides an ethnographic example of such distortion. Then, the emphasis of the chapter is an ethical one, recalling Enlightenment expectations of anthropology as a discipline and drawing on the later ethical hypothesizing of Emmanuel Levinas. In a situation of ignorance and likely misapprehension concerning the sense being made by an individual's human fellows, what is a 'moral' vision of social engagement? It is suggested that a 'cosmopolitan politesse' represents a form of social exchange that an anthropologist might propose that best accommodates transference as an existential condition; so that the 'uneasy truce' between a diversity of individual world-views is, nevertheless, mutually gratifying.

The volume closes with a reflection by the honorary life president of the ASA, Marilyn Strathern, based on the Firth lecture she delivered at the conference. In 'Afterword: Becoming Enlightened about Relations', she ponders what Enlightenment thought addressed and what it omitted, and why:

> Some sixty years ago Raymond Firth thought it necessary to point out that social relations could not be seen by the ethnographer; they could only be inferred from people's interactions. Abstraction was necessary. At the same time Firth unproblematically talked of relations in the abstract when he was comparing, for example, economic and moral standards. The issues would have not been unfamiliar to Hume, and other luminaries of the Scottish Enlightenment, who dwelt on the power of relations in (human) understanding and (scholarly) narrative, as well as interpersonal sympathy. It seems appropriate to draw in John Locke and an antecedent period in the European Enlightenment at large, at least for certain peculiarities in the English language that many Scots were making their own. These usages thickened the plot as far as 'relations' go, with implications that still tease us. The burden of the account is what happened then – or more accurately what did not happen – in the course of particular philosophical disquisitions. A third figure, artist and naturalist Maria Sibylla Merian, is a concrete reminder that that there was never only one view, and that we can obviously recover quite divergent echoes from the past.
>
> Here is a conversation, as I have contrived it between these figures, which concerns the characterization of relations, how connections are made in the imagination and the kinds of examples one might bring to mind. Kin connections were common in discourses of the time (and had a long history), and Hume draws on familiar/familial examples just as Locke did before him. However, they are used as examples of proximate relations, as any other example would be, and kin are not singled out as being any different in this regard from close acquaintances. (This tells us something about kinship.) More significantly, in discussions of the moral person and personal identity there is no reference to relations, let alone kin relations. In this chapter I make of this omission an 'event' that did not happen, or a non-event that had repercussions. Indeed it can only be known by its after-effects.

V

As intimated, Amos Oz's claim for social structure to be seen as essentially a matter of emotion goes against how we have thought to consider social structure, at least since the days of Radcliffe-Brown. Surely, here is an external institutional framework for the ordering and reproduction of social life that undercuts or bypasses the emotional, and purposely so. A social structure ensures a way of public life independent of its particular functionaries and their dispositions. Ideally, emotional states and particular lives become irrelevant. Alternatively, emotion is one of the things to which a social structure gives birth, along with cognition and behaviour. To say that emotion is the essence of social structure is tautological and redundant – as it would be to query whether a particular social structure was or was not 'moral'. Amos Oz offers us a challenge, therefore, but it is one that this volume would take seriously.

As we have seen, Adam Smith set up the puzzle – on the one side the richly self-educating power of sentiment, on the other the ongoing but morally indifferent social division of labour – but he did not solve it. For some decades the Radcliffe-Brownian model of equilibrating society has lain in tatters (Strathern 1996). Recent commentators have gone further – the Enlightenment presentation of 'human exceptionalism' on which social science was founded is now 'unthinkable' given our awareness of the symbiosis of human beings with all the other biological entities; the concept of 'Anthropos', and the 'imperializing eighteenth century' from which it sprung, have become a fundamental hindrance to knowledge, Donna Haraway (2016) amongst others have claimed. All of which entitles and perhaps demands of anthropology that it should revisit Enlightenment questions and ask them anew. What role does/should/ may emotion play in moral social relations? How does moral recognition of fellow human beings (as individuals and in groups) – extending 'sympathy' towards them, institutionalizing humane norms of social interaction – actually take place? Are moral sentiments 'naturally-occurring' in the ethnographic record, and can anthropology hope to promote a moral vision? Is anthropological practice itself moral?

These are old questions, we have seen. A key feature of the Enlightenment that subsists, however, is the way that these questions become scientific questions to which human beings might, in their freedom, find answers – free from the dictates of religion and other dogma, and free from the habituality of custom and culture – and find answers that might then provide avenues of progress along which all of humanity might proceed. 'Anthropology' was born here: the word Immanuel Kant coined to describe that cosmopolitan project of finding how the life of the whole – the human species – and the life of the part – the individual human being – might come closest to reflecting one another, both rationally and morally. For Kant and Hume alike, the need was to avoid cultural specificities of caprice, arbitrariness, ignorance and partiality.

The particular point of departure for this volume, it has been explained, is Adam Smith and his *Theory of Moral Sentiments*. For Smith, a moral practice begins through extending an imaginative sympathy towards fellow human beings and placing oneself in their situation, and also through becoming an impartial observer of one's own littleness and the dishonour one does oneself through a disproportionate self-love. 'Moral self-consciousness requires that I divide myself as it were into two persons', Smith wrote. Societies were held together by this form of emotional trade between participants – a mutual impartiality and sympathy – such that an appropriate attunement of individual emotions became automatic. How do the insights of Kant, Hume and Smith look today? The questions remain fundamental ones to an anthropological science. What is it to be human? How best to know the human and to write the human? What are the origins of moral human behaviour and how can these be given a universal authority? How to secure the rights of the human to a fulfilling self-expression in each precious individual life? A second major work of the volume is to address these Enlightenment notions from the perspective of contemporary comparative ethnography and analysis.

If in this volume the immediate key is Smith, then the wider question involves forging connections to the Enlightenment in order to reconnect contemporary academic anthropology with the primary concerns of the present. Anthropology may continue to abide in a state of 'crisis' as it attempts to substantiate knowledge while feeling itself yield yet more terrain to the 'social technicians'; but it remains the discipline that has dealt for longest with what is now recognized as the hyper-diversity that prevails globally in human practices and ideas. Anthropology has been methodologically (in its encounters), if not theoretically (in its paradigms), 'cosmopolitan' for longer than any other modern academic discipline. If, under these conditions, a concern with human sentiment, imagination and freedom are not at the centre of contemporary anthropological inquiry, then, what is?

Notes

1   Cf. Dell Hymes's edited collection 'Reinventing Anthropology' which grew out of a 1969 seminar on 'Rethinking Anthropology'.
2   Recent controversies surrounding the retesting of a range of psychology studies led to the summary headline in *Nature* 'Over half of psychology studies fail reproducibility test' (Baker 2015).
3   Paul Romer, chief economist at the World Bank, has recently accused econometrists of introducing variables into economic calculations that are the scientific equivalent of 'phlogiston': 'macro models now use incredible identifying assumptions to reach bewildering conclusions', he proposes (Romer 2016).

References

Baker, M. 2015. 'Over Half of Psychology Studies Fail Reproducibility Test'. *Nature Online*, 27 August. Available online: www.nature.com/news/over-half-of-psychology-studies-fail-reproducibility-test-1.18248 (accessed 11 July 2018).
Beck, U. 2004. 'The Truth of Others: A Cosmopolitan Approach'. *Common Knowledge* 10(3): 430–49.
Berreman, G. 1972. '"Bringing it All Back Home": Malaise in Anthropology'. In *Reinventing Anthropology*, D. Hymes (ed.). New York: Random House 83–98.
Erickson, P., Klein, J., Daston, L., Lemov, R., Sturm, T. and Gordin, M. 2013. *How Reason Almost Lost Its Mind: The Strange Career of Cold War Rationality*. Chicago: University of Chicago Press.
Evans-Pritchard, E. 1976. *Witchcraft, Oracles and Magic among the Azande*. Oxford: Oxford University Press.
Firth, R. 1936. *We the Tikopia*. London: Allen & Unwin.
Forman-Barzilai, F. 2010. *Adam Smith and the Circles of Sympathy*. Cambridge: Cambridge University Press.
Geertz, C. 1970. 'The Impact of the Concept of Culture on the Concept of Man'. In *Man Makes Sense*, E. Hammel and W. Simmons (eds). Boston, MA: Little, Brown.
Geertz, C. 1983. *Local Knowledge*. New York: Basic.
Geertz, C. 2000. *Available Light*. Princeton, NJ: Princeton University Press.

Gellner, E. 1964. *Thought and Change*. London: Weidenfeld & Nicolson.

Gellner, E. 1993. 'The Mightier Pen? Edward Said and the Double Standards of Inside-out Colonialism'. *Times Literary Supplement* February 19: 3–4.

Gellner, E. 1995. 'Anything Goes: The Carnival of Cheap Relativism which Threatens to Swamp the Coming *fin de millenaire*'. *Times Literary Supplement* June 16: 6–8.

Girard, R. 1978. *To Double Business Bound: Essays on Literature, Mimesis, and Anthropology*. Baltimore, MD: Johns Hopkins University Press.

Haraway, D. 2016. 'Tentacular Thinking: Anthropocene, Capitalocene, Chthulucene'. *e-flux* (75) (September). Available online: www.e-flux.com/journal/75/67125/tentacular-thinking-anthropocene-capitalocene-chthulucene/ (accessed 11 July 2018).

Hayek, F.A. 1944. *The Road to Serfdom*. London: Routledge.

Hayees, D. (ed.). 1972. *Reinventing Anthropology*. New York: Random House.

Kant, I. 2006. *Anthropology from a Pragmatic Point of View*. Cambridge: Cambridge University Press.

Kelty, C. 2016. 'Liberty and Lock-in: The Trouble with Freedom in Anthropology'. In *Freedom in Practice: Governance, Liberty and Autonomy in the Everyday*, M. Lino and H. Wardle (eds). London: Routledge, pp. 164–86.

Kohn, E. 2015. 'Anthropology of Ontologies'. *Annual Review of Anthropology* 44: 311–27.

Levinas, E. 1989. *The Levinas Reader*, S. Hand (ed.). Oxford: Blackwell.

Lino e Silva, M. and Wardle, H. (eds). 2016. *Freedom in Practice: Governance, Liberty and Autonomy in the Everyday*. London: Routledge.

Malinowski, B. 1922. *Argonauts of the Western Pacific*. London: Routledge and Kegan Paul.

Oz, A. 1975. *Touch the Water, Touch the Wind*. London: Chatto & Windus.

Polanyi, K. 1957. *The Great Transformation*. Boston, MA: Beacon Press.

Rapport, N. (ed.). 2017. *Distortion: Social Processes beyond the Structured and Systemic*. London: Routledge.

Romer, P. 2016. 'The Trouble with Macroeconomics'. Paper given to the Stern Business School, 14 September. Available online: https://paulromer.net/wp-content/uploads/2016/09/WP-Trouble.pdf (accessed 11 July 2018).

Sartre, J. P. [1948] 1963. *The Psychology of Imagination*. New York: Citadel Press.

Simmel, G. 1910. 'How Is Society Possible?' *American Journal of Sociology* 16(3): 372–91.

Smith A. 2004. *Selected Philosophical Writings*, J. Otteson (ed.). Exeter: Imprint Academic.

Strathern, M. 1996. 'The Concept of Society Is Theoretically Obsolete. For the Motion'. In *Key Debates in Anthropology*, T. Ingold (ed.). London: Routledge.

Viveiros de Castro, E. 2012. 'Cosmological Perspectivism in Amazonia and Elsewhere'. *HAU: Masterclass Series* 1: 45–168.

Williams, B. 1978. *Morality*. Cambridge: Cambridge University Press.

Wittgenstein, L. 1978. *Philosophical Investigations*. Oxford: Blackwell.

1

After Sympathy, a Question

Anne Line Dalsgård

'Here! Read this book and you will know everything about me'. Evinha handed me a small paperback with almost yellow pages and a worn out cover. 'Julia', the title read. I took it with me and made sure to read it before meeting her next time. I was interested in Evinha's life, had known her since she was 15, and now – 32 years old – she was one of the key informants in my fieldwork. The novel told the story of a young woman in the United States, who worked as an interior designer. She had recently started her own company when she met a man, whom she first found to be a superficial, rich playboy, but in time came to love deeply. Julia was slim and blond (was that in the book or in my imagination?), she definitely wore jeans and flat shoes, and she looked breathtaking in the silk dress she wore at the wedding at the end of the book. She was perky, chic and independent. It is probably needless to say that the novel was very predictable, and yet I was totally absorbed in it. What needs mentioning, though, is that I did not see any similarity between Julia and Evinha. Why did Evinha give it to me? Trying to answer that question, I became aware of another.

In the following I will describe how I found my way to a kind of understanding of Evinha's statement and where that left me. I will present a small piece of fictional writing (you could call it sympathetic imagining) and Evinha's reaction to it; then I will discuss Adam Smith's notion of sympathy and its relevance for anthropological fieldwork and understanding; and finally I will return to Evinha and the question she left me with – a question which has to do with friendship and the proper posture towards a friend's distress. You could say that it reaches beyond anthropology and is a matter of personal, moral judgement; you could also say that friendship has nothing to do with the anthropological endeavour, as every relation between the anthropologist and the people he or she studies is inherently unequal, instrumental and temporary; but, obviously, this all depends on how we understand friendship and how we practise anthropology. In the following I locate the question within a discussion of ethics and the moments in fieldwork when typifications like 'fieldworker' and 'informant' are destabilized (Throop 2012: 164) or simply made irrelevant. I then return to this discussion later, at the end of the chapter.

The particular fieldwork that I draw upon took place in a low-income neighbourhood on the outskirts of the city of Recife in northeast Brazil in December

2013. I have conducted fieldwork in this neighbourhood over periods of varying length since 1997, when I first arrived there as a PhD student (see Dalsgård 2004; Dalsgård and Frederiksen 2014).

Ethics and fieldwork: An old discussion

The discussion of ethics is not new to anthropologists. How often have we not discussed the notion that the ethical questions of our profession cannot be answered by rules and guidelines, but need to be an integrated part of our research practices (Hastrup 2009: 7)? That ethics in our kind of research is not a matter of 'abstractly correct behaviour, but of relations between people' (Patai 1991: 145), as we repeatedly find ourselves in situations in which we are forced to consciously consider the correct ethical response. This is seldom just a response to a practical matter; often it concerns our intervention into people's self-understanding and sense of agency. Though in the 1960s it was still possible to ask whether anthropologists were only 'playing an intellectual game in which nobody outside our own tiny circle is interested' (Gjessing in Caplan 2003: 6), we have had to acknowledge since then that our interlocutors in the field may be readers, perhaps also of our research if we publish in their language, and we can no longer pretend that we do not have a responsibility towards these readers. Even without reading our analyses, our interlocutors may be provoked by the anthropological approach to reflect upon their own lives, perhaps by comparing life situations (Gay y Blasco and de la Cruz Hernández 2012), perhaps just through the questions we ask face to face, which may touch upon matters otherwise unquestioned.

In her essay 'U.S. Academics and Third World Women: Is Ethical Research Possible?', Daphne Patai writes on ethnographic interviewing that 'part of what those interviewed "get" from the process is precisely the undivided attention directed at them by another individual' (1991: 142). Doing fieldwork among low-income women in Brazil, Patai observed that the opportunity to talk about one's life, to make sense to oneself and to another human being of choices made and actions taken (or not) seemed to be 'an intrinsically valuable experience' (1991: 142). Like Patai, I have found that my so-called informants often appreciate interviews as meaningful occasions for reflection, and not only in Brazil. Doing fieldwork among accountants in Denmark, we noticed that 'most informants appreciated the opportunity to share experiences and their possible meaning with a couple of outsiders, and a question like "Why did you become an accountant?" seemed to allow for thoughts that were rarely touched upon in the daily hubbub' (Dalsgård 2008: 147, my translation).

The inequality of social status, however, makes the intervention into women's lives in Brazilian low-income neighbourhoods more ethically dubious, or at least this is what we usually think: the attention and 'comparatively non-judgemental acceptance' (Stacey 1991: 117) that ethnographic interviews may offer interviewees may lead to a level of intimacy on false premises, as 'the lives, loves, and tragedies that fieldwork informants share with a researcher are ultimately data – grist for the ethnographic mill' (Stacey 1991: 113) and the researcher can leave the field much more freely than the research subject, without leaving any intimate revelations behind in exchange for the 'data' she carries away (Patai 1991: 142). The conclusion to be drawn may very well be that truly ethical research cannot be done in an unethical world (Patai 1991: 150). From that perspective, any illusion about friendship necessarily withers away. However, knowing that I risk being judged and being regarded (at best) as naïve, I wish to present a different conclusion: that some encounters in the field force us to step out of the safe framework of research and accept friendship with all that it involves in terms of affection and commitment. In *If Not the Words* Keith Ridler places 'the dense fabric of friendship, its close-woven texture, multiple – sometimes conflicting – role expectations, its emotional weight in carrying us beyond the conceptual boundaries of self' at the heart of the ethnographic encounter as it is experienced in fieldwork (Ridler 1996: 250). Ridler's background is one of long-term, repeated fieldwork and practical engagement in everyday activities of the field, and it may be the difference between just interviewing and participant observation during longer periods that evokes these different perspectives on fieldwork.

At least, the question of ethics that I address in the following is likewise tied to the kind of fieldwork in which you live with the people you study over lengthy periods and to whom you return for subsequent fieldwork, thereby affirming that your relationships in the field are more than just instrumental and temporary. You meet the same people in many different life situations, and you yourself change over the years. Life stories get intertwined when – as in the case of Evinha – the girl whom you once met as the timid daughter of one of your informants grows up and works with you as an assistant in order to earn money for entering nursing school; subsequently taking part in your research as an informant when she is a young mother. Her projects have changed along the way, as have my own. We have helped each other: *she* once told me that I was the first person in her life to trust her capacity to work (when I gave her a job as an assistant); and *I* have asked her a lot of questions for my research, because I like her sincere answers and the way she confronts my ignorance. We have also simply spent time together, often sitting on her sofas, which over the years have improved in quality. While much more has passed between us, I will focus upon a particular occurrence in the following, which I shall call a moment of mutual sympathy.

The concept of sympathy that I employ is Adam Smith's concept of the sentiment of an impartial and well-informed spectator, by way of whom one may imaginatively put oneself in the situation of another. His is thus not necessarily a caring sentiment; just a feeling along with someone. I argue that writing fiction based on ethnographic data may be a sympathetic experiment in which the situation of another can be explored, and I describe how such an experiment may be received by the other person whom it sets out to understand. Moreover, I will argue that friendship is a potential realization of such a sympathetic imagining. This argument involves, as we shall see, a definition of friendship which is based on the mutual recognition of difference. It also involves a question of responsibility, which transcends the framework of research and moves us into 'the "poetics" of fieldwork', i.e. the construction and performance of relationship (Ridler 1996: 246), and shows us that fiction can be real (including the fiction of anthropological field research identified by Clifford Geertz) because it has real consequences. Evinha, who is at the centre of my argument, is a young woman of Afro-Brazilian descent, who grew up in a house in illegally occupied territory in a so-called *favela* with parents who could only afford the most basic necessities. Today she lives with her husband and two children, and her days are full of activities, as she has a job in town and also takes care of kids and does the housework. She and her husband have their difficulties. I have always found Evinha beautiful with her lively movements and infectious laughter. Over the years she has acquired a slightly more ample girth, but that does not prevent her from squeezing into a pair of tight shorts to go for a stroll in the neighbourhood in the evenings. Evinha is not the person I write about in the story below, but her story along with others formed part of the empirical foundation for my writing. After telling the story I shall explain how it changed my relationship with her.

A fictional story

It's been a long time since Betty last cried. She feels an urge to give in and sob until she's inside out. She pulls her legs up and gets the rocking chair moving. Yes, she is sad and she needs to be held. The rain is dripping down between the roof tiles, which have always leaked. She can hear the heavy splashing on the concrete below. The sounds have come closer and the mosquitoes have settled on the wall. The rocking of the chair is making her calm. She keeps it going to hold back the tears. Like some kind of spell. 'Betty! Hurry. The key!' She isn't getting up. 'Beeetty!' He keeps going but she doesn't want to get up. Doesn't want to go outside, open the gate and let her father in. All of a sudden she feels faded. Just rocking. 'Betty, meu Deus! Come out and open up!' She takes the key, steps out into the soggy courtyard and opens the padlock on the gate. The hinges squeak, and the gate has to be lifted back into place. She pulls the chain back around the bars and puts the padlock on. Click! 'Have you eaten?' he asks on his way in. He hurries through the rain. She immediately knows that he's been drinking, the white in his eyes always goes a little brown. She is hungry, but still says yes. 'You need to eat well, my girl. I've brought some bread.' Betty doesn't reply. She returns to the rocking chair and turns on the TV. It's very small and the image is so fuzzy. It's actually hard to see anything at all, but it's an excuse for not listening. The eight o'clock novela is on. Some middle-class wife gets a visit from her son. Their voices are shrill, one fast line after the other. An unimportant argument.

Her father is rummaging around in the kitchen, the sound of eggs being fried. And then the smell of steamed cuscuz that spreads to the living room. That dented steamer is her childhood. The lid doesn't really fit anymore, allowing the smell to move more freely around the house. It carries with it the happiness of being at home back then when she still didn't know who she was. When she still didn't know that she was going to live such a predictable life. Back when she thought that everything belonged to her and that she had a choice. The worst thing wasn't the disappointment, but the fact that no one had told her the truth.

Whistling, shouts and laughter by the gate. 'Bettiiiii!!' Her father goes to open. Comes back in, accompanied by her sister. 'What terrible rain! I almost floated all the way down to the highway, had to take off my sandals so they didn't leave me behind.' Nonsense and laughter as always. Anita's shorts and legs are covered in sprays of mud from her sandals. She gets a towel from the kitchen. As she's wiping herself off, she looks at her sister. Severely. But quickly changing to a teasing look. She can't help it. It's tiresome, but somehow protective. It's almost impossible to talk about problems when Anita is around. Betty gets up from the rocking chair to check on the boy. Her breasts tighten. She straightens the little blanket without knowing if she wants him to wake up or not. She runs a hand through her hair and pulls her nightgown into place. She's been wearing it all day. Anita has sat down by the table. Betty takes a seat next to her. There are crumbs of bread left from this morning. She hasn't wiped the oilcloth and the dishes aren't done. Anita, my dear sister with the long nails and cheeky smile, can't you for once just be quiet and take my hand? A puddle of water on the tablecloth. Betty dips her finger and draws a line. Her father puts a plate of cuscuz, bread and eggs in front of her and takes a seat in the rocking chair with his own full plate.

She sits up a bit straighter and starts picking at the food. Anita tells them about her new job at the telephone company. The mobile customers keep calling with stupid questions. It's easy to spend too much time on them and she has started simply cutting them off if the call drags out. It's piecework. Her wrist is aching from using the mouse. She spends too much time in front of the computer every day. Maybe she'll have to quit soon. Even though she's doing a good job. So they told her the other day. Talk, talk, talk. But then a break: 'You need to find a job soon, sister, or you'll go mad! You can't just let father support you.' Anita glances at her father, he's eating and watching TV. In a lowered voice she adds, 'People have started gossiping about you.' Anita knows about gossip, she's been the subject of it herself. You walk down the street with a shiver on your back and a thundering silence in your ears whenever gossip surrounds you. It's evil and without intention at the same time. Anita used to cry a lot when people said that she had been a loose woman, that her daughter had many fathers, that she'd spread her legs for anyone. Most of all she cried because she had loved once and she knew that happiness is possible.

Why is Anita talking about the gossip? Doesn't she know that you have to let it pass? That there's no room in life for concerning yourself with gossip? People can think what they want. We all have our own inner world to take care of, and the outer world only exists so that we can survive. We need it, but only because we need food, a place to sleep, work, sex. What's real is the abyss inside each of us. The condensed desire, beauty and pain that is tearing at our bodies. This is where she lives. Betty is watching her sister's hands move through the air, the long fingers with the nails that make them even longer. Her hands look like insects, long legs, sharp claws, the bending joints. Anita lives a different life than she does. Anita is good, Anita is loving, Anita believes that you can change the past by loving another person. Anita keeps insisting that her child was planned. A love child.

A sex child? That term doesn't exist. But the children exist. It's believed that young women get pregnant out of stupidity. But Betty wasn't stupid. She was wild. Her body vibrating and strong. The darkness surrounded her, pounding through her and pulling her down. In the light at the doctor's, when the test confirmed her situation, everything was different and too late. She ended up as expected. Just one of a large number of young mothers who had been careless and didn't use protection. Typical for her economic status and her home in a poor neighbourhood. She and Anita are both part of the same statistics. Now Anita is standing, holding the boy. He's crying with a dry rattle in his tiny voice. Anita walks around for a while trying to calm him down by making small noises, but he's clearly hungry. 'You should have eaten something yourself, Betty,' says her father as he takes her plate to the kitchen. Betty gazes at him, wondering what he wants from life. She also wonders what she's going to do. How is she going to support the baby and herself.

She stands up and goes to take the boy. He's so small, his bottom is no more than a handful and his tiny body is strangely loose. She has to keep it together, close to her own. The boy is sucking, greedily, attached to her breast. The pull on her uterus is close to painful but she lets him suck. She knows that she will be all right. The two of them can nourish each other, she'll make him grow, walk, talk, he'll make her mature, plan ahead and take responsibilities. They are each other's ladders. It's a long fall, but they'll stick together. Nobody knows the story from here, but it's a relief to no longer be fighting against expectations. Betty rocks the chair slowly. The boy is sleeping and she leans her head back and lets the sounds calm down around her. There's nothing to fear. It happened. Anything can arise from that.

A real story

I wrote the story above back home in Denmark and had it translated into Portuguese. I wished to return some of my insights to the young women whom I had interviewed during my fieldwork on youth and futurity (Dalsgård 2014). I thought there was a need for literature describing their reality which was unlike 'Julia' and the other novels about romantic love, which seemed to be the only books they had access to. Upon returning to my fieldwork I asked some of the young women in the neighbourhood to read my amateurish attempt at literary fiction. The first person to read my text was Evinha's sister Patricia. After reading it she slapped her 3-year-old daughter, who kept asking for something, and then wearily told me that she had to go. She was going to work and Nici, her daughter, was going to be looked after. No comment on the text. I never understood why Patricia had come to see me, and I regretted using the occasion for my own benefit. When I asked Evinha if she would read it, I made sure the moment was more appropriate. It was a lazy afternoon, we were just chatting and had plenty of time, and she agreed to read while I switched on my recorder and then asked: 'Could this happen, Evinha, or is it not realistic?'

Evinha answered:

Yes, it could – the story gives a good impression of what happens in real life. The romance novels are more like a fantasy about a life that doesn't exist. Whichever problems the characters might have are quickly resolved; there is always a person that helps out, but in reality that doesn't happen. We have babies; have to live with our parents. But you need to add something to the story: Here you could write something about her appearance, something to identify her, her face, 'Betty is a slim woman, beautiful eyes, her lips … ' If it has to be realistic? Then she's not a woman with a perfect body. She's 1.6 metres tall, black hair, brown eyes, a sad look on her face, light or dark skin, thoughtful. You should describe her age too.

When I was reading about her, I pictured her as being young, a teenager who had made a mistake [*que errou*]. At the point where her father enters and calls her, you can write a few lines about her thoughts … 'Betty listened thoughtfully to the rain. My God, I gave myself to this man, believed in him, was thinking that I was going to be happy. Now I'm here, what should I do? Who can help me?' We need to know what she's thinking, so we'll get caught up in the story. How does it continue? Well, she finds a job and sends the child to kindergarten. And at this job … here comes my part [Evinha changes her tone and lowers her voice], my dream of perfect love: My friends from work invite me to a party. I'm thinking that I'll arrange for a babysitter and stop by, but I can't stay long because I have to catch the last bus home. Suddenly she needs to go. Her friends are saying that they'll drive her home, but they've been drinking and she prefers to go alone. She misses the bus and decides to walk. She realises that someone is walking behind her, two men, and she starts getting anxious. She doesn't know the street and isn't sure what to do. Then she spots some young men talking in front of a house. She acts fast and hurries towards them as if she was planning to meet up with them. She goes to the one who's the most handsome – in my opinion – light skinned with blue eyes and brown hair, Michael [pronounced in English]. She gives him a kiss, 'hey my love, sorry I'm late', and whispers in his ear, 'sorry, two men are following me, could you help?' and he takes her inside the house. She meets his parents, and they let her stay until the morning. He's sleeping in the living room, and she is in his bed. She's wearing nothing but panties [Evinha draws out the sentence, building tension with her tone of voice], she prefers to sleep like that, and during the night she wakes up and hears the rain on the roof. She wants to take a shower in the rain – I enjoy doing that too. He's still wide awake in the living room, because the kiss made him all confused, and he lends her a T-shirt. So she's standing there in the rain in panties and a T-shirt and she gets completely wet, her clothes are clinging to her body. In the morning I wake up after sleeping like a princess and leave without talking to anyone. The following days I don't know what to do. My friends notice that I'm sad, so they take me out and I tell them the story. One of them tells the guy who I am, he looks me up and we start dating … That's how the story could continue! She meets someone either through the kindergarten or through work. But the most beautiful thing would probably be if it were the baby's father. He goes through a tough time, maybe he gets sick or has an accident – a lot of people get hurt on motorcycles – and she's the only one who comes to see him in the hospital and takes care of him at home. All his friends that he used to party with are suddenly gone, and she's all he's got. He realises that she's his woman, his love, for life. He recovers, loves her, witnesses the baby's first step, hears the baby say 'Papai!'

When I asked Evinha if those kinds of stories ever really happen, she answered in a disheartened tone of voice:

Well, I'm not the best person to answer that question because I don't believe it. I like to read about it, I like to leave my own reality. I wish it were real. I know there are people living happy lives together. But I also know that most couples have struggles that end up with one of them giving in. And it's often the woman. Like me. I thought that I was going to be the happiest person in the world, that I had *O Marido* [husband], *O Michael*. He exists, but he's not for me. Well, if you like that suggestion, feel free to put it into your story.

Evinha's proposition made me ponder. How should I understand first her expressed identification with Julia ('Read this book and you will know everything about me') and now, in her continuation of my story, her moving away from what *could* be reality into this same fictional universe of romantic love, only to land on a pessimistic note by saying 'he exists, but he's not for me'?

Fictional writing as sympathetic experiment

The story I wrote about Betty is not far from Evinha's and Patricia's everyday life, as I have mixed their stories with details from other stories in my field data. I connected interview quotations and observations and invented a figure I called Betty, while allowing myself to imagine the thoughts and feelings that made these quotations and observations meaningful. I wrote the story close to my understanding of their lives, as I thought that kind of literature was needed and that it might be a way to return my work to the young people and perhaps evoke some reflections upon life, as it is and as it could be. I was very aware that I could not write real, identifiable stories, hence the fiction, but I learned that my fiction intermingled with other kinds of fiction. Through Evinha's contribution to my story I got to know her longing for romantic love and a husband who cares for her, and I got a glimpse of how she lives with these dreams: when proposing ideas for the continuation of the story, she alternated between 'she' and 'I', as if the story was occasionally her own. Through the writing and her response, I thus moved closer to an understanding of Evinha's situation, while – at the same time – I also grew more puzzled. You could say that I moved from a register of empathy to one of sympathy.

In the article 'Meaning and Feeling in the Anthropology of Emotion' (1996), John Leavitt writes that 'emotions are no more purely private than are acts of cognition. While we do not know what someone else is feeling, this is true only in the same sense that we do not know absolutely what someone else means when he or she says something. In both cases we interpret: we postulate meanings for the words, gestures, or tears' (Leavitt 1996: 529). Leavitt goes on to state that 'this means that ethnographers of affect must work upon their own feelings, modifying them to model the emotional experiences of people of another society' (Leavitt 1996: 530), and he proposes the use of sympathy at the expense of the often stated significance of empathy for ethnographic fieldwork:

empathy, while perfectly real, is not an end to understanding but the beginning of a search. The problem with empathy is not that it involves feeling but that it assumes that first impressions are true. Instead of adhering to first impressions, however, it should be possible to re-examine and rework one's initial empathic reaction in light of a better grasp of the culture one is seeking to understand [...] This kind of reworking of one's own affect is a very different thing from the spontaneity of empathic communion. It is an activity that might be called sympathy rather than empathy: not a feeling *inside* what someone else is feeling (*em-pathia*), but a feeling *along with* (*sum-pathia*), a realignment of one's own affects to construct a model of what others feel. (Leavitt 1996: 530; original emphasis)

Leavitt does not draw directly on Adam Smith, but Smith's thoughts upon the role of sympathy as a moral sentiment are relevant here. Smith places imagination and a good deal of effort at the core of sympathy, and in his description of sympathy as a moral sentiment he rejects 'any simplistic notion of sentiment as a purely individualistic emotional response to moral problems' (Throop 2012: 153). Our senses alone, Smith writes, cannot tell us what another suffers: 'They never did, and never can, carry us beyond our own person, and it is by the imagination only that we can form any conception of what are his sensations' (Smith [1790] 2006: I.I.1.2).[1] At the same time, 'even our sympathy with the grief or joy of another, before we are informed of the cause of either, is always extremely imperfect [...] Sympathy, therefore, does not arise so much from the view of the passion, as from that of the situation which excites it' ([1790] 2006: I.I.1.9–10). The kind of effort that Smith sees as a precondition for sympathy is thus a willingness to let oneself be moved by the situation of the other, which implies a thorough insight into all that this situation consists of.

A mother's feelings for her child depend on how she experiences motherhood, how she experiences her child and how she understands her task in relation to this child (an understanding that may be out of step with her specific experience), and all these things are necessarily shaped by her social circumstances, her ideas of infants, of responsibility and of many other things. Hence, the feeling another person is obviously experiencing can never be taken for granted. It is not only a question of how we name that feeling; it is the web of relations in which the feeling arises that we must regard from without, as an impartial observer, neither 'me' nor 'her'. The point is not to make oneself feel the same way as the other person but as an impartial spectator to imagine her situation and, then, in Smith's word, bring the case home to ourselves (Smith [1790] 2006: I.I.I.4). As Emily Brady writes, 'there is a "double movement" of imagination where we first project ourselves into the shoes of an impartial spectator and then, from that position, imaginatively put ourselves into the shoes of the other. This impartial standpoint is not abstract or dispassionate, rather it involves affective engagement with the situation or person at hand' (2011: 100). However, as the movement is not one of empathy, that is, feeling the same, but rather one of imagining what it would be to be in the other's situation, there is a space between oneself and the feelings of the other person, which is only transgressed by the imagination (Brady 2011).

To understand the situation of the other, as I read Smith, is an ideal which is impossible to reach. What we can do is to listen, observe and stretch our imagination – and then admit that light also falls upon ourselves. Upon our own lack of impartiality, 'the limitations of our imaginative abilities and the fact that we are who we are' (Brady 2011: 101). Thus, Jason Throop writes:

Seeing sympathy as oriented not only toward the acts and experiences of others, but also reflexively back toward how those same others view the actions and experiences of the self, Smith views the mutuality of the sympathetic imagination as located at the heart of moral experience [...] Entailing what seems to be a significant intersubjective orientation, Smith's notion of sympathy is thus necessarily a social affair, although one that always expects there to remain important asymmetries of experience between individuals who work to coordinate their actions and reactions with one another through time. (Throop 2012: 153)

Leavitt proposes that we, anthropological observers, let this reworking and translation of affect take place in our writing, thus providing a sense of possible ways of feeling – 'not, as in literature, primarily to please us or to make us better or wiser in general but to give a sympathetic (this is, constructed) sense of what others experience' (1991: 531). What I did in the story about Betty was something else: I tested my understanding of the young women's situation by writing down the connections I imagined existed between the fragments of subjective life that I had observed. Like a mirror I held the story up and asked them as well as myself: 'Could this have happened?' What was shown was my qualified guesswork – or sympathetic imagining – and hence my view of their situation. I could have shown them my anthropological analyses and they would probably never have read them (except for interview extracts), but *here* there was no way to avoid understanding what I had seen. I had seen a lack of someone to trust, a suffering from low external expectations and a lack of trust from anyone else, as well as a possibility for newness once the situation is accepted.

In Evinha's and Patricia's reactions to my text I also saw my own judgement of their attitude to their situation, as I proposed acceptance as the appropriate stance and precondition for newness ('It happened. Anything can arise from that'). I had, unequivocally, written the fictional piece in response to the dreams of romantic novels like 'Julia'. According to Smith, we are ultimately forced to rely on our own experience when judging the appropriateness of the other's action or attitude:

Every faculty in one man is the measure by which he judges of the like faculty in another. I judge of your sight by my sight, of your ear by my ear, of your reason by my reason, of your resentment by my resentment, of your love by my love. I neither have, nor can have, any other way of judging about them. (Smith [1790] 2006: I.I.III.10)

In this case he was right.

An ethical moment

The anthropological project may be to understand what *is*, not what ought to be (Wolcott 1999: 181), and hence it should have nothing to do with judgement and appropriateness. Simultaneously, every anthropological analysis could be said to include a judgement. Not necessarily an explicit judgement; but by choosing one analytical perspective (for instance agency) instead of another (habitus, social reproduction), we conclude on the deceptiveness or potential innovative action of our informants' hopes for the future (Dalsgård and Frederiksen 2013). As long as we see our work as purely academic, we may not need to reflect upon the consequences of our thinking, in particular for the people whose lives and projects we try to understand. But once our thinking becomes part of the world it seeks to describe, it enters the narrative activities of the people who are being described and hence their efforts to create continuity between past, present and imagined futures (Ochs and Capps 1996: 22).

When Evinha handed me 'Julia' and said 'Here! Read this book and you will know everything about me', she did not ask me to believe that she was Julia. The book does not describe her, but the fact that she had read it was a hint to me and telling me was a gesture or narrative claim. She might just as well have said 'I know life could be different!' At least this is how I understood her after that lazy afternoon with my fictional piece. In Evinha's edition of the story, Betty listens to the rain on the roof and thinks 'Now I'm here, what should I do? Who can help me?' and later she stands in the rain while Michael, who probably still cannot sleep, desires her. Evinha had previously told me about her crying in rain showers on gloomy days, but I knew that beside such moments where the rain hid her tears, the thoughtful and longing person did not have much room in Evinha's daily life. She is like Anita, Betty's sister, who is rarely caught in a moment of seriousness. She lives an everyday life full of worries, dishwashing, an unreasonable financial situation, food that is never satisfying and troublesome relatives. But when she walks the street she strolls so that people know that she is more than wear and fatigue, and in her dreams of love she is desired as a thoughtful and loving person.

My attempt at sympathetic imagination regarding young women's experiences of motherhood was methodologically effective, as I learned more about the distress and emotional management involved. But it was also ethically challenging. I believe I looked into the pain of being exposed, when that which you struggle with in your personal life is not particularly wanted and when you wish that your potential for another life was recognized. Patricia hit her daughter after reading my text, while Evinha changed the story by adding a romantic ending. If seen within a framework of fieldwork ethics, I could be accused of transgressing the border to the unethical by creating such friction in two young women's lives. Who am I to expose the daily pain of motherhood in these difficult circumstances? You could say that I had certainly led Patricia and Evinha into 'intimacy on false premises', letting them tell me about their everyday sorrows and joys only to later expose them publicly, a betrayal which they now very clearly objected to. But if seen within a larger framework of ethics, where ethics is a normal part of social life as a necessary conscious task or search for moral rest (Zigon 2009: 263), the fictional text and its counterpart, Evinha's story, could also be seen as such a moment of 'work' in which a question was alive between the two of us. Or perhaps two questions facing each other: hers and mine.

My question was how to respond to the sadness I heard in Evinha's dream and disillusion, which she most often kept to herself. Her question – which led to the expression of both sentiments – was, as I understood it, how to respond to my judgement of her situation. Sympathy, understood as the effort to transport oneself as an impartial spectator into the situation of the other, may evoke the same in response, according to Smith. When you are considering the appropriateness of another's action, the other is also 'led to imagine in what manner he would be affected if he was [...] the spectators of his own situation' (Smith [1790] 2006: I.I.IV.8). And to me, this is what took place between us: being aware that I saw her situation and judged it, Evinha was moved to reflect upon it herself. My question mattered to me, because at that moment I realized (as I had done before) that I care for Evinha. Whether the whole thing mattered to Evinha I do not know; she has so much else to think and worry about. Nothing further happened that afternoon, as I remember it, but it has left me with a sense of responsibility towards Evinha which, however, does not evoke any clear answer as to what to do. This had led me into considerations upon friendship.

Friendship in the field

Within philosophy, Aristotle's view that friendship is based on mutual recognition and likeness has formed most subsequent definitions. In the *Nichomachean Ethics* Aristotle writes: 'How could they be friends when they neither approved of the same things nor delighted in and were pained by the same things. For not even with regard to each other will their tastes agree, and without this (as we saw) they cannot be friends' (in Cocking and Kennett 1998: 506). Adam Smith, too, saw the 'common' as constitutive of friendship: the new kind of friendships that he identified in the growing English commerce of the eighteenth century were based on the recognition among virtuous men of each other's virtues (Smith [1790] 2006: VI.II.I.18), and hence the recognition of the other as another self (Griswold and Den Uyl 1996: 623). Other philosophical writers have taken this idea of likeness even further in what is sometimes called the 'mirror view of friendship', where friendship is based on seeing one's own traits reflected in another (Cocking and Kennett 1998: 506–14).

Anthropological cross-cultural examination shows that nothing essential can be said about friendships. Much has been written on the topic from an anthropological perspective (for instance Grindal and Salamone 1995; Bell and Coleman 1999; Desai and Killick 2010); but generally friendship is found to be an elastic category (Cocking and Kennett 1998: 502), varying from place to place and over time according to dominant concepts of personhood. As Ridler writes:

> Friendships are of all relationships those, which play most freely in the interspace between individual intention and cultural constraint, between agency and structure, in the lifeworld as it is concretely experienced. In this sense, they are by nature indeterminate, open to future possibility in unpredictable ways, and finally, enigmatic. (Ridler 1996: 255)

However, even an open statement like Ridler's needs some kind of definition, since 'friendships' cannot be discussed if we do not know what the category includes. Ridler finds revelation, 'ambiguous and nuanced as it may be' (1996: 255), to be crucial for such relationships; revelation as it happens in shared practical activities where you walk, work or engage in something else for its own sake and beyond instrumentalization.

I have described another kind of exposure, one in which judgement, dreaming and sadness stand forth without conclusion. On that background, I will argue that if we abandon Smith's idea that friendship is based on virtue and likeness and return to his notion of sympathy, a definition of friendship that works well with fieldwork is possible. Sympathy, as we have seen, is based on a particular effort to distance oneself from one's immediate identification with the other through empathy; and to try, by way of imagination, to put oneself as an impartial spectator in the position of the other. If friendship is then based on a responsiveness to the other, and a willingness to stretch one's imagination and be shaped in the encounter (Cocking and Kennett 1998), sympathy may very well be a prelude to friendship.

In *Fieldwork in Morocco* Paul Rabinow describes his relationship with his friend ben Mohammad as one of difference, including 'a crucial space' between ben Mohammad and himself (1977: 143) and an effort to reach out towards each other:

> Through mutual confrontation of our own situations we did establish contact. But this also highlighted our fundamental Otherness [...] I could understand ben Mohammad only to the extent that he could understand me – that is to say, partially [...] Different webs of signification separated us, but these webs were now at least partially intertwined. But a dialogue was only possible when we recognized our differences. (Rabinow 1977: 162)

In *In Praise of Love* Alain Badiou asks: 'What is the world like when it is experienced, developed and lived from the point of view of difference and not identity?' (2012: 19). Badiou's answer is love, a love that also involves the surrendering of one's body to the beloved and is, therefore, nothing to do with what I have described here. Friendship, Badiou writes, is different – it is the most intellectual sentiment, as it has no resonance in bodily pleasure (2012: 28). But, even so, Badiou seems to think that experiencing from the point of view of difference characterizes friendship too. That makes sense to me. My relationship with Evinha is not one of love, but it is certainly one of care and concern, and that moment of our mutual recognition of my judgement of her situation only tied me closer to her. I consider her a friend. However, this does not change the fact that I still do not know how to respond to her distress. Beyond being a witness and accepting the fact that she can see me in return.

Note

1   All Smith [1790] 2006 references are in the format I.I.I.2 = part I, chapter I, section I, paragraph 2.

References

Badiou, A. with Truong N. 2012. *In Praise of Love*. New York: The New Press.
Bell, S. and Coleman, S. (eds). 1999. *The Anthropology of Friendship*. Oxford: Berg.

Brady, E. 2011. 'Adam Smith's "Sympathetic Imagination" and the Aesthetic Appreciation of Environment'. *The Journal of Scottish Philosophy* 9(1): 95–109.

Caplan, P. 2003. 'Introduction: Anthropology and Ethics'. In *The Ethics of Anthropology: Debates and Dilemmas*, P. Caplan (ed.). London: Routledge, pp. 1–34.

Cocking, D. and Kennett, J. 1998. 'Friendship and the Self'. *Ethics* 108(3): 502–27.

Dalsgård, A. L. 2004. *Matters of Life and Longing: Female Sterilisation in Northeast Brazil*. Copenhagen: Museum Tusculanum Press.

Dalsgård, A. L. 2008. '*Verfremdung* and Business Development: The Ethnographic Essay as Eye-opener'. I: *Being Seen: Paradoxes and Practices of (In)Visibility*. EPIC conference proceedings, American Anthropological Association, Copenhagen, 15–18 October 2008. 146–59.

Dalsgård, A. L. 2014. 'Standing Apart. On Time, Affect, and Discernment in Nordeste, Brazil'. In *Ethnographies of Youth and Temporality: Time Objectified*, A. L. Dalsgård, M. D. Frederiksen, S. Højlund Og and L. Meinert (eds). Philadelphia, PA: Temple University Press, p. 22.

Dalsgård, A. L. and Frederiksen, M. D. 2013. 'Out of Conclusion: On Recurrence and Open-Endedness in Life and Analysis'. *Social Analysis* 57(1): 50–63.

Den Uyl, D. and Griswold, C. L. 1996. 'Adam Smith on Friendship and Love'. *Review of Metaphysics* 49(3): 609–32.

Desai, A. and Killick, E. 2010. *The Ways of Friendship: Anthropological Perspectives*. New York: Berghahn Books.

Gay Y Blasco, P. and de la Cruz Hernández, L. 2012. 'Friendship, Anthropology'. *Anthropology and Humanism* 37(1): 1–14.

Grindal, B. and Salamone, F. 1995. *Bridges to Humanity: Narratives on Anthropology and Friendship*. Prospect Heights, IL: Waveland Press.

Hastrup, K. 2009. *Mellem mennesker. En grundbog i antropologisk forskningsetik*. Copenhagen: Hans Reitzel.

Leavitt, J. 1996. 'Meaning and Feeling in the Anthropology of Emotions'. *American Ethnologist* 23(3): 514–39.

Ochs, E. and Capps, L. 1996. 'Narrating the Self'. *Annual Review of Anthropology* 25: 19–43.

Patai, D. 1991. 'U.S. Academics and Third World Women: Is Ethical Research Possible?' In *Women's Words: The Feminist Practice of Oral History*, S. B. Gluck and D. Patai (eds). London: Routledge, pp. 137–53.

Rabinow, P. 1977. *Reflections on Fieldwork in Morocco*. Berkeley: University of California Press.

Ridler, K. 1996. 'If Not in Words: Shared Practical Activity and Friendship in Fieldwork'. In *Things as They are: New Directions in Phenomenological Anthropology*, M. Jackson (ed.). Bloomington and Indianapolis: Indiana University Press.

Smith, A. [1790] 2006. *The Theory of Moral Sentiments*. 6th edition. São Paulo: MetaLibri. Available online: https://www.ibiblio.org/ml/libri/s/SmithA_MoralSentiments_p.pdf (accessed 11 July 2018).

Stacey, J. 1991. ' Can There Be a Feminist Ethnography?' In *Women's Words: The Feminist Practice to Oral History*, S. B. Gluck and D. Patai (eds). London: Routledge.

Throop, J. 2012. 'Moral Sentiments'. In *A Companion to Moral Anthropology*, D. Fassin (ed.). Chichester: John Wiley & Sons.

Wolcott, H. F. 1999. *Ethnography: A Way of Seeing*. London: AltaMira Press.

Zigon, J. 2009. 'Within a Range of Possibilities: Moral and Ethics in Social Life'. *Ethnos* 74(2): 25.

2

His Father Came to Him in His Sleep:
An Essay on Enlightenment, Mortalities and
Immortalities in Iceland

Arnar Árnason

Introduction: Visitation from beyond the Great Mist

His father came to him in his sleep. They were at the time somewhere over the North Atlantic, on a flight to New York from Iceland.[1] It was a journey he had made many times before, once in reverse as a permanent and triumphant return home having established his scientific reputation in the United States; a return made to establish one of the most remarkable scientific and economic endeavours in Iceland's recent history (Pálsson 2007). His father had come to relate to him a poem: a poem amounting to a reflection on the state of their 'nation', its language, its culture, its past and its future. It was a poem he was to share, along with a description of its provenance, with their 'nation' a few days later in an opinion piece in one of its leading newspapers. On the poem and the authority of his father, he built arguments for his particular vision of the immediate and more long-term future of their 'nation', the possibility, even, of its survival.[2]

He at least was over the Atlantic; the whereabouts of his father were somewhat more mysterious. For his father had not bought a ticket for this plane, had not presented his identification papers or undergone the security checks at the airport in Iceland. For his father had been dead for more than twenty years. Such visits as this, visitations from beyond the Great Mist (*móðan mikla*) as the locals might have it, are commonplace in Iceland. Sometimes they occur while the host is awake but more often they happen in dreams (Heijnen 2005: 117 onwards), or at least when the host is in a limbo of one sort or another. To be in a dreamy sleep on a plane travelling over a vast ocean, is of course to occupy a place of significant ambiguity, a place of double liminality, if not a non-place (Augé 1995). The general ethnographic literature speaks of dreaming of the deceased (Malinowski 1916; Hollan 1995; Lohmann 2000; Heijnen 2005; Niehaus 2005; Stewart and Strathern 2003; Traphagan 2003). It appears that these dreams are, in Iceland and elsewhere, understood by many to be real, to be experientially of the same quality even as waking life. The dreams often reveal the special knowledge the deceased have access to and communicate to the living in dreams, a process of communication in which a certain collapse of time seems to happen.[3] The sharing of accounts of these visits in a relatively public forum is a reasonably common occurrence in Iceland, something that might happen over a morning cup of coffee, for example. Still, not many would take to the national press to do their sharing. Then again the messages received from beyond the mist are not always of such general 'national' importance as in this case and not everyone is in the position, or of the inclination, to intervene so publically in matters of the 'nation's' future, as the host on this occasion was.

Professor Kári Stefánsson, founder and CEO of the Iceland-based biotechnology company DeCode, is undeniably one of the foremost scientists in Iceland, irrespective of which of the common scales for measuring such achievements is used. With possibly one or two exceptions, he is also the best known Icelandic scientist worldwide. More importantly in the presence context, Kári is one of the most prominent scientists in the country to engage in public political debates specifically as a scientist. During the summer of 2016, in the run up to general elections in Iceland, he challenged the finance minister of the country to a televised debate on the future of the national health service. This was the culmination of a campaign, calling on the government to fund the health system properly that Kári organized, collecting in the process over 80,000 signatures in a country of less than 350,000 inhabitants. By this Kári, certainly in my view, cemented his status as the most important, the most telling and the most insightful political opposition in Iceland. In his interventions, Kári draws on his background in medicine. In seeing his science as having very clearly a role in improving his society and the lives of its members, and often as the source of his authority in political debates, Kári thus embodies in many ways more powerfully than anyone else, the legacy of the Enlightenment in Iceland.

Given this status it is interesting that Kári would openly rest his argument for what is most important for the immediate future of his 'nation', on a poem received in a dream on a plane from his deceased father. How – to ask as Barbara Johnson (1994: 38) did – does this haunting signify? How does a ghostly intervention in matters of such importance mean? (see Gordon 2008). I think that we should take this ghostly appearance seriously. Anthropologists are of course only too familiar with the mixing of such things that Western thought is oft the times said to want to separate, and separate crucially through a temporal logic: mythos and logos, hauntings and science (Gordon 2008). To simply point out the coexistence of the two would surely be to state what anthropologists now take as blindingly obvious. However, the origin of the poem that Kári shared and his purpose in sharing it do not simply point to the coexistence of two different 'world views'. The poem was offered to claim authority in a hugely important debate, one that Kári himself, despite all his well-known humour, clearly took deadly seriously. In speaking of haunting, Avery Gordon explains: 'What's distinctive about haunting is that it is an animated state in which a repressed or unresolved social violence is making itself known, sometimes very directly, sometimes more obliquely' (2008: xvi). Gordon goes on to add:

> Haunting raises specters, and it alters the experience of being in time, the way
> we separate the past, the present, and the future. These specters or ghosts appear

when the trouble they represent and symptomize is no longer being contained or repressed or blocked from view. The ghost, as I understand it, is not the invisible or some ineffable excess. The whole essence, if you can use that word, of a ghost is that it has a real presence and demands its due, your attention. (2008: xvi)

In what follows I draw on Gordon's insight into hauntings. My immediate task, if you like, is to seek to understand how the foremost scientist of the 'nation' could in part at least rest his argument in such an important matter as the future of his 'nation' on such a ghostly source. Seeking that understanding, I suggest, takes us to the way in which haunting 'alters the experience of being in time, the way we separate the past, the present, and the future', as Gordon has it. Appreciating the importance of this alteration, in turn, requires a reflection on the legacy of the Enlightenment in Iceland. In doing that I am aided by well-known works on speech, or voice, and writing, or text, by Jacques Derrida (1978), Michel de Certeau (1984) and Barbara Johnson (1994). The tension between voice and text draws me to Marilyn Ivy's (1998) anthropological interpretation of Jacques Lacan's 'thing'. Through this discussion I seek to illuminate the ambiguity of the Enlightenment ambition in Iceland. This discussion, I hope, may in turn offer insights into the entangled relations between anthropology and the Enlightenment, anthropology meaning the enlightened attempt to explain human social affairs that necessarily has adopted the unenlightened at the heart of human sociality. However, before proceeding I need to begin by saying something about the Enlightenment in Iceland.

The Enlightenment in Iceland

In Icelandic the Enlightenment is *upplýsingin* or *upplýsingaröldin* if referring specifically to the time period of the age of Enlightenment (Sigurðsson 2010: 372–3). The Icelandic here is very clearly drawn from the Danish *oplysning* and has almost exactly the same meaning as the English word enlightenment. The connotations are of light, *lýsing* meaning light, and of illumination, *lýsa upp*, to throw light on. To be enlightened is to be *upplýstur*, as the dictionary form goes. Even so, probably the most common use of the term in contemporary Iceland is in the plural *upplýsingar*. Here the meaning is somewhat different. *Upplýsingar* is information in the most everyday and mundane sense. This shift in meaning is interesting and important and it may come back to haunt another paper, but not this chapter.

When *upplýsingin* arrived in the eighteenth century, Iceland was part of the Kingdom of Denmark and its arrival and its spread throughout the country, according to the leading Icelandic historian on the Enlightenment, was initially largely driven by the Danish authorities (Sigurðsson 2010: 374). Even so, it is important to note that Icelanders themselves engaged enthusiastically in the effort of enlightening and referred to *upplýsingin* as a cultural and social movement. As part of Enlightenment efforts, expeditions were sent to investigate and map 'the island in the north' with a particular emphasis on achieving a clear overview of its resources and the possibilities of their exploitation. For this purpose, and in this spirit, two Icelanders, Eggert

Ólafsson and Bjarni Pálsson, were given the mission to explore the country in the mid-eighteenth century, their account of their travels being published in Danish in 1772. The purpose of mapping resources in such a way was of course the possible enrichment of the kingdom itself but simultaneously the hope of improving the living conditions, the health and well-being of the island's inhabitants, most of whom suffered terribly from persistent hunger and frequent plagues. It was understood by the government, historians have later observed, that the strength of the state depended on the vitality of its population (Björn Þorsteinsson and Bergsteinn Jónsson 1991: 246) in what Michel Foucault, of course, later termed biopolitics (Foucault 1991).

The efforts of the Danish authorities were supported by Icelandic officials, themselves almost always educated in Denmark. Their aim was similarly to improve the general level of education in the country largely, but not exclusively, for practical purposes. This involved the printing and publication of books on improvements in agriculture in particular. Of central importance here is the book *Atli* (the Icelandic version of the name Attila) written by the country vicar Björn Halldórsson and published in 1780. The book was distributed for free to farmers in Iceland with the support of the Danish king and was widely read for its educational merit but also because it was considered an entertaining read. The book takes the form of a dialogue between a young farmer, Atli, and an older, experienced and importantly unnamed farmer. Atli asks the older farmer questions while the older farmer dispenses advice, admonishes and encourages. Unlike Kári's father, this voice is unnamed but like him clearly speaks with the accumulated wisdom of the past. The older farmer's is literally the voice of experience, a voice from the accumulated past that points towards changes and improvements for the future that Atli, standing in for all young farmers of the country, can hope to reap for himself and his country if he heeds the advice he is given.

Publications aimed at securing improvements in agriculture were accompanied by treatises of philosophical interest and scientific merit, most often European classics translated into Icelandic rather than works written originally in Icelandic. These were mostly printed and published by the same enterprise as the book *Atli*. A case in point here is another country vicar, Jón Þorláksson, who lived at the church farm Bægisá in the north of Iceland. There, almost as far away from any cosmopolitan centre as it was possible to be, he translated both John Milton's *Paradise Lost* and Alexander Pope's *Essay on Man*, in addition to writing his own poetry. In his translations, Þorláksson looked back to the form of the ancient Eddic poems, the so-called *fornyrðislag* (*forn* meaning ancient) rather than to the poetic language of his day. This resurrection of an old and long unused poetic form was an attempt to capture the language of the works he translated. At the same time this going back to the old poetic language in an ode of optimism for the future, such as an *Essay on Man*, is important. While the Eddic poems feature the voices of the Nordic gods, their allies and their adversaries, they themselves of course do not have an author; their source is unnamed.

As elsewhere, the Enlightenment in Iceland entailed a certain expectation of, even at times demand for, progress. Part of this process were attempts to measure progress, already evident amongst Icelandic historians at the time, that drew contrasts and comparisons with descriptions of the country during the time of settlement and before it became subject to a foreign power (see Sigurðsson 2010). The efforts to secure progress were frequently undermined by natural catastrophes – volcanic eruptions, drift ice and cold summers, plagues – which meant, for example, that by 1786 the population of Iceland had fallen to 38,000 people, 10,000 fewer than it had been a few years before. In this context the perceived need for economic progress, for progress in terms of the health and well-being of the population, was great, progress deemed crucial for the future of the nation. At the same time, it is important to note that the demands for progress were rarely, if ever, directed at the social organization or the governing structures of the country (Björn Þorsteinsson and Bergsteinn Jónsson 1991). Rather the improvements that were hoped for, expected and even demanded, had to do with economic production, trade, consumption, education and health, to be achieved without social change as such.

Serious and sustained demands for a political change, specifically political independence from Denmark, only became prevalent as the Enlightenment spirit was further infused by the German romanticism that arrived in Iceland via Denmark itself around the mid-eighteenth century (Sigurðsson 2010). I say infused because it may be unwise to draw too sharp a distinction between the Enlightenment and national romanticism when it came to Iceland; indeed a significant degree of continuity is evident between them (Sigurðsson 2010). Even so it is usual to mark the arrival of national romanticism and the first clear battle cry for independence at the publication of the poem *Ísland* by Jónas Hallgrímsson in 1835. Jónas was one of the four so-called Fjölnismenn who published the journal *Fjölnir* for a few years from their base in Copenhagen. The poem *Ísland*, with a simple Eddic form and, at the time, unusually without rhyme exalted simultaneously the beauty of Iceland and the virtue of the characters whose stories are told in the *Icelandic sagas*, the (almost exclusively) men who found and settled the island. The poem asks pointedly what has happened to the heroism of old, what has become of Iceland in the course of its history, its fame of old, its freedom, its virtues. The poem appears to call for a future that is effectively a return to the past, the past as depicted in the *Sagas*. This signals an important aspect regarding the construction of history in Iceland, an issue I will come to shortly, but for now I would like to make a few further points regarding Jónas, the best-loved poet in all of Icelandic, as he has been called, the man whose birthday is now celebrated as the day of the Icelandic language. *Ísland* was one of many poems that Jónas wrote that were informed by romantic sentiments often of the nationalistic sort. Even so Jónas was also a natural scientist, arguably the first Icelandic geologist, who explored Iceland in as systematic a fashion as anyone had done to this point (see Jakobsson 2009) and in that carried on the Enlightenment endeavour in many respects. The first mineral collection from Iceland was carried out by Jónas in the mid-nineteenth century, brought by him to Denmark and lay there forgotten until the 1970s. Finally, I would like to note that Jónas was closely associated with the Enlightenment figure Jón Þorláksson mentioned before who schooled Jónas initially and supported him, at least morally if not financially, to seek the kind of education unusual for a poor farmer's son, moreover fatherless from an early age, in nineteenth-century Iceland.

The past, the future, of the 'nation': Voice

The themes of hauntings and voice have appeared a few times in this chapter largely without their relevance and their importance having been made explicit. What is the relationship between hauntings and voice, and what can that relationship tell us about the legacy of the Enlightenment in Iceland and the relationship between the Enlightenment and anthropology?

Let me start to address these questions more squarely by recalling that hauntings, as Gordon notes, call into question the ordinary ordering of the past, present and the future (2008: xvi). Ghosts challenge notions of temporal linearity in particular, of course, around life and death. That boundary between life and death is, furthermore, relevant to voice and writing. Barbara Johnson reminds us of the associations often drawn in Western thought between speech and life, on one hand, written language and death, on the other (1994: 18), associations that animated much of the work of Jacques Derrida (1978). Writing on deconstruction and psychoanalysis, Maud Ellmann recalls the logocentrism that Derrida claimed as the founding stone of Western metaphysics, a centrism that repressed writing in favour of speech, or voice (2000: 211). Writing, Derrida argued, has always been perceived as dangerous because it betokens absence in the same way that speech betokens presence. In speech the speaker must be present to the interlocutor; in writing, the writer may be absent from the reader; speech is associated with the breath of life, writing with the waste of death, the corpse of words (Ellmann 2000: 211).

The writer, Ellmann adds paraphrasing James Joyce, is necessarily 'a ghost by absence [… or] a ghost by death from the moment that the written word embarks upon its independent odyssey' (2000: 211). Johnson (1994) draws on Derrida's rereading of Paul de Man's essay on 'Autobiography as de-facement'. The 'essay analyses the structure of autobiography as a form of prosopopoeia, the fiction of a voice from beyond the grave' (Johnson 1994: 20). What is of interest here is the 'reversibility that in seeming to bring the dead back to life, threatens to strike the living dead' (Johnson 1994: 20). Johnson evokes de Man himself to this effect:

> The dominant figure of the epitaphic or autobiographical discourse is … the prosopopoeia, the fiction of the voice-from-beyond-the-grave … Such chiasmic figures, crossing the conditions of death and life with the attributes of speech and silence … evoke the latent threat that inhabits prosopopoeia, namely that by making the death [sic] speak, … the living are struck dumb, frozen in their own death. (de Man 1984: 75–8; quoted in Johnson 1994: 20–1)

As it turns out, says Johnson, the association between speech and life, the written word and death, cannot hold, as Derrida famously demonstrated (1994: 20). And if that is the case, then what is the haunting that is going on here and what does it have to do with voice?

It is not overstating things to say that the financial collapse, *hrunið* as it is referred to locally, has dominated, not haunted, Icelandic politics and general public discussions since the autumn of 2008. The financial consequences, the monetary restraints that *hrunið* necessitated, is the context in which Kári relates his father's poetry to their 'nation'. The Icelandic state, practically bankrupt as a consequence of the 'meltdown' (Pálsson and Durrenberger 2015) of the country's financial sector, was in the years after the collapse under tremendous fiscal strain. It has been widely agreed in the country that the health service, a significant part of public expenses, had suffered in particular. This is the point that Kári Stefánsson made. In a piece he wrote initially in the *Morgunblaðið* on 10 September 2013, he lists the various non-health related investments made by the then outgoing government. This includes a house for Nordic studies in Iceland that the government had started work on. This, he argues, has happened despite the government's general lack of funds that, he says, has plagued investment in the healthcare system. Evoking a famous question asked by the central character, Jón Hreggviðsson, in Halldór Laxness's celebrated novel *Iceland's Bell*, Kári's piece is titled: 'When does a man (government) kill a man?' His claim was that disinvestment in the healthcare system was reaching such a level that people were dying unnecessarily; people whose lives it should be possible to save were dying because of lack of funding in the healthcare system while funds were being made available build a house to store and study old manuscripts.

On 17 September 2013, Guðrún Nordal,[4] wrote a piece in the same paper as Kári had written in a week before. Without Kári or his article ever being mentioned it is clear that this is the context in which Guðrún writes. Indeed she starts by acknowledging the strain placed upon the healthcare system in Iceland following the collapse. However, she goes on to make a plea for the importance of other investment as well, specifically in the house intended to be the centre of Nordic studies in Iceland. Guðrún is the director of the Árni Magnússon Institute. It is named after the seventeenth-century Icelandic manuscript collector, generally credited with rescuing priceless medieval Saga and Eddic poem manuscripts that were gradually disintegrating in plagued and poverty-stricken Iceland. Árni Magnússon is a character in *Iceland's Bell*. Jón Hreggviðsson's life is saved by Árni's lover who frees Jón so he can carry a message to Árni. Árni forsakes his lover in order to dedicate himself to the rescue of the manuscripts, their personal happiness sacrificed for a greater good. Guðrún argues that while investing in healthcare is important, investment in the house where the priceless manuscripts will be kept and researched is vital. Icelandic, the language, she says is not a luxury. At a time of tremendous and rapid technological change, the language will not survive without the research that takes place in the institute. The Saga manuscripts, moreover, are, she says, the very embodiment of the 'nation's' proclaimed link with the past, the material manifestation of the 'nation's' uniqueness and hence the key to its future, its very continued existence.

This, finally, is what has prompted the visit from Kári's father. While Kári makes it clear that he agrees with Guðrún about the importance of the Icelandic language, he can not agree with her that the future of that language will depend on the building of a house, even if that house is there to keep the manuscripts save and studied. The language will survive and change irrespective of a house, he says. It lives in its use, by poets and writers, plumbers and farmers. The language will survive and change even if the institute is closed for many years. The manuscripts, he says, can wait. They are good at waiting, used to waiting. Here Kári relates the visit from his father, with which

I started this chapter. He reminds his readers of his father's love for and skill in using the Icelandic language. And before relating the poem itself Kári tells us that there are clearly some benefits in being dead, although overall it can not be a desired position. Even so, his father had clearly not only read the piece by Guðrún but also knew that Kári was going to write a response, even before Kári knew so himself. This is a voice from beyond the great mist that can speak of the future.

Hauntings and voice, again

Gordon (2008) describes haunting as an animated state in which a repressed or unresolved social violence makes itself known. She adds: 'The ghost, as I understand it, is not the invisible or some ineffable excess. The whole essence, if you can use that word, of a ghost is that it has a real presence and demands its due, your attention.' Death as a consequence of an underfunded healthcare system may perhaps be taken as an example of such social violence, not least seeing that its effects are likely to be felt differently by different social groups. In this, I might add, Kári, maybe unintentionally, invites a recall of those episodes of his 'nation' when it faced near extinction, as mentioned above. In local discourses the repeated catastrophes that led to the near disappearance of the 'nation' are usually attributed primarily to natural causes, volcanic eruptions, drift ice, the arrival of virulent contagious diseases. The Enlightenment endeavour in Iceland was not least to equip the country to meet such disasters. Rarely, but occasionally, are the catastrophes attributed to the violence of foreign oppression and exploitation or the very unequal and oppressive indigenous social system. Their violence tends to be repressed. Drawing attention to them takes us back to the voice.

In making his claims for how best to map the course for the future of the 'nation' Kári clearly works the distinctions between voice or speech and text. Speech is living language that will survive and change and even thrive irrespective of whether the dead language as recorded in books and manuscripts is studied now or later. Interestingly, then, Kári draws some of his authority here from the spoken words of his deceased father, the living speech of the dead, whose mastery over the language, and hence his authority, is demonstrated by his skills in the ancient arts of conjuring up a poem more or less on the spot. So here again we have the 'voice of experience', the one who can tell us that language will survive, an institution dedicated to its study or not. The nameless but experienced farmer in *Atli* has become a named figure, and not just any named figure. Stefán Jónsson, Kári's father, was himself a well-known public figure, something of a national treasure in Iceland, a man spoken of admiringly, lovingly. A politician and a writer, amongst many other things, he was famed for his humour and for his grasp of and love for the Icelandic language. Such grasp secured immense esteem in those days, to some extent still does. Stefán was also a much-loved radio broadcaster. He was thus experienced in appearing as a voice from, if not from beyond, the mist. Through his voice he was an absent, disembodied presence in many people's lives in Iceland until his death. He is a figure that is likely to evoke a sense of nostalgia in many in Iceland, as Guðrún Nordal noted in her response to Kári, turning Stefán's place in the heart of his 'nation' against the case his son was making.[5]

In his book *Ignorance*, Milan Kundera has noted that the 'Greek word for "*return*" is nostos. *Algos* means "suffering". So nostalgia is the suffering caused by an unappeased yearning to return' (1993: 3). Kundera adds that in Icelandic, one of the oldest languages in Europe, the equivalent word is *heimþrá*, literally the longing for home. Michel de Certeau asserted at some point that 'all returns to the past are a return to the voice' (quoted in Ivy 1998: 98). In *The Practice of Everyday Life* de Certeau makes 'the signal observation that an epistemological crisis arose as the view that all language and consequently all meaning originated with God was steadily eroded by sixteenth-century scholarship which by exposing the agency of authors in transforming and disseminating God's word eventually revoked the foundational resemblance between words and things' (Buchanan 2000: 77). With the rise of printing technology and the following proliferation of texts, which made the Enlightenment possible, a new question was asked: 'Who *wrote* the text?' (2000: 77). When God is known to be the author of a text, a sacred text of course, that text can be taken at its word, 'it has only to be read and understood, not made' (2000: 77). When the certainty of the identity of the author has been 'destroyed, then so too is the value of the word it expresses' (2000: 77). Hence the enormous importance of the question that according to de Certeau came to define the Classical Age: 'who speaks when there is no longer a divine Speaker who founds every particular enunciation?' (de Certeau 1984: 156).

It is, as Ian Buchanan points out, important to 'appreciate the nature of the crisis' here (2000: 77). If God 'is the undisputed source of all order and authority in the social world' then the loss of his 'credibility will be chaos and disorder' (2000: 77). A 'vacuum appears' and where 'once a mysterious and divine Other had served as the basis of all meaning, now there was only others – that is, man, a poor babbling substitute for the Supreme Being' (2000: 77). This, according to de Certeau, was felt as a loss, rather than liberation. But:

> Fortunately, the very instrument of the dissolution of the sacred text, writing, also provided the means of its replacement. Since writing is creation, and creation the province of God, writers occupy His place, or so it came to be thought by seventeenth-century scholars. And so the subject was born. The answer that was finally settled upon (which in the eighteenth-century served as the central moral and ethical pillar of the Enlightenment) was: it is the individual subject who speaks. (Buchanan 2000: 77; see de Certeau 1984: 157)

According to this, the identification between individual subject and voice is a relatively recent development, and it is a development that formed the pillar of the Enlightenment. The association between the individual subject and voice is, moreover, clearly a political development (de Certeau 1984: 157), part of what John and Jean Comaroff (1992: 26) call 'the biographical illusion'. They describe this illusion as 'a modernist fantasy about society and selfhood according to which everyone is, potentially, in control of his or her destiny in a world made by the actions of autonomous "agents"'. However, that association between individual subject and voice is not straightforward. The Comaroffs invite a questioning of the association between the voice and the subject and so I might ask now: who speaks when an old Icelandic cultural form, the short somewhat humorous poem, is used by a ghost of twenty odd years to comment on matters of grave contemporary national interest? Johnson, I have already noted, speaks of how the voice from beyond the grave signals a certain 'reversibility that in seeming to bring the dead back to life, threatens to strike the living dead' (1994: 20). Derrida's (1978) conclusion was of course that the distinction between speech and text and the association between speech and life, the written word and death, do not hold (see Johnson 1994: 20; Ellmann 2000). Stefán expresses his conviction of the survival of living spoken Icelandic through the dead form of the poem that is then related in writing by his son. Kári evokes the words of a character from the novel by Halldór Laxness, a character that has some historical foundation, to express the gravity of the consequences of the government's funding priorities. The old farmer that speaks to Atli at the outset of the Icelandic Enlightenment, is nameless, the embodiment of the accumulated wisdom of the nation, at least its male half.

Hauntings, voice and the language of genes

When Kári returned triumphantly and permanently to Iceland, as mentioned at the start of this chapter, he did so to establish DeCode Genetics, a genetic research and biotechnology company. This was in the mid-1990s. It is the success of this company that has secured Kári's status as one of the foremost scientists in the country. The purpose of the DeCode project was to research the possible genetic causes of common diseases by running together extensive genealogical records, genetic material acquired from tissue samples and health records kept by the Icelandic National Health Service (see Gísli Pálsson 2007). A number of characteristics were said to make Iceland a particularly suitable place for such research activity. Of particular importance to this chapter is the fact that the country had been settled initially by quite a homogenous group of people, and the further reductions in the genetic variation of the population brought about by natural disasters as mentioned before. The trauma of Icelandic history was in this context an advantage.

However, that trauma can only be an advantage because of further linkages. In communicating the work of DeCode, Kári has drawn on the association commonly made between genes and language. According to this idea, genes are to be understood as instructions written in a transmissible language that can be read. In an interview with the newspaper *Morgunblaðið* on 24 November 1996, Stefánsson began with a revealing reference. He said: 'In the beginning in the Holy Bible was the word, but in later editions it was forgotten that the word, the information, was written in DNA, in the genetic material. This is the information that is transferred from one generation to the next' (Pálmadóttir 1996). *Morgunblaðið* later published an article entitled 'The Search for the Genes' (3 October 1998). Here it says that: 'Alone the letters [of the DNA] tell us nothing but if we can read the words that they form (genes) and the sentences (chromosomes) that the words make then there is the prospect of understanding the language of genes' (Sverrisdóttir 1998). In Iceland such associations have particular power as the discussion of the debate between Kári and Guðrún is evidence of (see Pálsson 2007). As Guðrún suggested, Icelandic identity, independence, history and culture are almost unthinkable without the Icelandic language. Here then, genes, are established as a particularly powerful link between the past, the present and the future. DNA is the ancestors talking through the abilities and the ailments of their descendants, but talking primarily and importantly by foretelling the future, the likelihood of the emergence of common diseases. As such the DNA is a mechanism for collapsing time, guaranteeing a return to the origin.

The Icelandic 'thing'

Van den Abbeele (1991) writes on the importance of the journey as a metaphor in Western thought. He discusses in particular the fantasy commonly attached to the idea of the journey that suggests a return to the home as it was when the journey began. Here Abbeele draws a link with how Western metaphysics has made presence, as in the subject who originates speech, its starting point. *Heimþrá*, the Icelandic word mentioned by Kundera, means longing for home. When Iceland celebrated political independence from Denmark in 1944 the then prime minister claimed: 'Icelanders, we have arrived home. We are a free nation.' Historian Guðmundur Hálfdanarson remarks that in this formulation, the independent nation-state is 'not primarily a political form but a home where the nation can find peace in its own country' (Hálfdanarson 2000; cited in Helgason 2003: 17). Time had been collapsed, return to the origin achieved. If time has been collapsed, if the origin has been returned to, then that signals something other than a return to the past as such. Rather it signals a return to something beyond the past. It signals perhaps a return to what Slavoj Žižek has called the 'national thing'. Žižek, drawing on Jacques Lacan (Ivy 1998: 94), describes the national thing as 'the particular nexus of national identification that is organized around what he calls "enjoyment"' (Ivy 1998: 94). Žižek's seeks here to understand what cements a political community. He says:

> What holds together a given community can never be reduced simply to the point of symbolic national identification: A shared relationship with *the other's* enjoyment is always implied. Structured by means of fantasies, this thing-enjoyment-is what is at stake when we speak of the menace to our 'way of life' presented by the other [...] National [...] identities are determined by a series of contradictory properties. They appear to us as 'our thing' [...] as something accessible only to us, as something 'they', the others, cannot grasp; nonetheless, 'our thing' is something constantly menaced by 'them.' (Žižek; quoted in Ivy 1998: 94)

Not only is the 'thing' simultaneously beyond the others' grasp while always under threat from them: if we try to specify the 'thing' we end up with tautologies or empty lists. The 'thing' cannot be 'reduced to those details themselves; there is something more that causes them to cohere into a nexus of identification and belief, into "our" national thing as a fantasy of shared enjoyment' (Ivy 1998: 95). In the debates reported on above, Guðrún Nordal makes of language the mysterious thing. It is a thing that has frequently been seen under threat from 'others', foreign influence in one form or another (Björnsdóttir 1989). At the moment when DeCode was made to appear the 'thing' was also seen to be at risk, and DeCode was accused of being on the verge of selling the 'soul' of Icelanders – their very essence, their genetic make-up – to foreign interests (Árnason and Simpson 2003). But this danger, be it to language or genes, is also the moment when the 'thing' appears as such, in the engagement with 'the other', and appears as always already at risk – as Ivy speaks of it with reference to Japan.

Conclusion

Anthropology emerged out of the Enlightenment as an effort to understand collective human affairs. At the heart of that endeavour was, has been, the conviction that enlightened sense could be made of human affiliations. At the same time the continued relevance of anthropology, its claim to authority, has rested on the assumption of an unenlightened darkness at the heart of human associating, darkness that anthropology took as its task to illuminate. Many have of course questioned and criticized such an anthropology in recent years. Still its legacy lingers. The account of the Enlightenment in Iceland, past and present, was offered here to draw attention to the contradictions between Enlightenment and its residues. The haunting that this chapter began with speaks to a trauma that appeared to put the Icelandic 'nation' at risk. The haunting speaks to the importance of Enlightenment endeavours to secure the future of the 'nation'. At the same time the haunting speaks of the danger that Enlightenment endeavours place the immortality of the 'nation' and the 'Icelandic thing' in. The uncertain places of speech, voice, language and genes, I suggested, speak of the tension in the Enlightenment endeavour. Unveiling the genetic make-up of an individual exposes the risks they carry within even as such unveiling may make possible interventions to counteract those risks. Unveiling the origin of the 'nation' through its genetic history, or its common identification through language, risks exposing it to all the 'others' that make up the 'nation', putting its 'thing' fundamentally at risk. The prosopopoeia, the voice from beyond the grave, that I began this chapter with, spoke the living language of the past while speaking of the future. Even so, it could only do so through the dead form of the poem that would secure its authority. In post-Enlightenment times, the 'nation', the 'national thing', is simultaneously dead and alive. The darkness at the unenlightened heart of human associations is simultaneously revealed and necessarily obscured. Perhaps the future depends on it remaining so.

Acknowledgements

I would like to thank my brother Ómar Árnason for his help, and the editors of the book Huon Wardle and Nigel Rapport for their insightful comments and their patience. This chapter began as a presentation at a gathering organized by Bob Simpson and Rachel Douglas-Jones. The section on DeCode draws heavily on work I did some time ago with Bob Simpson. Indeed most of the ideas there are Bob's. My friends and colleagues Tanya Argounova-Low, Nancy Wachowich and Gro Ween have help enormously with the writing.

Notes

1   Kári Stefánsson, 'Íslenska'. *Morgunblaðið*, 19 September 2013.
2   Ibid.
3   I am indebted to Donald Lyon for this point.
4   'Íslenskan er ekki lúxusmál', *Morgunblaðið*, 17 September 2013.
5   Guðrún Nordal, 'Draumur og veruleiki', *Morgunblaðið*, 20 September 2013.

References

Augé, M. 1995. *Non-places: An Introduction to Anthropology of Supermodernity*. London: Verson.

Árnason, A. and Simpson, B. 2003. 'Refractions through Culture: Making Sense of the New Genomics in Iceland'. *Ethnos* 68(4): 533–53.

Buchanan, I. 2000. *Michel de Certeau: Cultural Theorist*. London: Sage.

Björnsdóttir, I. D. 1989. 'Public View and Private Voices'. In *The Anthropology of Iceland*, E. P. Durrenberger and G. Pálsson (eds). Iowa: Iowa University Press, pp. 98–118.

Comaroff, J. and Comaroff, J. 1992. *Ethnography and the Historical Imagination*. Oxford: Westview Press.

de Certeau, M. 1984. *The Practice of Everyday Life*, S. Rendell (trans.). Berkeley: University of California Press.

Derrida, J. 1978. *Writing and Difference*. Chicago: University of Chicago Press.

Ellmann, M. 2000. 'Deconstruction and Psychoanalysis'. In *Deconstructions: A User's Guide*, N. Royle (ed.). Basingstoke: Palgrave, pp. 211–37.

Foucault, M. 1991. 'Governmentality'. In *The Foucault Effect: Studies in Governmentality*, G. Burchell and P. Miller (eds). London: Harvester Wheatsheaf.

Gordon, A. F. 2008. *Ghostly Matter: Hauntings and the Sociological Imagination*. Minneapolis: University of Minnesota Press.

Hálfdanarson, G. 2000. *Íslenska Þjóðríkið: Uppruni og Endimörk*. Reykjavík: Hið íslenska bókmenntafélag.

Heijnen, A. 2005. 'Dream Sharing in Iceland'. PhD Thesis, Aarhus University, Aarhus.

Helgason, J. K. 2003. *Ferðalok. Skýrsla Handa Akademíu*. Reykjavík: Bjartur.

Hollan, D. 1995. 'To the Afterworld and Back: Mourning and Dreams of the Dead among the Toraja'. *Ethos* 23(4): 424–36.

Ivy, M. 1998. 'Mourning the Japanese Thing'. In *In Near Ruins: Cultural Theory at the End of the Century*, N. B. Dirks (ed.). Minneapolis: University of Minnesota Press, pp. 93–118.

Jakobsson, S. P. 2009. 'Steinasöfn Jónasar Hallgrímssonar' [The minerals collections of Jónas Hallgrímsson]. *Náttúrufræðingurinn* 77(3–4): 89–106.

Johnson, B. 1994. *The Wake of Deconstruction*. Oxford: Blackwell.

Kundera, M. 1993. *Ignorance*, L. Asher (trans.). Bath: Chivers Press.

Lohmann, R. 2000. 'The Role of Dreams in Religious Enculturation among the Asabano of Papua New Guinea'. *Ethos* 28(1): 75–102.

Malinowski, B. 1916. 'Baloma; Spirits of the Dead in the Trobriand Islands'. *Journal of the Royal Anthropological Institute of Great Britain and Ireland* 46(1): 353–430.

Niehaus, I. 2005. 'Witches and Zombies of the South African Lowveld: Discourse, Accusations and Subjective Reality'. *Journal of the Royal Anthropological Institute* 11(2): 191–210.

Pálmadóttir, E. 1996. 'Lesið í erfðaefnið' [Reading DNA]. *Morgunblaðið* 88(270) (24 November): 18–21.

Pálsson, G. 2007. *Anthropology and the New Genetics*. Cambridge: Cambridge University Press.

Pálsson, G. and Durrenberger, P. (eds). 2015. *Gambling Debt: Iceland's Rise and Fall in the Global Economy*. Boulder: University of Colorado Press.

Sigurðsson, I. 2010. 'The Icelandic Enlightenment as an Extended Phenomenon'. *Scandinavian Journal of History* 35(4): 371–90.

Stefánsson, K. 2013. 'Hvenær drepur maður (ríkisstjórn) mann' [When does one (government) kill a man]. *Morgunblaðið* 101 (210) (10 September): 23.

Stewart, P. J. and Strathern, A. J. 2003. 'Dreaming and Ghosts among the Hagen and Duna of the Southern Highlands, Papua New Guinea'. In *Dream Travellers: Sleep Experiences and Culture in the Western Pacific*, R. Lohmann (ed.). New York: Palgrave Macmillan, pp. 43–59.

Sverrisdóttir, R. 1998. 'Leitin að genunum' [Searching for the genes]. *Morgunblaðið* 90(225) (4 October): B1 & B6-9.

Traphagan, J. 2003. 'Older Women as Caregivers and Ancestral Protection in Rural Japan'. *Ethnology* 42(2): 127–39.

van den Abbeele, G. 1991. *Travel as Metaphor: From Montaigne to Rousseau*. Minneapolis: University of Minnesota Press.

Þorsteinsson, B. and Jónsson, B. 1991. *Íslandssaga til okkar daga*. Reykjavík: Sögufélag.

3

On 'Bad Mind': Orienting Sentiment in Jamaican Street Life

Huon Wardle

Every one thinks that the sovereign stamp of human nature is imprinted in him, and that from it all others must take their rule.

Michel de Montaigne 1845: 336

'Bad Mind!' … This chapter listens to a cry of exasperation heard anywhere and everywhere on the 'street' and in the 'yard' in Jamaica. Not just 'bad mind', but 'sympathy', 'love' and 'righteousness' are everyday words in the language of moral sentiment for Jamaicans deployed to value people's intentions. Here, then, is a chance to open a conversation between contemporary Jamaican street life and Adam Smith's theory of sentiment. For, as with Smith on 'sympathy', these words used by Jamaicans assert universal claims about human motivation and as such they offer a key toward a pathology and eudaimonology of everyday life (Hickling and James 2012). Indeed, claims about 'bad mind' are so widely voiced on the urban 'corner' in the Caribbean that it is unsurprising that the verb 'to badmind' tends to be glossed as acting jealously or grudgefully (Sobo 1993; Lewis 2015). This is not a wrong translation – much of the time that is exactly what people do intend – but nor does it provide a full account for reasons I will lay out.

It can help initially to think of the 'bad mind' person as a type and as the opposite of the 'good' person whose actions are guided by 'sympathy'[1] and who is aiming at 'righteous livity' or 'living good' with others. Seen this way, 'bad mind' indicates a distinct principle of motivated 'antipathy' or 'negative empathy'. Note that, as in other forms of English, in Jamaican patois 'mind' as a verb can mean 'think of' and 'care for'. 'No pay 'im no *mind*!' is a common invocation in patois (the translation 'don't pay her/him any *attention*!' loses some meaning). The 'mind' put in question by 'bad mind' can be a person and it can be a thing; an antagonist or the toxic presence they intrude into someone's life. And, so from this perspective 'sympathy' and 'bad mind' present a local figural variation on the general dynamic that Smith describes where human beings try to understand each other. As Smith explains in his *Theory of Moral Sentiments*:

> Every faculty in one man is the measure [...] of the like faculty in another. I judge
> of your sight by my sight, of your ear by my ear, of your reason by my reason, of
> your resentment by my resentment, of your love by my love. I neither have nor can
> have, any other way of judging them. ([1790] 2006: 13)

Smith does not develop an account of how shared symbols or local categories such as
'bad mind' may mediate this power of individual judgement. However, it is evident in
the Jamaican case, to paraphrase his mirroring perspective, that I judge of your 'bad
mind' by my 'bad mind', your 'sympathy' by 'my sympathy' – indeed, how could it
be otherwise? Likewise, on the Jamaican street, as with Smith, the mind of the other
is understood and judged in moral, sympathetic and motivated terms. As the phrase
suggests, 'bad mind' is the interior passionate essence of another's psyche wilfully
imagined, mirrored and judged from my own perspective. Understood this way, this
kind of judgement must summon and reflect my own capacities – it is egomorphic
(Milton 2005). At the same time, it is important to heed Edith Stein when she shows
how empathy is an 'act of understanding [...] in which the "foreign will enters into
mine" and still remains that of the other' ([1917] 1989: 35). My structuring of the
other's view may be inevitably egomorphic, but this does not lessen the 'foreignness' of
this other's will as it appears in my imaginative recomposition. Indeed, the 'foreignness'
of the other's 'bad mind' is crucial to how 'bad mind' makes its presence felt.

Attending closely to the work 'bad mind' and kindred phrases do in Jamaican daily
life we find that they offer clues, then, to how people understand the human psyche
– subjectivity and intentionality – to function. A first issue to raise, caught up in 'bad
mind' (when understood as a 'theory of mind'), is the idea that people are possessed
of a unique psyche, character and of singular 'gifts' or powers (cf. Wardle 2018a). The
individual's 'gifts' can be 'good', 'bad' and they may be 'two-fold' or ambivalent (Wardle
2016a), but they are not a matter of indifference. Likewise, this individual should 'make
a noise' so that her unique moral voice can be heard (Reisman 1974): moral order is
always acoustically (and politically) in the making. In this way a given person's moral
potency, as it is imagined, remains an open question or an enigma (even to the person
in question) and this has socially iterative effects that I return to later.

It is important to mention a further connotation: the pre-eminence of personal
powers on the street is indicative of the weak articulation of 'sovereign power' or
governmentality in the dynamics of everyday life. Sure enough, there is awareness of
'pressure' from above ('downpression') that keeps people trapped in the cramped space
of their interactions, pressuring some 'sufferers' toward evil acts. However, it is rare to
hear anyone argue that the state could solve the inter-psychic conflicts involved. To
draw on a central Enlightenment philosophical distinction,[2] the might (*potentia*) of
the state is acknowledged but its right to command (*potestas*) is not. On the corner and
in the yard, the state and its actors (the police, the army) are viewed as an aggressive
and alien force and as an immediate outflow point for the greater transnational
'Babylon system' or 'shitstem' as Rastafarians have titled it. Para-state gang violence
and the perceived 'prevalence of injustice' over many decades (to use Smith's phrase[3]),
have continued to trigger recursive revisions of trust and distrust, both in the overall
'system' and interpersonally. This is a nation-state of fewer than three million people

where, in 2016, 1,354 people were murdered, predominantly young men.[4] All this has undoubtedly invigorated a local stereotype of interpersonal 'bad mind' as somehow epidemic in Jamaican social life – 'we Jamaican are bad mind people!' – while simultaneously further erasing expectations of government by consent. However, the uses of violence and its blurred legitimacy in Jamaica is not an issue this chapter will pursue (it has been very extensively commented on both by anthropologists and others, though perhaps often in ways that confirm rather than disaggregate stereotypes (Wardle 2002: 258; Thomas 2011; James 2015).

What will concern us here is a puzzle both these features raise concerning the moral sentiment and moral powers of the individual as she affects those around her. The moral *potentia* of the individual is strongly acknowledged – 'You is a Power', people say categorically (see Wardle 2016a: 12) – but the character of their *potestas*, the 'righteousness' of someone's sentiments, always has a fractal and uncertain quality since it can break down reputationally under the gaze of others and their accusations of 'bad mind' (inter alia). Nonetheless, as in any social setting, moral sentiments and moral claims assert the possibility of order in a situation of recognizable disorder.

So, to grasp the fuller meaning of 'bad mind' and 'sympathy' we need to recognize how these terms are used to index and assign personal powers to individual others. But in what does this potence and *potestas* of the individual consist? Where do these powers come from to begin with and how are they shown? These are ideas that confronted Enlightenment philosophers metaphysically when they tried to figure the social effects of the human 'power of sentiment',[5] the circles of sympathy on which polities were constructed. They confront Jamaicans likewise. To comprehend the *potentia* of 'moral sentiment' as it appears in someone's 'bad mind' or 'sympathy' we need to consider other potencies of individuals (human and non-human); for extraterritoriality, transcendence and telepathy (emotional resonance at a distance), for instance. The powers under discussion are multiple and take diverse forms.

***

This chapter reconsiders, then, the puzzle Adam Smith bequeathed contemporary anthropology with his *Theory of Moral Sentiments* (see the introduction to this volume), by exploring the schemas and moments of self and sentiment that form an imaginative background to the 'sympathy', 'righteousness' and 'bad mind' foregrounded in Jamaican street speech. However, having generalized the terms in question '*sub specie aeternitatis*', as Malinowski would say,[6] a contrast appears: because the more care we take to look and ask, the more we can notice that the particular expectations, images and models involved, in fact, vary radically and fundamentally from one person to another where each individual considers themselves the ultimate 'sovereign' judge. Nevertheless, the ubiquity with which the terms are deployed shows their crucial coordinating or placeholder role in the map people are using to orienteer their passage through a society of their own imagining, aiming to 'live good' (or not) with others in their orbit (cf. Wardle 2018a).

Considering the stark contrasts of human inequality as these appear to city dwellers in Jamaica; the tangible prosperity of some and the dirt and misfortune of others, the rapidly shifting, mobile and unpredictable individual circumstances of most, we can begin to appreciate how often the maps or models we are talking about change and how difficult this good living or 'livity' is to achieve as a common sense experience. As Austin-Broos shows (1997), there is a 'politics of moral order' to be taken account in finding a good life which pits 'righteousness', 'sympathy' and impartiality against 'bad mind' in an interplay of images and expressions – the conjunctural artfulness of which people recognize and appreciate without it achieving any kind of final coherence or definitive meaning. Again, there is the core notion to consider – individuals are construed as wilfully acting on their own inborn and individually diverse spiritual or psychic-characterial potencies and personal gifts. Whether they are valued as doing so according to 'good' or 'bad' or 'two-fold' intention will have effects both for their perceived spiritual trajectory and also, hence, for their public 'reputation'.

Here are some typical uses of 'sympathy' from the urban context. The moral sentiment and imagery involved are not abstract, they are very closely connected to situations that have recurred many times in these lives:

> **Jeanette** You have to have sympathy for people in life. Like say … you have one madman that walk up and down the road hereabout. Every day me hear him walk up and down the road, and it come in like him bawl and 'cratch fi him face when him hungry [When he is hungry, it seems, he cries out and scratches his face]. Me now, if me hear him pass and me are eat, me would give him something to eat too; beca', you know, even if you help someone and even if they don't know you one are help them, it will come back to you a certain way—something come back to you even if that person don't even realise.
>
> **Marshy** All the time them come beg, you know? [come to Marshy's food stall and beg]. 'Beg you one breakfast, Mr Marshall!' 'Beg you three hundred dollar, Marshy!' Most times I give them and tell them 'go way'. Sympathy … you have to live good, you have fi gi' way—ca' are like, if you gi' way to people after a little while it run back to you [because it is as if, when you give things away, after a while those gifts come back to you]. My father was a kind man—a Wrap-Head [a Revival Shepherd].
>
> **Michael** It come in like I grow myself as a young boy pickney beca', see me now, my mother don't really feel no sympathy for me at all when me a little child. [In effect, I brought myself up when I was small because, you see, my mother never felt any sympathy for me.]

Here is how 'bad mind' is often deployed:

> **Marshy on other street-sellers** A bad mind people that! tscho! All the while them want me fi lef' from here and take it fi them own [they try to force Marshy out from his street stall and take the site for themselves]. 'nough time them are plan fi take it from me—them no rest 'til them have it. But me always are go on good with Mr B [get on well with the owner of the site] … bring come gi' him something from up in the hill and so [bring Mr B fruit or vegetables from Marshy's hillside farm plot].

Andrew on his co-worker And him are wear fi him earphone so [mimicking the
co-worker listening to music on his earphones] and him are go on so—'ugh'
and 'ehh' [series of inarticulate grunting sounds]. Come in like you cannot
talk to him: a pure bad mind something that! Me no know what the boss
them are deal with ... [I don't know why the bosses put up with it].

What these comments describe are discrete concrete instances of types of psychic
disposition known to have powerful effects. Note that when people talk about 'sympathy'
they sometimes place an explicit stress on its roundabout or circular causality – sooner
or later sympathy returns to the one who shows it. Sympathy ('minding' or 'paying
mind'[7] in this sense) is exemplified not merely by solicitude but also by actively 'giving
away' something of oneself or one's own to the others. 'Bad mind' reverses this: it is
defined behaviourally by a 'craven' desire to strip someone else of their goods. But it
is not the other's material possessions that are the ultimate focus, most significantly it
is their good standing or reputation that is being destroyed by the 'cravenness' of 'bad
mind'. This is why glossing 'bad mind' as 'jealousy' with gossip ('susu' or 'bad mouth' in
patois) as the basic technique is insufficient. Less emphasized, but nonetheless equally
present, is the idea that the toxic pathos that is 'bad mind' also finds its way back to the
person who practises it by way of some kind of final subtraction from their spiritual
well-being and as a distortion in their ability to act morally – people can be 'haunted'
by their own morally destructive intentions.

'Bad mind' like having 'sympathy' is a psychic state, then, but, as the descriptions
show, it also describes a kind of materializable *agency*. As people will explain, 'bad
mind' is more than simply 'ill will' because unchecked it is toxic – ultimately it can
kill the person it is directed at and it can 'mash up' the 'bad mind' person herself.
This is why the perception that 'bad mind' is being directed at oneself can provoke
so much fear (Cohen 1956; Sobo 1993: 101). At one end of the spectrum 'bad mind'
is formalized or ritualized via the practice of *obeah*, witchcraft, which, for all the
technical virtuosity that may go into its use of grave dirt and other paraphernalia, is
essentially 'bad mind' *in extremis* – an exercise in the reach and effects of evil thought
carried beyond everyday moral limits. This kind of 'bad mind' has its alter or mirror
in the curative sympathy of the 'medicine man/woman': note too that the practitioner
of 'medicine', 'obeah' or 'science' may be one and the same person, the same power can
be 'two-fold' in its effects. People sometimes make the prima facie paradoxical claim
that they don't 'believe' in obeah because obeah attacks will not harm them. Clarice,
who ran a small shop, told me this about the seamstresses next door. They, she stated,
were lighting candles and engaging in typical obeah activities: 'that can't harm me; me
no pay them no mind, I don't believe in that [obeah]'. But in saying this she was not
discrediting the reality of the spiritual power and intentionality involved: rather she
had to protect herself from its evil effects by mastering their own intentions against
it – what she describes as 'not believing' is better understood as a kind of active belief
in her own powers.

As concepts, 'sympathy' and 'bad mind' correspond to knowledge and potentials
that individuals possess which they can deploy to create effects on, between and
in, others. As we have seen, this type of power is mimetic and reciprocal – it has a

tendency to circle or mirror back to the individual herself (an even more literal or material turn than Smith's – 'I judge of [...] your reason by my reason'). Described in this way – what is wilfully given out pays itself back equally wilfully – we may see family resemblances with other kinds of reciprocal intentional effects described in anthropological literature, as when, for example, one Kula partner projects the consequences of receiving their valuable gift onto a distant other, or when Dobuan lovers anticipate the effects of their love magic (Fortune 1932: 217, 236–8). Discussed, variably or simultaneously, as a thing and a person 'bad mind' displays the general magical properties that Marcel Mauss ascribes to '*mana*': 'bad mind' is likewise 'not simply a force, a being, it is also an action, a quality, a state. In other terms the word is a noun, an adjective and a verb' (Mauss [1902] 2001: 133).[8]

We should not assume that 'bad mind' stops critical debate in this setting, though. On the contrary, it spurs it on – the street 'corner' is a space where debate about a good life is fervently pursued. The same virtues of justice ('righteousness'), prudence and beneficence that Adam Smith saw as primary are seen in the same light here too. Equally, it is perhaps not surprising that claims about 'bad mind' are more publicly voiced than those about 'sympathy'. Smith makes a similar case in his *Theory*; we humans tend to be more strongly concerned by other people's negative than their positive appraisals and intentions. As noted, it is not uncommon to hear derogatory or self-deprecatory generalizations such as that 'we Jamaicans are bad mind people' or 'it's bad mind that keep we in the ghetto' (See Lewis 2015). Psychological maxims like these run parallel with a more sociological awareness, promoted by Rastafarian 'reasoning' in particular, of other systemic aspects of the 'downpression' of the mass of Jamaicans (we will return to this later). Either way, claims about 'bad mind' are more strongly vocalized in everyday life than assertions of 'sympathy'.

Being addressed: Anticipating intentionality

We have seen that 'bad mind' and 'sympathy' describe an imaginative power (or powers) with real effects that enables someone to act on another. To experience someone's 'bad mind' or their 'sympathy' means to 'be addressed' in the spiritual sense that Buber describes (1958). The technical expertise of, for example, the Obeahman or Pentecostal preacher can help shape this power efficaciously toward curative or morbid ends (in addition, by paying a technical expert the protagonist may hope to avoid these powerful affects from returning back to them). There is also clearly a perspectival element to all this: one person's 'bad mind' can be another's 'sympathy', and an individual's own intentionality can cancel out the 'bad mind' that others direct at it. Nonetheless, other people's motives are understood to be hard to decrypt – it is often simpler to judge that they are 'just a bad mind somebody' than to figure their complicated or mixed motives.

The specific effects of being addressed in this way will vary with the quality of the network of relationships existing for that individual – the place and tone or intuitive sense. The parameters of concern are autobiographical and depend on the context of the situation. One thing to add at this stage is that the imaginative relations of 'sympathy' and 'bad mind' need not be limited to co-present living individuals (on a side note we must disagree with Anderson when he argues that 'imagination' only becomes relevant to community-formation beyond the level of face-to-face relations [1991]). In fact the power of sympathy or antipathy involved takes in a much more varied domain: the number of psychic forces affecting the individual in the city can be very large and it is not confined to the living or solely to human others.

Here, Benjie and Jeanette independently describe the antipathy of certain plants to being named, hence discovered and harvested. Jeanette elaborates on the motivated intentionality of plants as she has experienced it. Some people, she suggests, are able to sense this kind of intentionality, though not everyone. Here, again, the moral judgements involved should be understood, not as anthropomorphic but, rather, as egomorphic:

> **Mr Benjie** You see this here wis [liana, vine]: if you call out fi him name him will hide!

A few days later, searching in vain for a particular medicinal plant, dog blood (*rivina humilis*), Jeanette commented 'if you call fi him name, him no answer'. Somewhat inconsequentially, I asked what kind of voice plants have:

> **Jeanette** Some people who hear it … but like me now hear my plant tell me 'good morning' and me hear it and tell it back 'good morning'. Sometimes the plant … you come out and you hear a voice who say 'drink piece of this one' and sometimes you drink it—it is the sickness here coming … They have a voice. If you even cut in a tree. That is why they say don't cut a bearing tree,[9] like – me don't know if others, maybe others, [but] Revivalist hear it – if you cut in to it, or breaking the leaf, it is feeling the same pain you know.

The 'street', the 'bush' and the 'yard' are worlds crowded with addressive voices whose ambiguous motives can potentially be divined. Coming to know this complexity and plurality of forces and voices takes us some way to understanding the kind of reduction that the notion of 'bad mind' involves.

'Bad mind': Divining spiritual motives

Revival Zion churches are gaudily decorated with colourful flags that attract spiritual powers, and the various altars and stands may be covered with glass vessels of different colours. These vessels are filled with water and in this medium angels come to visit. Attending a Revival church in May 2016, at a certain point in the service, one of the Shepherdesses started to pray with the congregation. Since everyone was praying individually a low droning of voices began against which this Shepherdess' was loudest and clearest as she knelt by the altar.

> **Shepherdess** Lord, put a barrier against fi wi enemy them, Oh My God. Protect us from them bad mind, Lord. Praise God … Protect Daniel and Lorna that is

down at U.C. [hospital] tonight my Lord. Holy Jesus we pray you pass through
the ward tonight. Spray you blood on the ward them, dear Jesus. Spray the blood
from you healing hand on the ward; cleanse and protect the ward them with you
healing blood, I pray you Holy Jesus. (At the Revival Church, May 2016)

Who were the 'enemies' or 'bad mind' people described here? Spiritual forces are
multitudinous so they are likely to be manifold also.

Since 'bad mind' and 'sympathy' describe the uses the individual puts their spiritual-
psychic powers to in the world, it is not surprising that their presence is felt particularly
acutely in the organization of religion. Kingston, Jamaica, is home to hundreds of
bigger and smaller churches and spiritual followings. Here Andrew compares three –
Pentecostal, Seventh Day Adventist and Revival in terms of the kind of spiritual
orientation involved.

> **Andrew** Pentecostal and Revival it kind of similar. You would see the both of
> them dress with turban and so; it different, but it come in kind of similar.
> Pentecostal it root in black people' religion; you have to kinda look into
> the history. Seven Day now that is more stusch like [stuck up]: dress smart
> clothes, big themself up, look down on ordinary people – oof!
>
> When you look it don't matter if it is Revival or Pentecostal – you receive
> power from the holy spirit to do a work, it [is] up to you now to use that for
> good or bad – up to you how you use that power according to fi-you gift them
> [up to you how you use your gifts] ... What you see more now is people not
> going to the big church again. Can't take the too much gossip, you know what I
> mean? You have people come together make a new something, pray and so on.

Again, Andrew is here talking about the complicated terrain Austin-Broos describes
as the 'politics of moral order': affiliation with different churches is taken by the
self as a claim about one's place in a shifting set of hierarchical distinctions (1997).
However, the hierarchy is by no means uncontested, people who 'walk' another,
distinct, religious 'path' will not likely agree with one's own trajectory. This comes
out, below, when Jeanette describes her experiences as a Revivalist who goes to
the local Pentecostal church. In Andrew's account, Pentecostalism and Revival
are similar. Contrastingly, Jeanette tells how she is consistently informed that her
behaviour as a Revivalist is unwelcome since it is viewed as 'obeah' practice or close
to it – particularly in terms of the quite distinct bodily gestures that go with trance,
being 'caught by the spirit', that characterize Revival versus Pentecostal worship. For
Jeanette it is Pentecostals, not Seventh Day Adventists, who are 'stusch' – stuck up
– with their emphasis on dressing finely and making up for church; in contrast it is
she as a Revivalist who is the brunt of claims that Revival is simply another form of
obeah, witchcraft – 'bad mind'.

Urban Jamaica is a strikingly individualistic setting in a region well-known for the
sparseness of coherent norms, collective institutions and established communities (Mintz
1971). The problem of interpreting other people's motivations is widely commented
on in the ethnographic literature on Jamaica in terms of a lack of interpersonal trust

and sense of threat that results from this (Cohen 1956; Kerr 1963; Sobo 1993). This is also a creolizing context where expectations of epistemic plurality – and openness to diversity – are implicit in the manner of communicating (Wardle 2007). The many different churches offer partial elements of a spiritual community, but affiliation to a church is very much elective – individuals tend to shift from one church to another and this leads to a multiplication of churches and sub-denominations as we explore below. We can see from both Andrew and Jeanette's accounts that this perceived problem with church affiliation, and the tendency toward splitting, turns on the cryptology of powers and intentions in a highly individualistic milieu. Jeanette understands herself to have particular spiritual powers, and she deals with others whose spiritual powers (gifts) are equally unique – powerfully good or malign – but also equally contested.

In her 1938 classic, *Tell My Horse*, Zora Hurston gives a very striking extended description of a Jamaican wake ritual, or 'nine night'. Perhaps the most prominent aspect of this account is how those present disagree about the spiritual properties or qualities of the dead, the ghosts or *duppies*. She shows how a very long series of 'duppy stories' are constantly interrupted by dissension over the nature of the dead and their capacities. In one paragraph participants debate the effects of salt on duppies without reaching any agreement:

> 'A pickney duppy is stronger than the duppy of a man,' one said.
> 'Oh, no. A coolie duppy is stronger than all other duppies.'
> 'No, man, a Chinee duppy is strongest of all.'
> 'Well,' the man who started it all summed up, 'all duppies got power to hurt you.'
> (Hurston [1938] 1990: 44–5)

Indeed, after attending many Jamaican wakes or nine nights of the kind Hurston describes here and the preparation for them, it becomes clearer that one of the constants is this disagreement about what capacities spirits have; the plural character of their bodily presence and agency (Wardle 2000: 175–6). Why is this important? The answer is that what individual people are considered able to do is very much a variant of what their spiritual capabilities are. As to the eschatology and history of these capabilities, this is equally very much a matter of interpretation or divination.

The issue of interpreting another's psychic state becomes more sharply defined when it comes to the work of a specialist with divinatory powers. Jeanette told me how she had taken a relative, D, to her Revival 'Church Mother' to see if she could help cure D of his erectile disfunction:

> **Jeanette** When we reach now to the lady, she there are look 'pon him and say 'when you stand up top of the building you drop the cigarette paper and you see it float down – and you couldn' do it'. That time D gone pale up and start fi shake [started to shake] beca' she *see it*: after him kill the man, D did a go up at one high building and want to, see the paper are drop, and he couldn' do it; could not kill himself. She give him some herbs and so.

In Jeanette's account D's impotence could be traced back to a manslaughter he had committed in a foreign country, his subsequent desire to kill himself and his inability to carry this out. None of which facts he had revealed to the priestess, Jeanette said. 'Sympathy' (or 'empathy', a word rarely used by Jamaicans) becomes here the divinatory or diagnostic capacity to inspect someone's psychic state toward finding a cure – putting them back on track. There is a looping or cycling aspect to someone's actions and their psychic state – D's current sexual incapacity is his previous violence and subsequent impotence at the point of suicide returning to haunt him. Indeed, killers are often described as 'haunted' by actions in the past that cause them to murder again in an eternal return.

Presence, precedence and transcendence

'Bad mind' offers a publically available symbol, and a diagnosis, for the problem posed by the other's intrinsic power. Moral sense is understood as an already given quotient of who this other person is and what they can become, but is described as becoming active through the deliberate use of 'gifts' endowed at birth, or perhaps before. Here we may think of Levinas's assertion that 'morality does not belong to Culture: it enables one to judge it' (1964: 57). Or as, a Jamaican friend, the artist Leonard Daley put it to me, 'Out of the baby and the birth certificate which one is before the other?' (Wardle 2000: 94). Where gifts or powers come from is debatable (and is quite deliberately ambiguated – gifts, it is sometimes suggested, can come from the Devil or from spirits of the dead – but the orthodoxy tends to be that gifts are given by God, or the Holy Spirit at inception. On the other hand, what individuals do with their gifts is a matter of their own willing; good gifts can be used for bad, bad for good, ambivalent gifts for either good or bad work, etc. People are indeed sites of warring psychic forces and varied powers. They are also bodies, understood as conglomerations of entrances and exits, through which blood and other liquids travel: these must be kept in balance with dietary care to avoid 'pressure', for example, using various kinds of 'washout' such as purgation or catharsis (Sobo 1993). The social scene is often described in terms of toxic misunderstanding leading to bodily sensations of pressure. But the foods used for 'washout' or other purposes have psychic properties too as Jeanette's explanation above indicates: people are never just or primarily bodies.

The sense of entanglement in the antipathetic or sympathetic gaze, hence the psychic power, of the others contrasts with the variety of personal attempts at transcendence. It is no accident that the metaphor of transcendence deployed here involves acquiring a visa and a passport to go elsewhere:

> People who 'red eye' or feel envy toward a 'clean sober' neighbour's 'booked passage' to heaven try to 'spoil' her or him. They sully the reputation and the bodily cleanliness of the person who has his or her 'visa', 'passport', and other 'papers' for heaven in order. (Sobo 1993: 118)

The official or formal role of religion in offering a 'step up' or 'betterment' – a means or mode for transcending local antipathies that would 'drag you back down' – is recognizable here as elsewhere. The particular figuring of transcendence appears again in this wake night song:

> When my pilot come I'll take an aeroplane ride!
> I am feeling happy with Jesus at my side,
> Sun, moon and star shine so bright,
> When my pilot come I'll take an aeroplane ride! (Wardle 2000: 95)

And the analogy between the transmigration of the soul and the living body is clear: one kind of transcendence is clearly and centrally physical migration: taking a flight out of the immediate nexus of positive and negative sympathy and gaze. The capacity to move allows the self to gain an overview and to regain its own integrity.

If we look closely, though, the models of transcendence in play are many and varied. For example, for Jeanette, her world is full of diverse kinds of spiritual 'voices' each with its own moral tone and intentionality: in her case these include the voices of living people, angels, animals and plants – and the dead, such as her late mother, Aunt Erica. However, Jeanette describes a kind of 'timeless' transcendent state that comes over her when she is possessed by the Holy Spirit and made to 'prophesy' and 'warn' about forthcoming events (Wardle 2016a). With the sense of being caught intransitively within a situation of imbricated psychic conflict comes a capacity for ambiguating the boundaries involved and an openness to alternative ontological possibilities (Wardle 2007).

Rastafarianism, the most famous of Jamaican religious philosophies, is also strongly transcendentalist but its model of transcendence is distinctive. In fact, the differences provoked strongly hostile encounters between Rastafarians and Revivalists in the early days of the Rastafari movement. Rastafari also emphasize that it is not the antipathy of others immediately surrounding the self that is the real cause of suffering, rather it is the psychic 'downpression' of the 'Babylon system' or 'shitstem' on people that is key to psychic-bodily suffering. Hence the centrality to Rastafari of Marcus Garvey's famous statement that there is a need to 'emancipate ourselves from mental slavery because whilst others can free the body, none but ourselves can free our mind'.

In this regard, the most obvious index of a disjuncture between Rastafarian and other Jamaican understandings of self and willing, lies in the atypical use of the pronoun 'I' developed by Rastafarians in their creatively adapted version of patois referred to as *I-talk* or *I-yaric* (Amharic after the national language of Ethiopia). In Jamaican Creole (as in other anglophone Caribbean Creoles) the first person is indicated using 'me' even though speakers are likely to be aware that 'I' is the upper status usage. In this way, a Creole speaker might say 'me give him the something' knowing that an upper status speaker would say the equivalent of 'I gave him the item'. As a matter of ideological principle, Rastafarians reclaimed this use of 'I' in order to critique the mindset of a 'me' who is the object (rather than subject) of 'downpression' by 'Babylon' (Faristzaddi 1982).

Asserting the power of 'I' goes beyond simply adopting the first person: it extends into a radical and wider alteration of language use. These transformations and creativities in Rasta I-language have been very widely discussed (Faristzaddi 1982; Chevannes 1994;

Pollard 1999). Most recognizably, the initial syllable of words is replaced by I. Hence, for example; Essence – *I-ssence*; Divinity – *I-vinity*; Ethiopia – *I-thiopia*; Create – *I-rate*. But, perhaps most significant of all these creative transformations has been the Rasta use of *I n I* to denote the collective – We. As Faristzaddi puts it, the I-words pronounce 'a new perception of self as Man and as nothing less, as subject and not as object' (1982: 34). As objects become aspects of self, individual willing becomes metonymic of the will of God (*Jah Rastafari*) and subjective understanding is asserted as radically transcendent (Wardle 2000: 8; 2011). Hence, the way to 'livity' is through 'reasoning', taking the form of a Socratic style of street-debate. There are many spiritual utopias on view in urban Jamaica, but whatever their manner of differentiation, Rastafari and the other religious forms have one referent in common – the principle, again, that 'You is a Power' (see Wardle 2016a: 12).

Spirited selves in the Jamaican street

'Bad mind' gathers and focuses moral sentiment about others in a statement about the spirited intentionality of a given person in a specific situation vis-à-vis myself. Contemporary Kingston, Jamaica, is, however, a place of plural and fluctuating theories of the spirited self-in-the-world. While Pentecostals may argue that the self should better itself by modelling its life on the image of Christ, by way of contrast, Rastafarians have created a divinized 'I' that can encompass all around it in a collective immanent, 'I-n-I'. Meanwhile, for Zion Revivalists the self appears as a 'Me' surrounded, often beset, by many spiritual voices and actors. What do these divergent theories or models of the self suggest about understandings of community and sympathy in the city? Undoubtedly, they are the inheritors of a complex history of ideas shaped by slavery, emancipation and enlightenment (Wardle 2000), but their point of conjuncture is the present-day city with the divergent conceptions of moral order, might and right of its inhabitants. It is these diverse ideas and principles that are gathered up in the image of the self acting with 'good' or 'bad' mind.

Passing through a local park on a Sunday, Andrew and I notice a small group of about seven church-goers sitting on chairs under a tree listening to a preacher. Small church groups like this form all the time Andrew explains because people become frustrated with the 'bad mind' of others in the larger congregations – too much 'susu' (gossip), he adds; thus they break away to form a church in miniature ('where two or three gather in my name, there am I'). People are drawn to a church where they can 'feel the spirit' in the company of others, but at the same time they often come to resent the power of church officers and the 'red eye' of fellow congregationalists. As a result there are hundreds of these small congregations all over Kingston.

Jeanette describes how as a Revivalist, but after falling out with her original Revival church, over the last few years she has begun to visit a Pentecostal tent church set up on a site near her home. Jeanette does not feel welcome in this new church and she tends to see the Pentecostals as 'too show off', however, she tells her stories about what goes on there with amusement and gusto. Most of these tales turn on how the pastor deprecates her behaviour in the church which he considers as being too Revivalist in manner, hence as too close to obeah. But, for Jeanette, any church should be open to every kind of believer and to divergent 'manners'. She envisages a kind of struggle going on between herself and the pastor over which kinds of spiritual powers can be used and how they should be physically expressed or channelled in the church.

In this setting, where she feels herself spiritually to be an outsider, what is nonetheless important to Jeanette, as occasionally happens at this church, is when another person fortuitously confirms her distinctive spiritual-moral experience by reiterating the same spiritual messages that have been spoken to her. The possibility of this happening seems to provide a motive for her going to the church:

> **Jeanette** At that time [a year or so previously] them are plan fi build fire station where the church stand. And pure lamentation are go on; all the time them pray fi stay on the land, fi them no build on the church land, fi save the land and so it are go on. So, one time a voice tell me say 'them lament too much: them shoulda more pray for the people that come to the church than go on lament so'. And that time me stand up in the church and say 'I have something to tell you, you know say, it come in to me that you lament too much about the land. Would-a better you pray for all the people gather here at the church than lament so.' Now, not long after, a next woman come to the church – she come down from up in the hills, and she stand up and say 'I want to tell the congregation that you lament too much for the land and you should more pray one one [individually] for the people in the church. And they look 'pon her and they look back 'pon me.

The fact that another person enunciates the same words, for Jeanette, is a sign that that person has been 'moved by the spirit' for the same reason that she has: in other words a kind of telepathy (emotional resonance at a distance) and, hence, a confirmation that in the midst of an otherwise perplexing situation of moral-spiritual plurality, Jeanette has understood her gifts, and her path in using them, correctly.

> **Jeanette** One time, up at the church, I passing in front of Pastor and the Deacon when I hear a voice tell me 'I not ready yet' and when I reach the podium I start to shout out 'Weh hey!' and wave my arm them. When it come to time for prayer, now, the Pastor hold down my hand; it look like him angry beca' what I am doing that is Revival, that is not a Pentecostal something. Later, one boy, youth, did up at one gathering, and the Pastor ask the boy why him don't baptise yet and he say 'I not ready yet' and at that moment I start up on a 'Weh Hey!' [she moves her arms] and that boy come to church soon after and are baptise.
>
> From me in Revival and them have them Pentecostal something, fi them Revival come in as 'Obeah church', but you know my little Revival gift some time work better than Pastor. Pastor put on a big show when him cure someone, but some time me have my little way that work better and I don't put on the show that Pastor put on.

Jeanette is not looking for collective fellowship at the church; what she searches for are contingent moments of spiritual consonance that will validate the universal significance of her own gifts – the validation or 'sign' coming from a stranger who has otherwise no moral-intentional connection toward her at all. She talks about how she, using her own modest or 'humble' spiritual powers, her unique way of calling on the Holy Spirit, had done more good in some instances than the grand theatrics of the Pentecostal pastor who, nonetheless, continues to condescend toward her, telling her how she should, or should not, behave in church. In this complex setting of multiplex personal powers, these are moments when Jeanette's *potentia* can be justified as 'righteous', as *potestas*, a right to command.

Vox populi, vox dei

Vox populi, vox dei – 'the voice of people is the voice of god' was a popular slogan of eighteenth-century liberalism. In the early 1990s I witnessed this motto being stuccoed onto a street front wall on the Old Hope Road in Kingston – the words are still there. Taken literally (as it was by eighteenth-century antinomian Christians), it is a foundational idea on the Jamaican 'street corner' too – the voice of god is immanent in the moral voice of people. However transient human lives are, each individual is an instantiation of universal power one index of which is the capacity to show sympathy for others around them. If we compare the image of self that appears in the writings of Enlightenment thinkers, for example, Adam Smith in his *Theory of Moral Sentiments*, Adam Ferguson in his *History of Civil Society* (2011), or Immanuel Kant in his *Anthropology* (2006), with the ideas discussed here there emerges a key similarity. The Enlightenment thinkers and Jamaicans in the 'street' and in the 'yard' have a 'spirited' view of the self as a free-acting being – a *homo noumenon* endowed with faculties that it makes use of freely in the world and in time (Wardle 2016a).

> The administration of the great system of the universe [...] is the business of God not of man. To man is allotted a much humbler department, but one much more suitable to the weakness of his powers, and to the narrowness of his comprehension: the care of his own happiness, of that of his family, his friends, his country [...] [I]t has been entrusted to the slow and uncertain determinations of our reason to find out the proper means of bringing them about. (Adam Smith [1790] 2006: 238)

In *The Theory of Moral Sentiments* Adam Smith offers a startlingly prescient psycho-social theory of moral sentiment as the look of others acting within myself to constrain my psyche and its modes of moral expression. Allowing that the self can have no extensive understanding of the 'great system of the universe', moral sentiments nonetheless have as their object, 'the care of [the subject's] own happiness [...] of [...] family, [...] friends, [...] country'. Moral sentiment is something that is forever being replayed – in our perception of the gaze we receive from others, in the look we give others and how they may comprehend it; in an endless learning and unlearning and imaginative recursion of moral judgement understood as a type of seeing and being-seen-to-see both in our own thoughts and in the public domain and as a limit on understanding the situation. Out of the 'narrowness of

[my] comprehension' I learn from your looking at and judging of me, you learn from mine. Your look can reappear as a strange presence, an alien 'spectator', in my imagining-looking. Hence, I learn from you something of the moral limits set by your viewpoint, but this learning is what constitutes *my* proper capacity for looking and judging not *yours*. This is the theory and description that Smith offers more than a century before the great advances in phenomenology and interactional psychology. The fabric of social life, he argues, is woven out of individual judgements learnt in the awareness of witnessing and being judged. So it is on the Jamaican street. As Rastafarians put it, together there can be a fully subjective and agentive 'I and I', but not an objectifiable 'we'.

Smith clearly neither meant to say that for any given person moral sentiment as an imaginative 'measure' for judging others will fall within uncomplicated limits, nor that the fundamental relativity in the ability to 'judge' others' subjective state has no significant effects on the social situation. On the contrary, he envisaged moral sentiments as manners of feeling that are built up imaginatively by the self out of the duration and reiteration of face-to-face encounters over time. He saw clearly that this could lead to very diverse types of moral valuing and virtue surfacing in the local group, but also the potentialization of transcendent or 'impartial' moral viewpoints too. Consider, in brief contrast to the situation we are discussing here, how silence in a conversation can express sincerity, well-being or affirmation in Scotland or Denmark while 'making a noise' in a Jamaican yard or on the street is equally recognized and valued for comparable reasons; both offer a kind of impartial stance (Reisman 1974: 112).

The greater contrast emerges, not between Smith and Jamaicans, but with a spirited view of the self *versus* a mid-twentieth-century 'cybernetic' understanding of subjectivity. Whereas the social philosophers of the Enlightenment took it as self-evident that the self is simultaneously a soul, a mind and a body equipped with practical reason (but with only limited means to 'make sense' of the 'great system of the universe' as Smith put it), in the 'cybernetic' understanding 'consciousness' became a puzzling 'ghost in the machine' best comprehended in terms of a theory of logical types. In this approach the seeming coherence of subjectivity-individuality is an illusory byproduct of metasystems that are in principle predictable and manageable by human relations experts (Koestler 1967). As Erickson et al. neatly put it, the mid-to-late twentieth century was a period in which 'Reason Almost Lost Its Mind' in favour of a view of culture as a supra-human system akin to a computer program (see the introduction to this volume; Erickson et al. 2014). Arguably, Smith presages this integration of subjectivity and system in his teleologically framed *Wealth of Nations*. Here he does make a claim to comprehend an impersonal 'great system' existing beyond the partial knowledge provided by moral sentiment; this he posits as a grand scheme of political economy. His theory of sentiment pushes in the opposite direction, or at least it insists on another way of looking at society: because of how plural moral intentions are tangled in the individual's imagining of the other, the closest circles of human social life are simultaneously infused with passion, sympathy, pragmatism and reason.

***

What ultimately can we say of 'bad mind'? If the aim is to show the significance of Smith's notion of a common and universal sympathy at the basis of social life, why expend so much effort here in exploring the distinctiveness of 'bad mind'? 'Bad mind' is a ubiquitous descriptor in Caribbean street life, so it can appear to offer only banal descriptions, in particular a banal summation of human motivation as either 'malice' or 'benevolence'. But we have established that in its passionate intensity 'bad mind' inevitably points to something beyond a superficial outline of someone's character and disposition. The more complex claim concerns the psychic-spiritual powers of the person involved – and these can be multitudinous; Caribbean cultural life is profoundly open (Wardle 2018b). The close link between 'bad mind' and 'obeah' makes the connection clear. 'Bad mind' is not simply a momentary disposition, it describes a toxic misuse of the plural spiritual gifts that the individual in question brings to the situation. In the shadow of the 'good life' is the pathology of unchecked individual 'bad mind'. But, for all its seeming intensity, the passionate scrutiny of another's 'bad mind' stems from fundamental imaginative ambiguity regarding this 'theory of mind'. What the interior spiritual properties involved consist in and where they came from can never be answered with definitive agreement; even though awareness of the powers of the other's mind has a crucial place in knowing one's own.

Perhaps 'bad mind' is best understood, then, not as a self-evident proposition but, rather, as a strange attractor around which images and ideas take shape and reform in particular scenes of judgement of the kind that Jeanette and the others here narrate. Within the indexing of the other's 'bad mind' lurks awareness of an absence of knowledge of why they are who they are. Ultimately, the strength with which the phrase is uttered speaks to this deeper perplexity. Nonetheless, 'bad mind' also underscores the substantiveness of the individual's unique *potentia* in making the social situation with others and also their potential both for destroying it and transcending it. Drawing our dialogue between Smith and a Jamaican street to a close, then, it is the limits of sympathetic understanding that stand out; the constraints on our ability to understand others' intentions and how these fundamentally limit our reasoning about social life. Here we reach a complex point of convergence between the Caribbean everyday and the Enlightenment concerns of Smith's *Theory*.

Notes

1   Describing linguistic contrasts in Trinidadian Creole, Levison and Jogie (2015) refer to 'bad mind' versus 'good mind'. In the Jamaican street setting 'good mind' is rarely used.

2   The groundwork is laid in Spinoza's debate with Hobbes in the *Theological-Political Treatise* (e.g. Spinoza [1670] 1999: 173–84). See Overing for a comparative ethnographic treatment of key Western notions of power and polity (2012).

3   See the chapter by Austin-Broos, in this volume.

4   Of these murders, 1,220 were men, 134 were women. Source; Jamaica Constabulary Force, Statistics Department (courtesy of Laura Obermuller).

5   Lisa Douglas uses this phrase as the title for her ethnography of upper status Jamaican kinship (1992).

6   'In the field one has to face a chaos of facts […] [which] are absolutely elusive, and
     can be fixed only by interpretation, by seeing them *sub specie aeternitatis*, by grasping
     what is essential in them and fixing this […] field work consists only and exclusively
     in the interpretation of the chaotic social reality, in subordinating it to general rules'
     (Malinowski 1916: 419).
7   See 'no pay 'im no mind' in the introduction. Mind can in this sense be 'paid' out and
     returned.
8   We may pause to consider how in Euro-American secular settings 'emotional neglect'
     and 'psychological abuse', which may otherwise be thought of as purely 'mental'
     phenomena, are known to cause physiological harm (e.g. Johnson and Gunnar 2011).
9   Cutting a tree that is bearing fruit can be understood as dangerous to the person who
     does so.

References

Anderson, B. 1991. *Imagined Communities*. London: Verso.

Austin-Broos, D. 1997. *Jamaica Genesis: Religion and the Politics of Moral Orders*. Chicago: Chicago University Press.

Buber, M. 1958. *I and Thou*. New York: Charles Scribner's Sons.

Chevannes, B. 1994. *Rastafari Roots and Ideology (Utopianism and Communitarianism)*. New York: Syracuse University Press.

Cohen, Y. 1956. 'Structure and Function: Family Organization and Socialization in a Jamaican Community'. *American Anthropologist* 58(4): 664–86.

Douglas, L. 1992. *The Power of Sentiment: Love, Hierarchy and the Jamaican Family Elite*. Boulder, CO: Westview Press.

Erickson, P. et al. 2014. *How Reason Almost Lost its Mind: The Strange Career of Cold War Rationality*. Chicago: Chicago University Press.

Faristzaddi, M. 1982. *Itations of Jamaica and I Rastafari*. New York: Grove Press.

Ferguson, A. 2011. *An Essay on the History of Civil Society*. Fairford: Echo Library.

Fortune, R. 1932. *Sorcerers of Dobu*. London: E. P. Dutton.

Hickling, F. H. and James, C. 2012. 'On the Phenomenology of Red Eye, Bad Mind and Obeah'. In *Perspectives in Caribbean Psychology*, F. W. Hickling, B. K. Matthies, K. Morgan and R. C. Gibson (eds). Mona: CARIMENSA, University of the West Indies.

Hurston, Z. 1990. *Tell My Horse: Voodoo and Life in Haiti and Jamaica*. New York: Harper Collins.

James, M. 2015. *A Brief History of Seven Killings*. London: One World Publications.

Johnson, D. and Gunnar, M. 2011. 'Growth Failure in Institutionalized Children'. *Monographs of the Society for Research in Child Development* 76(4): 92–126.

Kant, I. 2006. *Anthropology from a Pragmatic Point of View*. Cambridge: Cambridge University Press.

Kerr, M. 1963. *Personality and Conflict in Jamaica*. London: Sangster's Books.

Koestler, A. 1967. *The Ghost in the Machine*. London: Hutchison.

Levinas, E. 1964. *Emmanuel Levinas: Basic Philosophical Writings*. Indianapolis: Indiana University Press.

Levison, C. and Jogie, R. 2015. 'The Trinidadian "Theory of Mind": Personhood and Postcolonial Semantics'. *International Journal of Language and Culture* 2(2): 169–93.

Lewis, J. 2015. 'A So Black People Stay: Bad-mind, Sufferation, and Discourses of Race and Unity in a Jamaican Craft Market'. *Journal of Latin American and Caribbean Anthropology* 20(2): 327–42.

Malinowski, B. 1916. 'Baloma: The Spirits of the Dead in the Trobriand Islands'. *The Journal of the Royal Anthropological Institute of Great Britain and Ireland* 46 (July–December): 353–430.

Mauss, M. and Hubert, H. 2001. *A General Theory of Magic*, R. Brain (trans.). London: Routledge.

Milton, K. 2005. 'Anthropomorphism or Egomorphism? The Perception of Non-Human Persons by Human Ones'. In *Animals in Person: Cultural Perspectives on Human-Animal Intimacies*, J. Knight (ed.). New York: Berg, pp. 255–71.

Mintz, S. 1971. 'The Caribbean as a Socio-Cultural Area'. In *Peoples and Cultures of the Caribbean*, M. Horowitz (ed.). New York: Natural History Press.

Montaigne, M. 1845. *The Works of Michel de Montaigne*, W Hazlitt. (ed.). London: C. Templeman.

Overing, J. 2012. 'Adiwa! Piaroa Philosophies of Power, Violence, Ingestion, Excretion, Blood and Beauty'. Unpublished conference paper for the Institute of Cultural Analysis, Vienna. Available online: www.academia.edu/24430774/Adiwa_Piaroa_Philosophies_of_Power_Violence_Ingestion_Excretion_Blood_and_Beauty (accessed 21 April 2017).

Pollard, V. 1999. *Dread Talk: The Language of Rastafari*. Montreal: McGill-Queen's University Press.

Reisman, K. 1974. 'Contrapuntal Conversations in an Antiguan Village'. In *Explorations in the Ethnography of Speaking*, R. Bauman and J. Scherzer (eds). Cambridge: Cambridge University Press, pp. 110–125.

Smith, A. 2006. *The Theory of Moral Sentiments*. London: Penguin.

Sobo, J. 1993. *One Blood: The Jamaican Body*. New York: State University of New York Press.

Spinoza, B. [1670] 1999. *Ethics*. Ware: Wordsworth Editions.

Stein, E. 1989. *On the Problem of Empathy: The Collected Works of Edith Stein*, Vol. 3. Washington, DC: ICS Publications.

Thomas, D. 2011. *Exceptional Violence: Embodied Citizenship in Transnational Jamaica*. Durham, NC: Duke University Press.

Wardle, H. 2000. *An Ethnography of Cosmopolitanism in Kingston, Jamaica*. New York: Edwin Mellen.

Wardle, H. 2002. 'Marshy and Friends: Informality, Deformalisation and West Indian Island Experience'. *Social Identities* 8(2): 255–70.

Wardle, H. 2007. 'A Groundwork for West Indian Cultural Openness'. *Journal of the Royal Anthropological Institute* 13(3): 527–78.

Wardle, H. 2011. 'I, Me, Myself y los Dilemas de la Voluntad en Kingston'. *Jamaica, Maguaré* 25(2): 11–39.

Wardle, H. 2016a. Times of the Self in Kingston, Jamaica'. *Ethnos* 82(3): 406–20.

Wardle, H. 2016b. 'John Brown: Freedom and Imposture in the Early Twentieth Century trans-Caribbean'. In *Freedom in Practice*, M. Lino E Silva and H. Wardle (eds). Oxford: Routledge, pp. 63–86.

Wardle, H. 2018a. '"Characters … Stamped Upon the Mind." On the A Priority of Character in the Caribbean Everyday'. *Social Anthropology* 29(1).

Wardle, H. 2018b. 'Caribbean Cosmopolitanism: The View from Ethnography'. In *Routledge Handbook of Cosmopolitan Studies*, G. Delanty (ed.). London: Routledge.

4

Westermarck, Moral Relativity and Ethical Behaviour

David Shankland

Edward Westermarck (1862–1939) is known but scantily in the modern anthropological consciousness. His name appears, if it does at all, usually in a passing comment or perhaps a footnote, often rather disparagingly.[1] This, I would argue is quite wrong, all the more so as he fits in precisely with the topic. He is, I would say, an unheralded bridge between the Scottish Enlightenment and modern anthropology, a person whose work far from being played out, deserves to be at the absolute centre of our understanding of the development of our discipline.

Who, then, was this Westermarck? He was, in brief, a brilliant Swedish-speaking Finnish anthropologist and philosopher who – according to his autobiographical account – having fallen out with the German thinkers, decided rather that he preferred the British.[2] Already when a young man, he made trips to Britain, to the British Library, and his doctoral thesis drew heavily on his researches there. Expanded, it appeared in English as *History of Human Marriage* in 1891. In it, there are found two arguments which resonate still today: that there has never been a human society in which regular bonds have not formed between partners and that proximity in childhood inhibits mating, that is, he claims to have solved the 'incest taboo'. The first was absolutely essential to the creation of kinship studies as we know them, because it removed the necessity to view human society as having passed through a series of historical stages, from promiscuity to marriage.[3] The second, his explanation of the incest taboo, is more controversial but there is a growing body of evidence suggesting that he may be correct, as has been argued consistently, for example, by Arthur P. Wolf.[4]

Not just brilliant but hard-working and cordial, Westermarck obtained university positions quickly in Finland, but he wished to pursue fieldwork, arriving ultimately in Morocco, where he stayed for part of the year, aided in doing so by the purchase of the Swedish consul's house in Tangier. He was also active in the independence movement, beginning – even whilst still busy with fieldwork – by travelling to England to help create a petition to the czar to withdraw Russian influence over Finland.[5] His fieldwork is sometimes regarded as being not very useful, because it is written in effect as a regional study rather than one focused in a single community, as was to become fashionable even during his lifetime.[6] This I believe is quite wrong: it is quite true that the level of abstraction is greater than we are used to dealing with today, but the collected essays in *Ritual and Belief in Morocco* (1926) are remarkable. They give an insight into the dense religious context of life in North Africa that is unparalleled until Bourdieu – and to my mind anticipated him and even, perhaps, influenced him in his conception of *habitus*.[7] It is also interesting – even if not directly relevant to my arguments here – that he always fully acknowledged the support he received from his closest informant, taking him with him back to Europe, and naming him as a contributor in his published work.[8]

He was equally successful in creating a social base in London. He became a Fellow of the Royal Anthropological Institute, receiving its Rivers Medal, and eventually the Huxley Medal, its highest honour.[9] Sponsored by Martin White, who believed that MPs should know something of sociology, he began lecturing at the London School of Economics (LSE), eventually in 1906 being awarded the Martin White Chair. He stayed at LSE for thirty years, dividing up his time between LSE, Morocco and Abo, in the north of Finland, where he was invited to become rector of a new private, Swedish-speaking university.

At the LSE, he became Malinowski's teacher, then friend, then colleague. Indeed, I have slowly come to realize the enormous influence that Westermarck had on Malinowski. Today, I am clear that the topics taught and discussed by Westermarck, such as the analysis of social institutions or the relationship between the social and the biological basis of behaviour, later were to become fundamental to Malinowski's vision.[10] Westermarck too, was thoroughly at home in discussing 'survivals', and was firmly on the side of scepticism at too free a belief in them.[11] It is also the case that Westermarck was teaching at the same time as Malinowski, so that rather than conceiving that crucial moment at LSE as the 'Malinowski' seminar, we should rather say the 'Anthropology Seminars', for the students at the time would go to both Malinowski's and Westermarck's seminars. Nor is it the case that Westermarck was a dry teacher, or distant figure. All contemporary reports, whether of his teaching at Abo or his seminars at LSE, say that he was as charming as he was stimulating.[12]

As if this was not enough to lead us to reassess Westermarck and his place in the emergence of social anthropology, he also wrote three major works on ethics and morals. These were *The Origin and Development of the Moral Ideas* (1906–08); *Ethical Relativity* (1932), and *Christianity and Morals* (1939). In them, he both attacks vigorously those whom he believes are seeking a spurious moral universalism and puts forward his own theory for moral relativism.

The ethnographic material for such a claim is laid out in the two substantial volumes of *Origins*. Drawing both on his fieldwork in Morocco, and on very extensive library researches, he divides the different aspects of human life that may lead to ethical conjectures into chapters; so that there are descriptions of suicide, marriage, celibacy, adultery, homosexuality, cannibalism, property, homicide, human sacrifice, slavery and so on. His survey takes him to the immediate conclusion that there is no universally accepted ethical principle. How in turn then, do we explain the diversity of ethics and morals?

Westermarck's explanation is that moral behaviour is rooted in emotions which he refers to as 'retributive'. By this, he means that emotional reactions to a given situation may become retributive when they result in identifying with another person's actions, whether positively or negatively. In this work,

The theory was laid down that the moral concepts, which form the predicates of moral judgements, are ultimately based on moral emotions, that they are essentially generalisations of tendencies in certain phenomena to call forth either indignation or approval [...] We found that the moral emotions belong to a wider class of emotions, which may be described as retributive; that moral disapproval is a kind of resentment, akin to anger, and that moral approval is a kind of retributive kindly emotion, akin to gratitude.[13]

We should note that though the emotional reaction is experienced subjectively, it is at the same time collective, shaped by the institutions of society. Therefore, ethical behaviour can only be understood in terms of an interaction between society and the individual, and can only be induced if an individual has the capacity to feel empathy or sympathy for their interlocutor. For Westermarck, becoming moral does not just draw on collective understandings but assumes an almost disinterested quality, so that the ethical judgement becomes a reflection upon the interaction independently of the individual concerned:

> Society is the birthplace of the moral consciousness [...] Public indignation is the prototype of moral disapproval, and public approval the prototype of moral approbation. And these public emotions are characterised by generality, individual disinterestedness and apparent impartiality. Thus moral disapproval is at the bottom of the concepts bad, vice, and wrong; whilst moral approval has led to the concepts good, virtue and merit.[14]

Westermarck's clear style, detailed examples and readiness to enter into detailed disputation with other philosophers whom he believed were not seeing the problems with sufficient clarity, led him to be widely reviewed, both by academic colleagues such as Hobhouse or Marett who wrote the review in *Mind*, but also in the press as well, such as *Nature,* the *Athenaeum, Scotsman* and *Yorkshire Post*.[15] It then appears to have fallen largely from view until taken up in philosophy by Timothy Stroup many decades later, who has written a detailed analysis of his thought and stimulated a parallel collection of essays, both published in 1982. Things then appear to go quiet again, though there is further interest today from a group of young Finnish scholars writing in English, and it is likely that he will become more prominent in the next decade.[16]

As we have seen, Westermarck's first major treatment of the problem in *Origins* is divided thematically into different areas of social life, drawing on extensive ethnographic examples. These are, admittedly, difficult to read concurrently with any great pleasure because they are so disparate. It is possible that they could be read as separate short treatises, as indeed Benthall has found when he made the chapter on 'Charity' the starting point for his recent essay on the same subject.[17] Some twenty years later, however, Westermarck returned to the subject. In *Ethical Relativity* (1932) he attempts to draw out his theoretical framework more explicitly so that his underlying tenet, that his approach provides the possibility of appreciating that ethics are not universal, is rendered clearer. 'It appears to me that the present publication of a book in defense of ethnical subjectivism and relativity is the more timely, as the large bulk of ethical literature which has been produced in this country since the beginning of the century has championed the opposite cause' (1932: xviii). Largely discarding the notorious scissors and paste technique, which he himself writes he feared prevented the reader from seeing the 'wood for the trees',[18] he produces a work with a quite different tone. Much more abstractly, in six broad sections, divided into nine chapters, he lays out his argument afresh with great care.

He begins by sketching out his opposition to utilitarianism such as that put forward by J. S. Mill, which he regards as a form of 'normative' ethics, and continues in the second chapter to assert that there is nothing in the human mind that is in any straightforward essential way a 'moral' precept. Rather, (in chapters three and four) that morals always have an emotional foundation, whether expressing approval or disapprobation. These emotions, in turn, are embedded in societal perceptions of the way that we should behave toward one another, therefore, they cannot be individualistic in origin. Further, we can learn such behaviour because of the ability that human beings have to 'sympathize' or empathize with one another. Moral reactions are therefore generalizations (chapter five) based on what is regarded as appropriate, or inappropriate conduct, an analysis which he extends into intentionality (chapter six). This eventually takes him to the assertion (chapter seven) that there are, practically speaking, great variations in ethical behaviour across different societies and that these differences must be because of their emotional origin. The work concludes (in chapters eight and nine) with a further discussion, and refutation of universalist theories, particularly taking Kant as his exemplar. The work finishes on a defiant note:

> I have tried to show that in his [Kant's] alleged dictates of reason the emotional background is transparent throughout. And if I have succeeded in such an attempt in the case of the greatest of all moral rationalists, I flatter myself with the belief that I have, in no small measure, given additional strength to the main contentions in this book: that the moral consciousness is ultimately based on emotions, that the moral judgment lacks objective validity, that the moral values are not absolute but relative to the emotions they express.[19]

Westermarck cites a myriad of sources in outlining his theory, both ethnographic and philosophical, engaging with some of the most well-known names with relish. For Stroup, however, the principle influences can be reduced to four: David Hume, Adam Smith, Frazer and Darwin.[20] From Hume, Westermarck borrowed the crucial insight that at the heart of morals lies an emotional reaction. Westermarck is even more enthusiastic concerning Adam Smith, of whom he writes:

> I maintain that Adam Smith's *Theory of Moral Sentiments* is the most important contribution to moral psychology made by any British thinker, and that it is so in the first place on account of the emphasis it lays on the retributive character of the moral emotions.[21]

Indeed, the opening lines of Smith's *Theory* show immediately just how much Westermarck has drawn from him:

How selfish soever man may be supposed, there are evidently some principles in his nature which interest him in the fortune of others, and render their happiness necessary to him, though he derives nothing from it except the pleasure of seeing it. Of this kind is pity or compassion, the emotion we feel for the misery of others […] The greatest ruffian, the most hardened violator of the laws of society is not altogether without it.[22]

In the way that he sets his wider arguments, Westermarck is sometimes dismissed as a typical evolutionist.[23] It is true that the influence of Darwin is very strong, and has to be taken account in order to appreciate fully the approach that he is taking. The quality of empathy is, for Westermarck innate, something that is potentially part of the biological make up of *Homo sapiens*. In turn, he assumes that there is an evolutionary advantage to human groups which are able to make that identification with each other, for it is equally essential to cooperation as a group or as a family. The question, in turn, as to why this empathic quality should be present in human beings is not one that he feels is troubling to his argument. Given we have this capacity to socialize and to identify mutually with one another at all, he feels that he has demonstrated its importance to moral behaviour. Stroup offers the following summary, which I think can hardly be bettered:

As a result of our likes and dislikes, together with our propensity to sympathise (which has altruistic overtones) and the beliefs we have about matters of fact, we approve or disapprove of certain intentions in others and in ourselves, and this, when contemplated from a disinterested, impartial and general viewpoint, causes us to apply predicates of moral approval or disapproval to the agent who has the intentions.[24]

If the roots of Westermarck's thoughts are clear, what of his present eclipse? That he is ignored, and I think unjustly, there is little doubt. That is not to say that he is not occasionally mentioned. He is. However, he does not inhabit that central position that he deserves in our understanding. Excluding him from the canonical understanding of important anthropological thinkers means in turn, that he is not taken into account in the recent literature on anthropology and morals. For example, we may take the otherwise fascinating volume edited by Monica Heintz, which appeared first in 2009. Nearly all its respective, and distinguished, authors state variously that the study of anthropology and morality is new. Rather than set the anthropological study of morality into its Enlightenment context, to which Westermarck clearly belongs, they assume that it is in some way linked to the emergence of postmodernism reflexivity, and only a few decades old. Heintz, for example, in her introduction writes 'Can we preserve in our writings the dignity of other cultures even though we may perhaps – as individuals – disapprove of their values? These delicate questions lurk in postmodernist debates.'[25] Having made that assumption, almost every chapter regards the history of such anthropological enquiries as having a different starting point: almost invariably recent.

Why should this historical myopia be so acute? It appears to me to be dependent largely on the way that the editors, and the authors, approach the question of why they have become drawn to the study of morality. For Westermarck, relativism of morals is a factual matter that can be discerned through research and explained in ways that he would call scientific. Thus, for him the truth is simply that there is, in the world, no one moral way of doing things, and any universalist proposition, such as those put forward by Spencer or Mills, is not tenable for the reason that it is contradicted by the available facts which he, Westermarck, has marshalled. Thus, the relativism of Westermarck and the relativism of postmodernism apparently derive from quite different starting points: the one dependent on a single truth, the other denying its possibility.[26] It is hardly likely then, that those who regard relativity as emerging from a postmodern uncertainty with the existential status of reality should take as their starting point a text which appears at least to have a form of evolutionary positivism as its inspirational framework.[27]

Even if this is the case, it leaves us with a further problem. It doesn't explain a rather long gap: Westermarck's work appeared in 1906, it appears to have fallen out of favour long before the emergence of postmodernism. Here, I think that we can discern a number of shifts, all of them unfavourable to Westermarck, which are instructive to think through even if apparently straightforward. The first comes with his erstwhile pupil Malinowski. Though Malinowski was deeply influenced by Westermarck, and indeed carried over much of his preoccupation with the relationship between social behaviour and its biological basis, the kind of ethnography produced by Malinowski was already quite different from Westermarck's. Just as Gellner remarks in his *Anthropology and Politics* (1995), Westermarck simply did not, nor did he wish to, produce the functionalist monographs that resulted in such dense, interwoven ethnographies based on a single community that came to characterize his school. For him, comparison remained quite vital, and its pursuit an inevitable part of anthropology, whether or not acknowledged as such.

The shift to structural-functionalism, which came to dominate in the subsequent years reinforces this rejection twice over. The first is in the growing disinclination to follow Malinowskian functionalism, that is the putative link between societal institutions and the biological basis of behaviour, which Malinowski had in any case taken over from Westermarck. It is this rebuttal that seemingly united almost all the authors in the rejection of their teacher in Firth's edited volume *Man and Culture* (1957) that was intended to celebrate Malinowski's work.[28] Further, though, the turn to Durkheimian sociology which characterized the structural-functionalists impeded precisely those questions of the individual and their role in ethics that Westermarck found so important. As Laidlaw writes, in his Malinowski lecture 'For an anthropology of ethics and freedom'. 'Durkheim's conception of the social so completely identifies the collective with the good that an independent understanding of ethics appears neither necessary nor possible.'[29]

There are, then, multiple reasons for Westermarck's becoming unfashionable, as he himself outlined in his Huxley lecture, given toward the end of his career, which today reads very defensively.[30] Yet, there is perhaps even a further underlying reason for the rapid eclipse. By the time that Durkheim had been incorporated into British social anthropology through Radcliffe-Brown, anthropology itself had shifted position so that it regarded itself as practising a form of induction.[31] This, with its easy assumption of access to external reality makes it appear sharply contrasting to the later sophistication of postmodernism. Westermarck has been tarred, repeatedly, with the same brush. Yet, Westermarck is not quite as straightforward as this. Though he certainly believes that there is a reality, and that there can be such a thing as rational thought, in fact his approach to social life is constructivist.[32] This, combined with his readiness to offer clear, succinct hypotheses that are amenable to falsification means that he is in fact very close to a form of Popperian deductivism before his time.

Not just this. Westermarck's exploration of morals and individuality contains at the same time a social prescription. He believes, just as Popper in the *Open Society* (1945), that through understanding the social basis of ethics and morals, it is possible for the thinking – or the rational actor – to escape society's coils. How we are in practice to achieve that separation from the social life that has in the first place constituted our own ethical understanding he does not make clear, but he believes that it is possible. In other words, for Westermarck his moral enquiry is ultimately about individual freedom: the way that the individual actor can escape the moral pressures that society imposes upon them through rational reflection.

Thus, we come full circle, back to the Enlightenment. In claiming that society's restrictions on individuals can be overcome by a better understanding of the human condition, Westermarck is self-consciously linking himself to that earlier scientific tradition that assumed that it is, with effort, possible to become an independent thinker, that we are not always in the thrall of collective emotions, and the resulting moral judgements that ensue from them. His work, therefore, is as well as its ostensive intellectual arguments, a much more down-to-earth plea for individual freedom.

> The unanimity of opinion that originally characterized the members of the same social unit was disturbed by its advancement in civilization. Individuals arose who found fault with the moral ideas prevalent in the community to which they belonged, criticizing them on the basis of their own individual feelings […] In the course of progressive civilization the moral consciousness has tended towards a greater equalization of rights, towards an expansion of the circle within which the same moral rules are held applicable. And this process has been largely due to the example of influential individuals and their efforts to raise public opinion to their own standard of right.[33]

Conclusions

In this chapter, I argue several connected points. I suggest, at its simplest level, that we need to talk not about the Malinowski seminar but the anthropology seminars at LSE. Only then can we gain a nuanced understanding of the multi-stranded way that modern anthropology was formed. I suggest further that there is more than one kind of relativism, or rather that relativism can emerge from different philosophical positions, and that we need to take this into account when we look at the history of our discipline's approach to anthropology and morals.

Westermarck, in his readiness to look back at the great moral thinkers of the Enlightenment, whilst at the same time being a pioneering anthropologist, acts as a bridge between the two streams of thought in major, scintillating works which repay as careful study today as they did at the time that they were written. The reason he has not been built into our understanding as a pioneer of the discipline may be partially explicable in terms of changing fashion, as he appears to have been caught out by the rapid transformation as anthropology finally succeeded in institutionalizing itself as a major university discipline.

Yet this eclipse, even if it is partial, also must partly be to do with the way that the history of anthropology is written and experienced by each succeeding generation; there is a very strong tendency to regard the history of our discipline as a series of dominant ideas which have in each decade been replaced, rightly, by new ones. This might work well as a motif to secure recognition from one's peers but it results in very poor historical studies. In fact, disciplines are built through multiple, mutually-interacting centres and actors who overlap in time.[34] When one looks at the gradual development of anthropology in detail, it resembles a palimpsest more than a series of discrete layers with different practitioners coming to the fore and others still continuing in the background even if they are no longer prominent – still interacting and still influential in ways that only become clear if one looks for them. In archaeological terms, we can say that in reality the stratigraphy of disciplinary endeavour is mixed up, with all sorts of intellectual endeavours being pursued simultaneously rather than exclusively, and the internal chronology of the different layers can become intertwined as it is pushed and pulled by events. It is only the later interpreters who smooth it out into discrete step-by-step developments, where each is separated from its predecessor, and I fear that this last process is above all the reason why Westermarck is so little remembered as a founder.

Yet, if we do look at anthropology's historical trajectory through the Enlightenment thinkers into its modern period, it is to Westermarck we have to turn as an essential link. Is acknowledging this, in the end, such a bad thing from the point of our understanding anthropology today? I think not. Anthropology, whatever theoretical lens we may wish to use to bring to bear on our subject, is about our knowledge of the external world. Even if we may be concerned at being caught in Enlightenment rationalism, we owe modern anthropology to it, for without the Enlightenment we would hardly have been able to develop the relativist position that is essential to our discipline, whatever kind of relativism we may profess. As we can hardly deny the influence of the Enlightenment's precepts, it is far better to deepen our understanding of disciplinary trajectories that led from the eighteenth century to today, rather than neglect them.

Notes

1   Lowie writes in his *History of Ethnological Theory* 'With Westermarck the reader has the uncomfortable feeling that nothing interests him less than to comprehend primitive tribes ... Sweeping generalisations of his, chosen here and there, will illustrate his ethnographic inadequacy' (1937: 97). Fletcher writes 'Most nineteenth century sociologists are much talked about and little read. Westermarck is not

even talked about' (1982: 195). It may be noted that Westermarck is treated more thoroughly in Stocking (1995: 151–63), but – ironically given the author – in a rather presentist way that doesn't allow Westermarck's preoccupations to show themselves clearly, leading to the same result.

2   Westermarck (1929).

3   Evans-Pritchard writes, for example, 'One of the main causes of confusion, not only in McLennan's writings, but also in those of his contemporaries, is a blindness to the social priority of the family. Amongst all the most primitive peoples the institutions of marriage and the family are found irrespective of the wide diversity of the other institutions with which they may be associated; but McLennan's thesis depends absolutely on the dogma that neither exist in early society. This was an axiom of the time (Maine was a notable exception; the idea was not dispelled until Westermarck and Malinowski)' (1981: 67).

4   For a recent statement, see Wolf 'I am confident that we will hear again the applause with which the Westermarck Hypothesis was greeted. The reason is simple – Westermarck was right!' (1995: 101). We should note here also that Charles Stafford at LSE, perhaps influenced by Wolf's reworking of Westermarck's theories, does incorporate Westermarck into his thinking. See, for example, Stafford (2000).

5   This was published as *Pro Finlandia* (1899). See also Lagerspetz et al. (2017), and Lagerspetz and Suolinna (2014). Also Shankland (2014: intro), where a letter from Westermarck describing his desire to help the cause is reprinted.

6   See, for instance, Gellner (1995: 235–6) or Handler (1985; 684).

7   Bourdieu (1977). On Westermarck's ethnographic contribution, which I have not treated here, see Bourqia and Al Harras (eds). 1993, also the suggestive essay by Brown (1982).

8   For instance, his *Wit and Wisdom in Morocco: A Study of Native Proverbs* (1930) was published as being by Edward Westermarck 'with the assistance of Shereef 'Abd-es-SalamEl-Baqqali'.

9   Westermarck (1936).

10 Malinowski himself was aware of this. See Young (2004: 172–4) 'Malinowski developed an enormous liking for Westermarck, and the affection was mutual … After he had accomplished his own unique Trobriands fieldwork, Malinowski paid sincere tribute to Westermarck's achievement in Morocco … several years later he acknowledged this mentor as one "to whose work I owe more than to any other scientific influence"' (2004: 173).

11 See for example his Huxley lecture (Westermarck 1936) or his paper on survivals, reprinted in Shankland (2014).

12 This point is discussed in a little more detail in Shankland (2014: intro). See also Montague's recollection of the seminars (1982), and Malinowski's own comment on Westermarck (1913: 34).

13 Westermarck (1906–08: 738).

14 Westermarck (1906–8: 740).

15 Extracts from such reviews are frequently quoted from as a form of advertising within Westermarck's publications, for example, see the double-sided advert 'By the same author', following page 422 of Westermarck's *Marriage Ceremonies in Morocco* (1914).

16 See Lagerspetz and Suolinna (2014), as well as the relevant chapters in Shankland (ed. 2014).

17   In the *Wiley Companion to Moral Anthropology*, Benthall starts his essay 'No
      anthropologist has published a global comparison of charitable traditions since the
      chapter on "charity and generosity" in Edward Westermarck … This Frazerian collage
      of historical and ethnographic snippets, much less substantial than his monograph
      Ritual and Belief in Morocco, is bound to alienate readers a century later … But if we
      disregard this, the inferences he arrives at are a starting point for reflection' (2015:
      359).
18   The full phrase reads as follows; 'to give a more precise formulation of my views by
      corrections and additions; and to make them stand out more clearly by detaching
      them from the mass of anthropological and historical particulars, which seem to
      have disabled some of my readers from seeing the wood for the trees' (Westermarck
      1932: xviii).
19   Westermarck (1932: 289).
20   Stroup (1982b: 126–7). See also Stroup (1984).
21   Westermarck (1932: 71).
22   Smith (1759: 1).
23   For example, Handler (1985: 684).
24   Stroup 1982a: 186.
25   Heintz (2009:).
26   On this point, see the essays in Gellner (1985).
27   In parallel fashion, see the remark by Fassin in his introduction to the Wiley
      Companion to Moral Anthropology; 'There is always an element of arbitrariness in the
      choice of founding fathers and one could have proposed, among others, Westermarck
      for his monumental *The Origins and Development of the Moral Ideas* … but [this]
      work [has] not significantly influenced the way we think about morality and ethics in
      the social sciences' (2015: 10).
28   See the comment to that effect by Gellner (1958) in his review of *Man and Culture*.
29   Laidlaw (2002: 312).
30   Westermarck (1936).
31   There are many ways to demonstrate this: for example, it is the position which Evans-
      Pritchard attacks in his famous 'Social Anthropology Past and Present' (1950).
32   On this aspect, see the comments on Westermarck and Hume in Douglas's 'How
      Institutions Think' (1998: 57–76).
33   Westermarck (1932: 112).
34   For a comment on this, see Shankland (2016).

References

Benthall, J. 2015. 'Charity'. In *A Companion to Moral Anthropology*, D. Fassin (ed.). Oxford:
      Wiley, pp. 359–75.
Bourdieu, P. 1977. *Outline of a Theory of Practice*. Cambridge: Cambridge University
      Press.
Bourqia, R. and Al Harras, M. (eds). 1993. *Westermarck et la société marocaine*. Rabat:
      Faculté des lettres et des sciences humaines de Rabat.
Brown, K. 1982. '"Curse" of Westermarck'. *Ethnos* 47(3–4): 197–231.
Douglas, M. 1998. 'How Institutions Think'. In *Developing Anthropological Ideas: The
      Westermarck Memorial Lectures 1983-1997*, Vol. 41, J. Siikala, U. Vuorela and T. Nisula
      (eds). Finland: Transactions of the Finnish Anthropological Society.

Evans-Pritchard, E. E. 1950. 'Social Anthropology Past and Present'. *Man* 50: 118–24.

Evans-Pritchard, E. E. 1981. *A History of Anthropological Thought*, A. Singer (ed.). London: Faber.

Fassin, D. (ed.). 2015. *A Companion to Moral Anthropology*. Oxford: Wiley.

Firth, R. (ed.). 1957. *Man and Culture: An Evaluation of the Work of Branislaw Malinowski*. London: RKP.

Fletcher, R. 1982. 'On the Contribution of Edward Westermarck. The Process of Institutionalisation: A General Theory'. In *Edward Westermarck: Essays on His Life and Works*, Vol. 34, T. Stroup (ed.). Helsinki: Societas Philosophica Fennica, pp. 195–218.

Gellner, E. 1958. '"Review" of Firth (1957)'. *Universities Quarterly* 13(1): 86–92 (reprinted in *Cause and Meaning in the Social Sciences*).

Gellner, E. 1985. *Relativism and the Social Sciences*. Cambridge: Cambridge University Press.

Gellner, E. 1995. *Anthropology and Politics*. Oxford: Blackwell.

Handler, R. 1985. 'Edward Westermarck: Essays on His Life and Works by Timothy Stroup'. *American Anthropologist*, new ser., 87(3): 684–5.

Heintz, M. (ed.). 2009. *The Anthropology of Moralities*. Oxford: Berghahn.

Lagerspetz, O. and Suolinna, K. 2014. *Edward Westermarck: Intellectual Networks, Philosophy and Social Anthropology*. Commentationes Scientiarum Socialium, Vol. 77. Sastamala: Finnish Society of Science and Letters.

Lagerspetz, O, Antfolk J., Gustafsson Y. and Kronqvist, C. (eds). 2017. *Evolution, Human Behaviour and Morality: The Legacy of Westermarck*. London: Routledge.

Laidlaw, J. 2002. 'For an Anthropology of Ethics and Freedom'. *Journal of the Royal Anthropological Institute* 8(2): 311–32.

Lowie, R. 1937. *The History of Ethnological Theory*. New York: Farrar and Rinehart.

Malinowski, B. 1913. *The Family among the Australian Aborigines*. London: University of London Press.

Montague, A. 1982. 'Edward Westermarck: Recollections of an Old Student in Young Age'. In *Edward Westermarck: Essays on His Life and Works*, Vol. 34, T. Stroup (ed.). Helsinki: Societas Philosophica Fennica, pp. 63–70.

Popper, K. 1945 *The Open Society and Its Enemies*, 2 vols. London: Routledge & Kegan Paul.

Pro Finlandia, Les adresses internationals á S.M. lémpereur-grand-duc Nicolas II. International Peace Conference. 1899. Berlin: Commission Chez Otto Mertz.

Shankland, D. (ed.). 2014. *Westermarck, Occasional Paper No. 44 of the Royal Anthropological Institute*. Canon Pyon: Sean Kingston Publishing.

Shankland, D. 2016. '"Review" of Kuper, Adam. *Anthropology and Anthropologists: The British School in the Twentieth Century* (Fourth edition). London, New York: Routledge, 2015'. *Journal of the Royal Anthropological Institute* 22(3): 739–40.

Smith, A. 1759. *A Theory of Moral Sentiments*. London: A. Millar.

Stafford, C. 2000. *Separation and Reunion in Modern China*. Cambridge: Cambridge University Press.

Stocking, G. 1995. *After Tylor British Social Anthropology 1881–1951*. Wisconsin: University of Wisconsin Press.

Stroup, T. (ed.). 1982a. *Edward Westermarck: Essays on His Life and Works*, Vol. 34. Helsinki: Societas Philosophica Fennica.

Stroup, T. 1982b. *Westermarck's Ethics*. Åbo: Publications of the Research Institute of the Akademi Foundation.

Stroup, T. 1984. 'Edward Westermarck: A Reappraisal'. *Man*, new ser., 19(4) (December): 575–92.

Westermarck, E. 1891. *A History of Human Marriage*. London: Macmillan.

Westermarck, E. 1906–08. *The Origin and Development of the Moral Ideas*, 2 vols. London: Macmillan.

Westermarck, E. 1914. *Marriage Ceremonies in Morocco*, 2 vols. London: Macmillan.

Westermarck, E. 1926. *Ritual and Belief in Morocco*, 2 vols. London: Macmillan.

Westermarck, E. 1929. *Memories of My Life*, A. Barwell (trans.). London: George Allen & Unwin.

Westermarck, E. 1930. *Wit and Wisdom in Morocco: A Study of Native Proverbs by Edward Westermarck with the assistance of Shereef 'Abd-es- SalamEl-Baqqali*. London: George Routledge & Sons.

Westermarck, E. 1932. *Ethical Relativity*. London: Kegan Paul, Trench, Trubner and Co.

Westermarck, E. 1936. 'Methods in Social Anthropology'. *Journal of the Royal Anthropological Institute of Great Britain and Ireland*, 66 (July–December): 223–48.

Westermarck, E. 1939. *Christianity and Morals*. London: Kegan Paul.

Wolf, A. 1995. *Sexual Attraction and Childhood Association: A Chinese Brief for Edward Westermarck*. Stanford, CA: Stanford University Press.

Young, M. 2004. *Malinowski: Odyssey of an Anthropologist, 1884-1920*. New Haven, CT: Yale University Press.

5

Saving Sympathy:
Adam Smith, Morality, Law and Commerce

Diane Austin-Broos

In both an academic and a public domain, Adam Smith[1] has been known principally for *The Wealth of Nations* first published in 1776. Termed the 'father' of political economy, he is especially regarded in that role by neo-classical economists. Of late he has also been a talisman for neo-liberal strategists known for libertarian positions on personal freedom, governance and markets. In turn, this stance has become a target for critique within the humanistic social sciences.

Independently, anthropologists and others, turning to the study of emotion in social life, have found Smith's *The Theory of Moral Sentiments* equally engaging. Increasingly, Smith has been recognized, like his friend David Hume, as a moral philosopher of note. Moreover philosophers have been at the forefront in offering new interpretations of Smith. Not only did Smith pursue Hume's interest in the 'passions'. He also showed a fascination with the nature of social life, both in its intimate aspects and in the context of global economics.

These two interests remain largely separate notwithstanding that many now underline the unity of Smith's work. Moreover, in neither of these milieux has there been great interest in his jurisprudence recorded in student notes. This chapter argues that for insights into moral systems, Smith's *Moral Sentiments* is best approached as part of a larger whole that also includes his work on law and economics. My contention is that this corpus holds most interest for anthropologists, and other humanistic social sciences, as a rendering of the good society and of the vexed relation between ethics and economics (see also Austin-Broos 1996).

This discussion is divided into two parts. The first is mainly exegesis concerning Smith's views on human nature, sympathy, virtue, jurisprudence and commerce. The second part discusses aspects of Smith's moral theory and his views on capitalism. Where his moral theory is concerned, I emphasize his sense of society. I discuss his views on commerce, or liberal capitalism, in terms of critiques by Marx, and some anthropologists. My concluding remarks return to the theme of Smith's integrated corpus and its significance for moral theory.

Adam Smith's social order

Human nature

Adam Smith's thought is framed by two observations on human nature. He notes, on the one hand, the 'fact' of human sympathy and, on the other, the pursuit of social 'betterment' or 'improvement'. Importantly, these are constants for Smith. Though circumstances vary, through both space and time, these attributes of human social being are with us always.

Smith's well-known words on sympathy begin *The Theory of Moral Sentiments*. Generally they are seen as an implicit response to Thomas Hobbes's and Bernard de Mandeville's stance on the primacy of self-interest among the motivating 'passions' or emotions of man. Whilst he was ready to concede man's selfishness, which he often railed against, still Smith sought a more nuanced account of human social life. 'Self-love' and sympathy were equally in play:

> How selfish soever man may be supposed, there are evidently some principles in his nature, which interest him in the fortune of others, and render their happiness necessary to him, though he derives nothing from it except the pleasure of seeing it ... That we often derive sorrow from the sorrow of others is a matter of fact too obvious to require any instances to prove it. ([1759] 1976: I.i.I.1, p. 9)

Later he remarks that Hobbes and his followers, including Mandeville, maintained that man seeks 'refuge in society' just for his own ends and not for the love of his kind ([1759] 1976: VII.iii.I.1, p. 315). Mandeville himself observed that 'the Sociableness of Man arises only from these two things, *viz.* The Multiplicity of his Desires, and the Continual Opposition he meets with in his Endeavours to gratify them' ([1732] 1924, I: 369). In sum, man is a selfish being.[2]

That 'opulence' or wealth came simply from selfishness was a theme that bothered Smith. His account of betterment is more optimistic and consistent with a kinder view of man. Both sympathy and betterment are natural propensities:

> Nature produces for every animal every thing that is sufficient to support it ... Such is the delicacy of man alone, that no object is produced to his liking. He finds that in everything there is need of improvement. Tho' the practice of savages shews that his food needs no preparation, yet being acquainted with fire he finds that it can be rendered more wholesome and easily digested ... the human skin cannot endure the inclemencies of the weather, and even in these countries where the air is warmer ... it must be stained and painted. ([1966] 1978: II.207, p. 487)

Smith furnishes numerous examples of betterment which include both material things and also aesthetical and abstract ones ([1966] 1978: II.208–13, pp. 488–9).

Just as betterment is natural, so are some of its constituent dispositions. One of these is the propensity to save:

the principle which prompts to save is the desire of bettering our condition, a desire which, though generally calm and dispassionate, comes with us from the womb and never leaves us until we go into the grave. In the whole interval which separates those two moments, there is scarce perhaps a single instant in which man is … without any wish for alteration or improvement of any kind. ([1776] 1982: II.iii.28, p.441)

Elsewhere in *Wealth of Nations*, Smith links this frugality to self-interest and accumulation. They provide the engine of economic life. Trade is integral to this process, 'the propensity to truck, barter, and exchange' which rests on 'the naturall inclination … to persuade' ([1776] 1982: I.ii.1, p.117; [1962–63] 1978: vi.56, p. 352). He notes that, unlike many animals, man is cooperative but cannot rely on benevolence alone. Therefore 'we obtain from one another the far greater part of those good offices which we stand in need of'. These comments usher in a notable remark: 'It is not from the benevolence of the butcher, the brewer, or the baker that we expect our dinner, but from their regard to their own interest' ([1776] 1982: I.ii.2, p. 119). Yet this 'interest' is also constructive, not simply the 'private vices' which Mandeville proposed produced 'publick benefits'.[3]

The prudent individual, in Smith's view, responds materially in interested ways so that he can practise beneficence. One barters and trades in order to secure oneself and improve the lot of those close at hand. Far from being mutually exclusive, both fellow-feeling and self-love inform betterment. Notwithstanding, Smith was deeply perturbed by the human tendency to be overwhelmed by self-interest producing both greed and corruption. He saw a perpetual struggle between constructive self-interest, and the personal and institutional damage that its excess brought. Consequently, he devoted himself to distilling the conditions that would contain these tensions: morality and law exercised in a prosperous milieu described by Montesquieu as '*doux* (sweet) commerce' ([1793] 1989). Smith began his investigation with the issue of morality.

Sympathy and virtue

Like philosopher David Hume, Smith sought an empirically relevant account of morality based neither in abstruse and conscious 'reason' nor in 'eternally valid' and perhaps divinely willed rules. Again like Hume, he grounded his view in the motivating 'passions' or emotions of human 'agents'. He addressed moral sentiment via a notion of sympathy or fellow-feeling sustained between individuals. Moreover, he noted that this sympathy is more than 'compassion'. It involves engagement with others across the range of positive and negative emotions. His method was also markedly social, and his fascination with man's sociality is evident throughout *Moral Sentiments*. Forman-Barzilai remarks,

Smith's central purpose […] was to identify an ordinary sociological process capable of ordering and unifying modern people without […] requiring archaic modes of coercion which would stifle modern (commercial) freedom and human progress. Smith challenged critics of progress and modernity who insisted that wealth and virtue were incompatible ends. (2010: 14)

Sympathy for him was integral to a sociality built by 'harmonizing' forms of feeling and cognition ([1759] 1976: VII.iv.28, p. 337).

From the outset, Smith observes that 'we have no immediate experience of what other men feel'. Rather, we use our 'imagination' to 'place ourselves in his situation', to 'enter as it were into his body … and thence form some idea of his sensations' ([1759] 1976: I.i.I.2, p. 9). Two features of his remarks reflect Smith's acuity. Firstly, he broadens sympathy's engagement. Sympathy is a response not only to the feeling of an agent, which the spectator may never quite grasp, but also a response to the agent's 'situation', to her relevant circumstance.[4] One asks of a person in the sway of emotion, 'What has befallen you?' The reply provides contextual knowledge, a narrative, which promotes a spectator's sympathy ([1759] 1976: I.i.I.9–10, pp. 11–12). Secondly, though one seeks to share an emotion, the spectator's effort is never simply a projection of the self. Smith here seems to grapple with the so-called privacy of feeling which, he suggests, also calls for a cognitive grasp. By way of demonstration he underlines that a spectator may sympathize with a situation beyond his experience. A man may sympathize with a woman in childbirth though he will never face that situation ([1759] 1976: I.i.I.13, p. 12).[5]

Next Smith explores the mutuality of sympathy, the manner in which it becomes a communication between individuals thereby shaping a social-moral self with conscience and a sense of duty; the latter involving rules derived by inference from experience. He explores this mutuality in terms of 'propriety'. He notes that the sympathy our friends express with us 'enlivens joy and alleviates grief' ([1759] 1976: I.i.2.2, p. 14). Moreover, when we approve another's opinion, we also adopt it and vice versa. This reciprocal approval confirms both agent and spectator in the rightness of their sentiments. These shared and proportional sympathies in turn define 'the propriety or impropriety' of subsequent action ([1759] 1976: I.i.2.2 & 5; I.i.3.2 & 6, pp. 14–18).

Smith elaborates on propriety in two ways. Firstly, it requires a certain levelling of the emotions. An agent is likely to take greater pleasure in his own good fortune than an onlooker would. Yet, that spectator knows that she should respond to the agent appropriately. Smith observes of the agent,

> He longs for that relief which nothing can afford him but the entire concord of the affections of the spectator with his own […] But he can only hope to obtain this by lowering his passion […] He must flatten […] the sharpness of its natural tone […] What [agent and spectator] feel will […] be […] different […] These two sentiments, however, may [correspond] with one another, as is sufficient for the harmony of society. ([1759] 1976: I.i.4.7, p. 22)

Smith remarks that although the two may never be in 'unison' they can be in 'concord'. He further suggests that two types of virtue derive respectively from the spectator's effort to sympathize, and from the agent's effort 'to bring down his emotions'. The spectator's effort fosters 'amiable' or positive virtues including 'delicacy'. The agent's response fosters 'awful' or negative virtues such as self-command ([1759] 1976: I.i.5, pp. 23–26).

A second and central elaboration comes when Smith considers 'self-love', 'conscience' and the need for 'general rules'. Propriety 'is a question of the aptness of a given action and its motive to its situation' (Haakonssen 1981: 56). But does this mean that morality is simply social convention? Smith remarks,

> Nature [has endowed the agent] not only with a desire of being approved of, but with … being what he himself approves of in other men. The first desire could only have made him wish to appear to be fit for society. The second was necessary in order to render him anxious to be really fit. ([1759] 1976: III.2.7, p. 117)

Smith points out that an agent asks whether or not others approve of his action. But he also must ask whether or not the action that is approved is actually a worthy one.

As agents and as spectators then, people 'endeavour to examine [their] own conduct [and] to pass sentence upon it'. In doing so, Smith proposes, we 'remove ourselves' from a situation and consider the issues 'at a certain distance'. One 'divides' oneself 'as it were, into two persons'. We try to examine our conduct as we 'imagine' a 'fair and impartial spectator' would ([1759] 1976: III.I.2 & 6, pp. 110, 113). Smith reflects on the marked propensity to selfishness in humankind. He notes that many would care less about 'myriads' in China 'swallowed up by an earthquake' than they would about a very slight injury to themselves. This circumstance requires the cultivation of conscience or principled judgement. Smith describes this human capacity in terms of an 'impartial spectator' that resides, more or less developed, within every person. He remarks,

> what is it which prompts [us …] to sacrifice [our] own interests to the greater interests of others? It is not the soft power of humanity [but rather] reason, principle, conscience, the inhabitant of the breast, the man within […T]he natural misrepresentations of self-love can be corrected only by the eye of this impartial spectator. It is he who shows us the propriety of generosity and the deformity of injustice. ([1759] 1976: III.3.4, p. 137)

Smith notes, therefore, that a sense of what is 'really fit' comes from within. Nonetheless, the self-command that pricks conscience and 'awakens' the 'man within the breast' needs support from others who can strengthen one's resolve ([1759] 1976: III.3.38, pp. 153–4).

Our 'continual observation' of such people 'insensibly lead[s] us to form […] general rules' founded on experience:

> We do not originally approve or condemn particular actions because […] they appear to be agreeable or inconsistent with a certain general rule. The general rule, on the contrary, is formed […] from experience, that all actions of a certain kind […] are approved or disapproved. ([1759] 1976: III.4.8, p.159)

Duty consists in regard for these rules which are secured by a sense of propriety. Though ordinary people believe themselves to be 'moved to decency' by reason, principle and belief in God, Smith proposes that a sense of rules, duty and propriety is in fact the product of sociality itself (Forman- Barzilai 2010: 18, 87).

Propriety is the shared and proportionate practice of sympathy which entails a concord concerning motives and actions. Smith shows how the consequent rules apply in the case of beneficence and justice, respectively 'positive' and 'negative' virtues due to the fact that one comes from a generous spirit, the other from righteous affront. He notes that we do not always sympathize with apparent generosity and gratitude. For example, we may not regard as beneficence the favours an indulgent prince lavishes on a fawning attendant ([1759] 1976: II.i.3.2, p. 72). And where justice is concerned, many sufferers deserve our sympathy but not the criminal who wilfully disputes his punishment ([1759] 1976: II.i.3.3, p. 73). This juxtaposition of beneficence and justice becomes a stepping stone for Smith to move from the sociology of moral sentiment to a discussion of justice, and thence to commerce and the 'wealth of nations'. The direction of his thought proceeds from ethics, through jurisprudence, to political economy.

Justice and property

Smith compares beneficence and justice remarking that beneficence and other positive virtues are 'free' or voluntary by their nature. Accordingly their rules arise from approbation. Justice, however, is demanded and can be 'extorted by force'. As a negative virtue, its rules stem from our 'resentment' at injustice. Sentiment alone, however, will not prevent injustice. 'Positive law' is required ([1759] 1976: II.ii.I.3, p. 78; VII.iv.36, p. 340).

> The rules of justice may be compared to the rules of grammar; the rules of the other virtues, to the rules which critics lay down for the attainment of what is sublime and elegant in composition. The one, are precise [...] and indispensable. The other are [...] indeterminate and present us rather with a general idea of the perfection we ought to aim at. ([1759] 1976: III.6.11, p. 175–6)

These different types of rule reflect a basic truth: that ultimately beneficence is 'less essential' to society than justice:

> Society [...] cannot subsist among those who are at all times ready to hurt and injure one another [...] Society may subsist though not in the most comfortable state without beneficence; but the prevalence of injustice must utterly destroy it. ([1759] 1976: II.ii.3.3, p. 86)

Smith asserts repeatedly that, within bounds, the pursuit of self-interest is central to society. Nonetheless, some men all the time, and all men sometimes trample others' rights and interests. This propensity necessitates a system of law ([1759] 1976: VII. iv.36, pp. 340–1)

The *Lectures in Jurisprudence* divide rights and law into three parts: individual, domestic and public matters.[6] The last concerns 'citizens or members of a state' ([1962–63] 1978: i.10, pp. 7–8; cf. [1966] 1978: 6–7, pp. 398–9). Public law includes international law and defence as well as the rights between sovereigns and citizens, among them personal liberty, taxes and services. Domestic law concerns husband–wife, parent–child and master–servant relations. The rights of individuals are in their person, their reputation and their estate. The last set of rights Smith divides into 'real' or 'personal'. Real rights include those bearing on property; personal rights, various types of contract and 'delinquency'. Laws concerning property rest on the 'reasonable expectation' of a possessor; on natural law, but also on the social conditions at hand (see Haakonssen 1981: 104–6). Therefore, Smith provides a stadial history to trace the development of jurisprudence. Though his debt to Montesquieu is clear, he presents a more expansive view of law, economy and social change (Winch 1978: 36–8; Skinner 1999a: 26–7).

There are various versions of the stadial history in Smith's work. Of the three more substantial ones, two occur in *Lectures on Jurisprudence* and one in Book V of *Wealth of Nations*. In the first of these, Smith begins in an interesting way:

> If we should suppose 10 or 12 persons of different sexes settled in an uninhabited island, the first method they would fall upon for their sustenance would be [...] by wild fruits and wild animals. ([1962–63] 1978: i.28, p. 14)

He proceeds through the wild or '*hunting*' stage to the maintenance of '*herds* and flocks', also called 'the age of shepherds'. Population pressure would bring *agriculture* and an interest in plants that proffer 'agreable and nourishing food'. A division of labour would grow as groups produced a surplus and turned to other 'arts' exchanging various commodities with each other. These changes culminate in *commercial society* wherein,

> This exchange of commodities extends in time not only betwixt the individualls of the same society but betwixt those of different nations [...] To Spain and Portugal we send our superfluous corn and bring from thence [their] wine. Thus at last the age of commerce arises. ([1962–63] 1978: i.31–32, pp. 15–16)

In his various accounts, it is common for Smith to linger over one or another variation: the 'Tatars and Arabians' who remain as herders due to limitations in their natural environment; or republican Greece and Rome with their slaves, freemen and city states ([1966] 1978: 30, 37, pp. 408, 411).

Nonetheless, his 'island' imagining suggests that the stadial history is schematic and constructed mainly for an analytic purpose. In particular his hunting or primitive society serves as a 'base-line', exhibiting the absence of all those features that would, for Smith, mark civilization: primitive society is small-scale and vulnerable to outsiders. Technology is minimal, and there is little accumulation. Property is limited and therefore there is little that requires formal governance and law. Because they are poor, these societies are egalitarian (see Haakonssen 1981: 155–6; cf. [1776] 1999: V.i.a.2, p. 279). A real divide comes with the advent of herds and especially cattle which can provide the source of substantial property and 'families revered and honoured on account of their descent' ([1776] 1999: V.i.b.10, p. 301). Smith traces the development of property through livestock and its products, to personal moveable goods and the advent of common, then privatized land. Feudalism waxes and wanes. New types of legal constraint emerge with the advent of mercantilism including restrictions on trade.An interest in these events encouraged Smith's liberal views

> Wherever there is great property there is great inequality [...] The affluence of the rich excites the indignation of the poor, who are often [driven by want and envy] to invade his possessions [...] The acquisition of valuable and extensive property therefore requires the establishment of civil government. ([1776] 1999: V.i.b.2, p. 298)

Yet with reference to rent-seeking merchants perhaps, he also remarked,

> Civil government, so far as it is instituted for the security of property, is in reality instituted for the defence of the rich against poor, or of those who have some property against those who have none at all. ([1776] 1999: V.i.b.12, p. 302)

Smith's views were influenced by Hobbes and Locke. In significant part, liberty meant protection of private property rights. Yet the state was there to integrate and defend society both against outsiders and its more rapacious self, so that trade might flourish.

Sweet commerce

It is, therefore, no exaggeration to suggest that 'the principal drama in Smith's account of the progress of opulence consists in the victory of the individual spirit over the oppression of legal institutions' (Rothschild and Sen 2006: 335). Prosperity went together with freedom from unjust regulation. To the degree that freedom was realized Smith saw prosperity in Europe. Hence his rather startling remark: 'Whenever commerce is introduced into any country, probity and punctuality always accompany it. These virtues in a rude and barbarous country are almost unknown'. He cites the Dutch as being 'most faithfull to their word', not due to national character but rather to 'self interest'. 'When a person makes 20 contracts in a day ... the very appearance of a cheat would make him lose' ([1966] 1978: 327, p. 538). Though Smith here underlines self-interest, the situation he describes is also one of dense sociality, of desire for respect and propriety as much as probity ([1759] 1976: VI.I.3, pp. 212–3). Morality, law and commerce were working in each other's favour and improving the labourer's lot. This optimism informed Smith's view of the division of labour and 'stock' or capital accumulation. Trust in commerce shaped his critique of mercantile practice and his opinion of colonialism ([1759] 1976: I.iii.2, pp. 50–1).

Smith characterized the division of labour in terms of three innovations: the first of these was improvement in the dexterity of workers; the second was the time that specialization saved by reducing the need to pass between forms of work; and the third involved 'the application of proper machinery', sometimes the 'inventions of common workmen' and sometimes the product of specialist machinists. Smith observed with some enthusiasm,

> It is the great multiplication of the productions of all the different arts, in consequence of the division of labour, which occasions, in a well-governed society, that universal opulence which extends itself to the lowest ranks of the people. ([1776] 1982: I.i.10, p. 115.)

Here he linked both law and increasing wealth to improved conditions for workers. Society could be free and become more equal.

The third innovation involved accumulation, a central prerequisite for a continuing division of labour. Smith was a relentless advocate for progress and increased productivity ([1776] 1982: II.iii.32, p. 443). This required annual net savings to employ more workers or acquire the means to equip them with better 'machines and instruments'. Accumulation was for Smith a social process that had both technical and moral dimensions. As Skinner explains, Smith's assumption was that each successive annual saving, available in that same year, would lead to 'higher levels of saving and investment in subsequent years, thus generating further increases in output and income'. Smith's annual flow was in fact a 'spiral' that would vary from year to year with production costs while still persisting on its upward path (Skinner 1999a: 73).

In the midst of his technical account, Smith also expanded on the virtue of saving or, as he termed it, 'parsimony':

> Capitals are increased by parsimony, and reduced by prodigality and misconduct [...]
> Parsimony, and not industry, is the immediate cause of the increase of capital [...]
> Parsimony [...] puts into motion an additional quantity of industry, which gives an additional value to the annual produce. ([1776] 1982: II.iii.14–17, p. 437)

Parsimony then is the principal tool available to man for accumulation. It is not by accident that in this chapter of *Wealth of Nations* Smith makes one of his important remarks on human nature: that parsimony, or 'the principle to save', 'the desire of bettering our condition', 'comes with us from the womb, and never leaves us [till the] grave'. Here Smith's notions of economy and moral virtue intertwine.

For this very reason, the sources of 'prodigality and misconduct' that impeded growth drew harsh words from Smith. Two were notable. One was the tail end of the landed 'great proprietors' who had populated feudal society. In Smith's view, their self-indulgence fostered unproductive labour. He remarks of such a proprietor,

> having nothing for which he can exchange the greater part of the produce of his lands [... he] consumes the whole in rustic hospitality at home [...] He is at all times, therefore, surrounded with a multitude of retainers and dependents, who, having no equivalent to give in return [...] must obey him.

Examples are provided from England, Scotland, Europe and Arabia and Smith tartly remarks that these practices 'were common in all nations to whom commerce and manufactures are little known' ([1776] 1982: III.iv.5, pp. 508–9).

The more notable targets, however, were the sovereigns, governments, corporations and merchants involved in the mercantile system at home and abroad. Smith's concern was first and foremost with practices that precluded free trade; that sought to accumulate treasury wealth; and indulged in nation- and empire-building, often using trading companies as commercial and political tools. He was riled by the 'laborious and plodding' ignorance shown by defenders of mercantilism ([1776] 1999: IV.ix.3, p. 248). He was also critical of their greed which he saw as a threat to opulence and to a beneficent society. Of some he remarked, 'to widen the market and to narrow the competition, is always the interest of [these] dealers'. They comprised a group 'who have generally an interest to deceive and even to oppress the public, and who accordingly have upon many occasions [done so]' ([1776] 1982: I.xi.10, pp. 358–9). For Smith, the reach of commerce was international and intimately linked with Britain's colonies, foremost among them 'America'. His discussion of the New World reflects much of his stance on the mercantile system and his analysis of the transition from agrarian economies to an expanding system of commerce.

Smith also had views on New World African slaves and the Indian 'savages' of America. He allowed both subject peoples a certain moral integrity. Their propriety should not be judged simply in terms of one or another 'particular usage', such as infanticide. He compared the 'magnanimity' of the 'negro' slave favourably to 'the soul of his sordid master' and described the self-command of the North Americans ([1759] 1976: V.2.9,15, pp. 205, 210). More generally, he contested that slaves cost less than the free and proposed that 'tyranny and not utility was the basis of slavery' (Salter 1996: 225; see [1776] 1982: I.i.38, pp.183–4). Nonetheless, he passed lightly over the legalized oppression of the slaves and even more lightly over the fact that the welcome 'cheapness' of land in America, a stimulus to economic growth, derived in the final analysis from indigenous dispossession ([1776] 1999: IV.vii.c.50, p. 192; see also Tully 1994). This brings into sharp relief his discussions of Stoic philosophy and its notion that beneficence, through quietude, might extend universally (see Forman-Barzilai 2010). Smith suggested that such aspirations were 'the business of God and not of man', to whom 'is allotted a much humbler department [...] the care of his own happiness, of that of his family, his friends, his country'. Notwithstanding his regard for sympathy, he assigned distant sufferers to providence ([1759] 1976: VI.ii.3.6, p. 237).

Drawbacks to the division of labour provided another and more immediate domain where sentiment and self-interest clashed. Smith was well aware of the darker side to his opening gambit in *Wealth of Nations*: that a superior division of labour could increase from one to many thousands the number of pins made in a day ([1776] 1982: I.i.3, pp. 109–10; see Heilbroner 1973). It also involved the constricted and meaningless tasks to which industrial labour was condemned. Therefore, he recommended state-funded basic education for those 'bred to the lowest occupations' before they were employed ([1776] 1999: V.i.f.54, p. 371). Smith explained the need:

The man whose life is spent in performing a few simple operations [...] has no occasion to exert his understanding or to exercise his invention [...] He naturally loses, therefore, the habit of such exertion and generally becomes [...] stupid and ignorant [...] The torpor of his mind renders him not only incapable of relishing or bearing a part in any rational conversation, but of conceiving any generous, noble, or tender sentiment, and consequently of forming any just judgment concerning many even of the ordinary duties of private life. ([1776] 1999: V.i.f.50, pp. 368–9)

Smith's proposals were progressive for his time though they were only modestly ameliorative. Moreover, his concern jars with his optimistic accounts of the division of labour. There were no such proposals for slaves or for the indigenous dispossessed.

Discussion

Of sympathy and self-interest ...

Does Adam Smith succeed in his attempt to demonstrate that humankind is not simply selfish? In his view, morality can and should inform economic life. Even though this is often not the case, the opening remark in *Moral Sentiments* makes the point that 'how soever selfish' a person may be she sustains some interest in another. As such, sociality entails sympathy. Moreover, sympathy requires imagination because it involves more than a simple assimilation (see Griswold 2006). Through an imaginative act the spectator draws on her experience, *and yet steps beyond it*. The German philosopher, Max Scheler, puts well the type of point Smith was making: 'Fellow-feeling proper [...] presents itself in the very phenomenon as a *re-action* to the state and value of the other's feeling – as these are "*visualized.*"' One visualizes another and then reacts oneself. Two moments are involved. For a current reader, Smith's ideas stand in need of semiosis and a notion of symbolic constructs. In Scheler's words again, concerning the other, 'we treat their bodies as a *field of expression* for their experiences' and this is a '*symbolic*' relation (Scheler 1992: 55, 50–1).

The mutuality between social beings that Smith describes in his accounts of propriety, conscience and rules is captured in a mid-twentieth-century social science that spoke of the '*complementarity of expectations*' forged by the '*double contingency*' between an ego's chosen response and an alter's own chosen response to ego. The need for '*stability*', or predictability, brings shared symbolic systems, and with them the 'mutuality of normative orientation' (Parsons et al. 1951: 15–16). Smith's discussion captures in his own transactional terms this passage from the immediate to the socially normative. Society is the 'mirror' through which man knows himself ([1759] 1976: III.3, p. 110).[7]

And what of the supposed contradiction between two works respectively concerned with sympathy and self-interest; '*das Adam Smith problem*' (Teichgraeber III 1981)? *Moral Sentiments* and *Wealth of Nations* barely refer to each other and seem to proceed in different registers; the one praising virtue, the other built on 'an edifice of vice' (Griswold 1999: 260). Arguments for conceptual continuity now outweigh this image of discord due not least to the 1978 publication, in one volume, of the earlier (1762–3) and later (1766) student notes that comprise *Lectures on Jurisprudence*. The movement from morality through justice to commerce can be read as a punctuated exploration of the conditions for 'civilization' *as a good society*; one informed by everyday virtue, commutative justice and a modest 'universal opulence' that mediates inequality and allows even the 'lowest ranks' some capacity for benevolence. Each major work is different and, like Marx, Smith became engrossed in the system that would be liberal capitalism. Nonetheless, Enlightenment optimism reinforced his central point that law and configurations of economy had moved in tandem to generate a more beneficent and equal society (see Fleischacker 2013).

More analytically, the central place of betterment, not just sympathy, in Smith's thought points to renderings of interest, and sentiment, which are variable and nuanced. This self-interest is the one of saving, manufacturing and specialization; 'bettering' through the ages. Smith is clear about the perversion of self-interest in commercial life that, in his view, explained the corruptions of mercantilism. He also notes the 'deceptions' of wealth that ironically, in his view, kept 'in continual motion the industry of mankind' ([1759] 1976: IV.I.9, p. 183). He implies that the prosperity so achieved seldom brings personal 'tranquillity'.

Smith moved beyond David Hume when he deployed a consistent empiricism in his study of emotions and morality. His method is a transactional account of the genesis of value as much as virtues. More Aristotle than Kant, Smith's ethics is undeniably social. His impartial spectator might be Durkheim's *conscience collective* made immanent in the breast of everyman. Both are context specific and ethically relative (see Fleischacker 2004: 53). Most illuminating in this regard is Forman-Barzilai's (2010) critique of the stance that would have Smith reinterpreted, via his reflections on Stoicism, as a precursor of contemporary cosmopolitanism. She also contests the position in Smithian studies that would claim for his ethics an objectivist, 'transcultural' reach (2010: 166–92). She documents Smith's uncaring descriptions of those who had drawn the concern of some Christians and others: 'the many wretches … in the languor of poverty [or] in the agony of disease'. Injunctions to care for them came from 'whining and melancholy moralists' who would 'damp the pleasures of the fortunate' ([1759] 1976: III.3.9, p. 139). Smith's response to this comfortable compassion was cynical, even as he hoped for a 'commercial cosmopolis' as Forman-Barzilai terms it. She is right to describe him as a 'troubled particularist' whose work reflects how local ethics often is in capitalism's impersonal world.

… and the grander department

Though Adam Smith excoriated 'the man of system' with his 'ideal plan of government', by reputation he became such in the twentieth century. George Stigler (1971: 265), of the Chicago School of Economics, announced that Smith had built a 'stupendous palace' on the 'granite of self-interest'. Long before this era, and this political orientation, Karl Marx saw Adam Smith as a man of system and attacked his views on the division of labour. Although it is inconsistent with his historical materialism to ascribe an ethics to Marx, nonetheless, his accounts of accumulation, alienation and the more diffuse 'commodity fetishism' involve a notion of 'man' as elaborate and value-laden as Smith's. Marx too constructed a stadial history based on 'modes of production' with tribal, 'ancient communal' and feudal stages (Marx and Engels 1970, 42–6). Where Smith spoke of 'betterment' Marx referred to need that is socially constructed: 'the first need [...] leads to new needs; and this production of new needs is the first historical act' (Marx and Engels 1970: 49). Marx's history lacked 'moral sentiment' as an effective cause. In its place he furnished a lack in Smith's work: the dispossessions and ontological reconfigurations that reflect relations of power (see also Hirschman 1977).

The contrast is most marked when Marx discusses 'primitive accumulation' (Marx [1887] 1967: I, Pt.8). This notion was deployed by both Montesquieu and James Steuart, Smith's Scottish predecessor in political economy, but barely touched on by Smith (see Perelman 1983). In colourful language, Marx likens Smith's account of the parsimony required for accumulation to a 'history of economic original sin'. A 'frugal élite' triumphs over 'other lazy rascals' (Marx [1887] 1967: I, p. 713). Importantly, Marx traces the dispossessions of use rights in land, and leisure, which accompanied the formal 'freeing' of feudal agricultural labour. He also notes the dispossession of indigenous peoples that enriched early European industrialists in the colonial plantation world. Following his list of such dispossessions, which culminates with the Dutch in Java, Marx exclaims 'Sweet commerce!'

Contrary to Smith's account, this dispossession was not for Marx a mere prior amassing of wealth that advanced the division of labour. It was also ongoing and involved the 'estrangement' or 'alienation' of industrial labour (Marx 1964: 106–19). Once more, the contrast is striking. Smith proposes that the division of labour 'alone accounts for' increasing consumption among 'the lowest of the people' ([1962–63] 1978: vi.29, p. 341). Marx's view rests on a more developed (and mistaken) labour theory of value but also on a different rendering of man through a phenomenology that constitutes persons in terms of their relations to the material world, and one another. The factory labourer becomes estranged from his product and from nature. He is also alienated from himself, from those who dispatch his products, and from fellow-feeling with his kind (see also Ollman 1976: 136–56). Marx's concept of 'commodity fetishism' extends this notion of social relations objectified in things to interpret a commodified world (Marx 1967: I, pp. 71–83; see also Fromm 1966: 43–6). Possibly galvanized by Smith's account of the division of labour's adverse effects, Marx provided his own account of class cruelty. Accordingly, he was unimpressed with Smith's advice to the state on education for the 'very poor'. In his view, this would be merely a potion dispensed 'prudently and in homeopathic doses' ([1887] 1967: I, p. 362).

In an excited fashion, both Smith and Marx grasped the systematic nature of economy, its materiality and its sociality, for better and for worse. Both saw in it the possibility of a 'universal opulence' with benefits for all. Marx's unclaimed ethic lay in his critique of the dispossessions and inequalities that capitalism brought. The analytic power of this position resided in his structural account. It is hard to deny that both dimensions of his work augmented subsequent views of capitalism. Notwithstanding, Marx did not trace convincingly the steps by which man would become unalienated in an enduring world of commodities and wealth accumulation. And where the division of labour is concerned, his remarks on its demise were at best utopian critique (Marx and Engels 1970: 53). Notwithstanding his own limitations, Smith saw a role for ethics, justice and law in relation to commercial practice. Marx, on the other hand, saw himself as a theorist of change and definitely not a moral philosopher. Despite his accounts of capitalism's degradations, he had little interest in ethics or liberal ideologies of justice and right unless it was to note their obfuscating role. Not so subsequent social historians who have often portrayed the moral self-conceptions of those engaged in forms of resistance (e.g. Moore 1978; Thompson 1980; Scott 1985; see also Richards 1985).

The position of humanistic social science has been to critique capitalism, with some debt to Marx, and the liberal individual that Smith was, and which he portrayed. Yet criticism of liberal economics has not been accompanied by much systematic thought regarding non-liberal forms of theory that ground issues of equality and justice in a compelling and systematic ethics. A little like Marx perhaps, this critical thought most often suggests that morality is either sentimentality or else an imposition of the state. There is little reflection on everyday practice that, in conjunction with larger institutional change, might subvert market excess from within.[8] A proliferating politics of rights tends to fill the space along with a generalized critique of materialism or economics itself. As the following examples show, anthropologists have been such humanistic critics. But should this be their last word?

Philosopher Charles Griswold argues that in Smith's view, the 'worker who sells his labor [...] is not harmed by doing so' because it is the worker's 'property' to which he has a 'sacred and inviolable' right (1999: 299). C. P. Macpherson identified the source of these ideas in the philosophies of Hobbes and Locke. He critically re-rendered them as a 'possessive individualism' in which man is free by virtue of his 'proprietorship' of his person. But where freedom involves 'domination over things', men are forced to alienate themselves in the fight for possessions (Macpherson 2011). Theoretical works in anthropology (Sahlins 1976; Dumont 1977), and in regional ethnography, have referenced Macpherson's critical stance, especially as it bears on change in small-scale societies (e.g. Sykes 2007; Macintyre 2011).

In his account of 'the genesis and triumph' of economy as ideology, Louis Dumont questions modern individualism, egalitarianism and materialism. He identifies Mandeville, Smith and Marx as proponents of this ideology. Irrespective of their differences, Dumont sees all three as apostles of 'self-love' (Dumont 1977: 67). Two themes inform Dumont's discussion: one concerns individualism and the 'revolution in values' whereby the holism of traditional societies is relocated in each person. In egalitarian society, every individual is 'an embodiment of humanity at large'. His second theme concerns the manner in which materialism reconfigures relatedness. 'Relations between men and things' become more important than 'relations between men' (Dumont 1977: 4–5). Both similar and different to Smith and Marx, Dumont's idea is to celebrate dependency, which he calls 'hierarchy' (Dumont 1977: 118). The political economists welcome its demise.

Another intriguing work returns to fellow-feeling and self-interest, this time in northern Italy. In *The Moral Neoliberal*, Andrea Muehlebach provides an ethno-historical account of volunteering in a declining industrial community located on the outskirts of Milan. She also traces the passage of caring from nineteenth-century charity, through the social service provisions of the welfare state, to a reprivatization of these services in the hands of unpaid volunteers, as commodified 'ethical' citizens (2012: 42–4). Muehlebach treats morality and the market as 'dual ontologies' of liberal capitalism; as two distinctive 'economies', of fellow-feeling and self-interest – as exemplified in the work of Adam Smith. Albeit with great insight, she writes from the dystopic world of state coerced self-fashioning and suggests that Smith was a sentimentalist. On this view, morality can only ever be ideology (2012: 27–30).

Conclusion

Because justice is itself a virtue and law is required to keep avarice in check, Smith saw an inextricable link between the practice of everyday morality and the limits that should be placed on monopolies, merchants and commercial practice. Some of these constraints were personal and, as a consequence, his work on commerce has a marked ethical bent. Still, law had the major role in ensuring a just world, including a capitalist one. Smith's liberal individualism led him to an optimistic and limited view of capitalism's excess and its ability to subvert the law. He could not have imagined the institutional power and impersonalism that would mark global capitalism today. As Rothschild and Sen (2006) observe, however, he makes a poor talisman for neo-liberalism. His own good society would have been different; one in which the self-interest involved in the pursuit of betterment would be curtailed by sympathy, the bedrock of human sociality as such. In itself, *Moral Sentiments* is a useful conceptual guide for ethnographies of moral order that focus on a taken-for-granted sociality. Yet from the standpoint of anthropological critique, it is even more rewarding to make the types of connection that Smith did for a current generation: to interpret liberal capitalism anew and the relations, via law, that can obtain between moral systems and economies.

Notes

1   Reference Key to Adam Smith's Works:
    Lectures on Jurisprudence ([1962–63/1966] 1978)
    i.28, p. 14 = Volume 1. Section 28, page 14.
    The Theory of Moral Sentiments ([1759] 1976)
    II.ii.3.3, p. 86 = Part 2. Section 2. Chapter 3. Section 3, page 86.
    The Wealth of Nations ([1776] 1999 and [1776] 1982)
    V.i.a.2, p. 279 = Book 5. Chapter 1. Part 1. Section 2, page 279.
2   Throughout this essay, I largely use the terms 'man' and 'mankind' as they were used by Smith and others. Substituting terms produced a far less readable text.
3   From Mandeville's *Fable of the Bees, Private vices, publick benefits* ([1732] 1924).
4   Smith uses the terms 'agent' and 'spectator' to refer to the subjects of an interaction.
5   On issues of imagination see Griswold (2006) and Haakonssen (1981, 45–8).
6   Haakonssen (1981:100) remarks that Smith transitioned from discussion of 'injury' in *Moral Sentiments* to 'rights' in his *Lectures on Jurisprudence*.

7   I am not convinced by Forman-Barzilai's (2010: 63) use of Foucauldian notions of 'surveillance' and 'discipline' to render the social symbolic process. This seems to me conceptually forced.

8   Possibly Harvey (2012) is an example, and Erik Olin Wright's ideas on 'real utopias' (pers. comm. Sydney, 21 May 2015).

References

Austin-Broos, D. 1996. 'Morality and the Culture of the Market'. In *Economics and Ethics*, P. Groenewegen (ed.). London: Routledge, pp. 173–83.

Dumont, L. 1977. *From Mandeville to Marx: The Genesis and Triumph of Economic Ideology*. Chicago: University of Chicago Press.

Fleischacker, S. 2004. *On Adam Smith's* Wealth of Nations: *A Philosophical Comparison*. Princeton, NJ: Princeton University Press.

Fleischacker, S. 2013. 'Adam Smith on Equality'. In *The Oxford Handbook of Adam Smith*, C. J. Berry, M. Pia Paganelli and C. Smith (eds). Oxford: Oxford University Press, pp. 485–500.

Forman-Barzilai, F. 2010. *Adam Smith and the Circles of Sympathy: Cosmopolitanism and Moral Theory*. Cambridge: Cambridge University Press.

Fromm, E. 1966. *Marx's Concept of Man*. New York: Frederick Ungar.

Griswold, C. L. 1999. *Adam Smith and the Virtues of Enlightenment*. Cambridge: Cambridge University Press.

Griswold, C. L. 2006. 'Imagination: Morals, Science, and Arts'. In *The Cambridge Companion to Adam Smith*, K. Haakonssen (ed.). Cambridge: Cambridge University Press, pp. 22–56.

Haakonssen, K. 1981. *The Science of the Legislator: The Natural Jurisprudence of David Hume and Adam Smith*. Cambridge: Cambridge University Press.

Harvey, D. 2012. *Rebel Cities*. London and New York: Verso.

Heilbroner, R. 1973. 'The Paradox of Progress: Decline and Decay in *The Wealth of Nations*'. *Journal of the History of Ideas* 34(2): 243–62.

Hirschman, A. 1977. *The Passions and the Interests: Political arguments for Capitalism before Its Triumph*. Princeton, NJ: Princeton University Press.

Macintyre, M. 2011. 'Money Changes Everything: Papua New Guinea Women in the Modern Economy'. In *Managing Modernity in the Modern Economy*, M. Patterson and M. Macintyre (eds). St. Lucia: University of Queensland Press, pp. 90–120.

Macpherson, C. B. 2011. *The Political Theory of Possessive Individualism: Hobbes to Locke*. Ontario: Oxford University Press Canada.

Mandeville, B. [1732] 1924. *Fable of the Bees: Or, Private Vices, Publick Benefits*, F. B. Kaye (ed.). Oxford: Clarendon Press.

Marx, K. 1964. *The Economic and Philosophical Manuscripts of 1844*, D. J. Struik (ed.). New York: International Publishers.

Marx, K. [1887] 1967. *Capital*, Vol. 1. New York: International Publishers.

Marx, K. and Engels, F. 1970. *The German Ideology*, Pt. I, C. J. Arthur (ed.). New York: International Publishers.

Montesquieu, C. de Secondat, baron de. [1793] 1989. *The Spirit of the Laws*, A. M. Cohler, B. C. Miller (trans.) and H. S. Stone (eds). Cambridge: Cambridge University Press.

Moore, B. 1978. *Injustice: The Social Bases of Obedience and Revolt*. London: Macmillan.

Muehlebach, A. 2012. *The Moral Neoliberal: Welfare and Witizenship in Italy*. Chicago: Chicago University Press.

Ollman, B. 1976. *Alienation: Marx's Conception of Man in Capitalist Society*. Cambridge: Cambridge University Press.

Parsons, T., Shils, E., Allport, G., Kluckhohn, C., Murray, H., Sears, R., Sheldon, R., Stouffer, S. and Tolman, E. 1951. 'A General Statement'. In *A General Theory of Action*, T. Parsons and E. Shils (eds). Cambridge, MA: Harvard University Press, pp. 3–29.

Perelman, M. 1983. 'Classical Political Economy and Primitive Accumulation: The Case of Smith and Steuart'. *History of Political Economy* 15(3): 451–94.

Rothschild, E. and Sen, A. 2006. 'Adam Smith's Economics'. In *The Cambridge Companion to Adam Smith*, K. Haakonssen (ed.). Cambridge: Cambridge University Press, pp. 319–65.

Richards, D. 1985. 'Book Review: "Marx and Justice," "Marxism and Morality," "Equality and Liberty"'. *New York University Law Review* 60(6): 1188–201.

Sahlins, M. 1976. *Culture and Practical Reason*. Chicago: University of Chicago Press.

Salter, J. 1996. 'Adam Smith on Slavery'. *History of Economic Idea* 4(1/2): 225–51.

Scheler, M. 1992. *On Feeling, Knowing, and Valuing*, H. J. Bershady (ed.). Chicago: University of Chicago Press.

Scott, J. C. 1985. *Weapons of the Weak*. New Haven, CT, and London: Yale University Press.

Skinner, A. 1999. 'Analytical Introduction'. In *The Wealth of Nations* [1776], A. Smith, A. Skinner (ed.). London: Penguin, pp. 8–96.

Smith, A. [1759] 1976. *The Theory of Moral Sentiments*, eds D. D. Raphael and A. L. Macfie. Oxford: Clarendon Press; New York: Oxford University Press.

Smith, A. [1962–63/1966] 1978. *Lectures on Jurisprudence*, R. L. Meeks, D. D. Raphael and P. G. Stein (eds). Oxford: Clarendon Press.

Smith, A. [1776] 1982. *The Wealth of Nations*, Bks I–III, A. Skinner (ed.). London: Penguin.

Smith, A. [1776] 1999. *The Wealth of Nations*, Bks IV–V, A. Skinner (ed.). London: Penguin.

Stigler, G. J. 1971. 'Smith's Travels on the Ship of State'. *History of Political Economy* 3(2): 265–77.

Sykes, K. 2007. 'Interrogating Individuals: The Theory of Possessive Individualism in the Western Pacific'. *Anthropological Forum* (Special Edition) 17(3): 213–24.

Teichgraeber III, R. 1981. 'Rethinking *Das Adam Smith Problem*'. *Journal of British Studies* 20(2): 106–23.

Thompson, E. P. 1980. *The Making of the English Working Class*. London: Penguin.

Tully, J. 1994. 'Rediscovering America: The *Two Treatises* and Aboriginal Rights'. In *Locke's Philosophy: Content and Context*, G. A. J. Rogers (ed.). Oxford: Clarendon Press, pp. 165–96.

Winch, D. 1978. *Adam Smith's Politics*. Cambridge: Cambridge University Press.

6

'Can We Have Our Nature/Culture Dichotomy Back, Please?'

Nigel Clark, Rupert Stasch and Jon Bialecki

Introduction (Jon Bialecki)

The Scottish Enlightenment is justly famous for upending fields as diverse as medicine, economics and philosophy – not to mention anthropology. But perhaps the greatest legacy of this intellectual awakening is the effect that one of its least known luminaries had on the seemingly inconsequential field of geology. In 1785, to an astounded gathering of the Royal Society of Edinburgh, James Hutton gave two lectures that were subsequently published as *A Theory of the Earth* (Hutton 1788). Hutton's radical thesis was that the earth's form had not remained unchanged since the seven days of Creation, and that the planet's topography was not the result of a singular catastrophic universal deluge or primary ocean. Rather, Hutton argued that the shape of the earth was the result of processes of constant but infinitesimally slow transformation. Hutton's claim was that erosion and volcanic uplift constantly worked together to remake the surface of the earth anew. This process, though, was so slow that it could only be inferred, occurring at the scale of not hundreds or thousands but, rather, millions of years. Hutton's conclusion was encapsulated in the famous final sentence of the paper where he first presented this argument: 'The result of our present enquiry is that we find no vestige of a beginning, no prospect of an end.'

Hutton's claim has accorded him the honour of being the founder of modern geology, as it states on the gravesite memorial that can be found in Greyfriars Kirkyard, located in Old Town Edinburgh, just minutes away from the original site of the University of Edinburgh. Hutton's theory accomplished more than that, however. It was also pivotal in laying the groundwork for the development of the theory of evolution. When Darwin toured the world in the HMS *Beagle* as the ship's naturalist, he brought with him all the then-extant volumes of Charles Lyell's *Principles of Geology* (1830–33); Lyell's book was a full-throated defence of Hutton's then still controversial geological theory. It was Lyell's book, credited in Darwin's *On the Origins of Species*, that opened Darwin's eyes to the vistas of time that he felt was necessary for natural selection to function as a means of speciation.

Hutton's work is therefore at once humanist *and* corrosive of any easy humanism. On the one hand, it champions human rationality as it presents our species as having a unique capacity, discipline and command of natural forces to deduce formative processes otherwise obscured through the passage of time – 'This subject is important to the human race, to the possessor of this world, to the intelligent being Man, who foresees events to come, and who, in contemplating his future interest, is led to enquire concerning causes, in order that he may judge of events in which otherwise he could not know' (Hutton 1788: 214). At the same time, the suggestion of ancient pre-human eras challenges the concept of the human as a privileged species. Not only do these vistas of time open the way for the 'cosmic outsideness' that terrified the American author H. P. Lovecraft, and haunts much of contemporary post-humanism (see Thacker 2011: 19–20), the stretches of long pre-human aeons implicit in Hutton's theory also eats away at the Kantian vision of human subjectivity that has been so influential to much of Euro-American modernity. Immemorial time taxes the epistemological conceit that (putting aesthetics aside) though we are walled off from the way objects are in and of themselves, we can know them as they exist 'for us'. Here, we have long-lost forces that are indifferent to the much later development of humanity. There is no 'for us' to be found (Meillassoux 2008).

When viewed from a strictly anthropological perspective, though, what is most striking is the way that Hutton's work at once reinforces one of the most foundational, and now problematic, oppositions in anthropology, and yet at the same time undoes that binary. Hutton's positing of an earth with unimaginably ancient beginnings helps validate a nature/culture dichotomy; if human history is just a slim swath of unimaginably vaster and more numerous ages, then it becomes possible to imagine a nature without a culture, a move which in turns suggest culture as something not identical to, or automatically following from, the natural order. At the same time, as the anthropologist Richard Irvine (2014a, 2014b) has recently suggested, Hutton's hypothesis in some ways is necessary for the Anthropocene to be conceivable in the first place. The human features and effects that constitutes the Anthropocene can only be truly visible when juxtaposed against a background of extended ages first charted in the West by Hutton. Thus, Hutton's work catalyses our conceiving of that most profound of nature-culture hybrids: an age forged, and perhaps destroyed, by *Homo sapiens sapiens*.

There is one more point that follows, though, when we juxtapose James Hutton and the Anthropocene. The apocalyptic anxieties that almost always arrive with the idea of the Anthropocene suggests that Hutton's claim that there is 'no beginning', may hold up much better than his presumption of there being 'no prospect for an end'. Indeed, Hutton's Uniformitarianism, set up in opposition to biblically dependent diluvian accounts of geological formation, may have blinded us to Catastrophism-leaning arguments regarding terrestrial or cosmic forces that could interrupt the Anthropocene – or which the Anthropocene may unknowingly unleash.

Thus, the quality and magnitude of the forces that we are playing with during the Anthropocene as a world-historical fact may exceed the capacity of the Anthropocene as a theoretical analytic to understand. In short, perhaps despite the critique that has been launched against it, the nature/culture opposition may still have much to offer.

It was these sets of concerns that contextualized the original plenary session at the ASA Decennial Conference in 2014 (convened by Magnus Course, Jamie Cross and me), and that was the precursor of this rendition of that session by Nigel Clark and Rupert Stasch. Nigel Clark, whose institutional home is at the Environment Centre of Lancaster University, is a sociologist by training but a geographer by profession. He has written not only on the vulnerabilities of human social and political forms to natural forces but also on the forms of collective human responses that those overwhelming terrestrial and cosmic forces may trigger. Rupert Stasch is a Cambridge socio-cultural anthropologist. He works on the Korowai of West Papua; in particular, on the role that the Korowai play in a media- and tourism-enflamed Western imaginary that is searching for a stabilizing 'primitive' other: a living specimen of the long-running occidental fantasy of humanity in some originary natural state. Given the way that their collective works not only straddle both sides of the nature/culture divide but also play with the generative differential forces expressed through and created by that divide, we (Course, Cross and me) turned to them at the ASA conference as we do here with a simple, heartfelt anthropological request: either because of, or despite, all that is on the table when we conjure with the concept of the Anthropocene, should we not also make use of the conceptual apparatus central not just to a prior anthropology but to an Enlightenment mode of Western thought? In short, 'Can we have our nature/culture dichotomy back, please?'

Part one (Nigel Clark)

Geologies of enlightenment

What planet are you on?

Long ago, in another hemisphere, perhaps even in a bygone geological epoch, I discovered the later writings of cultural theorist Raymond Williams. What drew me to Williams was his willingness, rare in the late 1970s, to fuse ecological thinking with radical social politics. 'In this actual world there is [...] not much point in counterposing or restating the great abstractions of Man and Nature', he wrote. 'We have mixed our labour with the earth, our forces with its forces too deeply to be able to draw back and separate either out' (1980: 83).

These words have since been copiously cited by critical social thinkers to support claims that the great modern binary – nature/culture and its variants – needed to be thoroughly undone. There are, at very least, several related factors motivating this task. One, perhaps Williams's prime aim, is to avert the tendency, familiar in the Western tradition, of conservative political forces evoking the referential force of nature in order to delegitimate undesired social change. Another is to prompt us to come to terms with the historical impact of social processes on the environment, especially valuable for problematizing the idea of wilderness and all its occlusions of the agency of non-Western peoples. A third is to undercut human exceptionalism and encourage us to take our place in the cosmos amidst a world of other beings and entities.

These are all imperatives I happily affirm. But has the project of effacing the nature/culture dichotomy become too routine, too strident, too totalizing? As social theorist Vicki Kirby cogently asks: 'Why has the critique of binaries been turned into a moral witch-hunt, as if oppositional logic is an error to be corrected?' (1999: 27–8). Without dismissing the practice of deconstructing dualistic thinking, Kirby argues that too hastily dismantled dichotomies have a habit of circling back and reinsinuating themselves in the very critical practices doing the demolition work. Moreover, she insists, making cuts or distinctions is not simply an error – a misguided partitioning of an otherwise continuous world – it is a productive process. Or rather, it *is* productivity, the very means by which processes of differentiation take place and are sustained (Kirby 1999: 28).

With this in mind, I want to take the current 'geologic predicament' of our species as an incitement to reconsider the nature/culture dualism – and question some of the prevailing modes of overcoming it. And then, in the context of a shifting and divisive earth, I will return to Kirby's provocations.

First, back to Williams. Just a few pages on from his influential encounter with the human/nature antinomy comes another prompt, much less cited. Williams calls upon his audience to 'to re-emphasize, as a fundamental materialism, the inherent physical conditions – a specific universe, a specific planet, a specific evolution, specific physical lives – from which all labour and all consciousness must take their origins' (1980: 108). The implications of this passage seem rather different from the first, and in the context of current planetary conditions, even more prescient.

It is noteworthy that Williams was writing not only in the midst of unfolding environmental problems but just behind a wave of momentous changes in the earth sciences. As historian John Brooke (2014: 25–8) reminds us, the years 1966–73 alone saw the emergence of four major new perspectives on the shaping of our planet. First came the confirmation of the theory of plate tectonics – the basis of a truly integrated view of the earth's crustal dynamics. Soon after came the thesis that evolution is punctuated by catastrophic bursts linked to major geophysical events, followed by a new appreciation of the role of extraterrestrial impacts in shaping earth history and, finally, the beginnings of the idea the major subcomponents of the earth work in collusion – as expressed in the Gaia hypothesis and earth systems theory (see Clark and Gunaratnam 2016).

Though quite a few dualisms or divisions in received ways of thinking about our planet began to take a tumble in this list, it is worth considering just how little these developments – and the successive transformations in the earth and life sciences that they unleashed – have impacted on the social sciences and humanities. Until very recently, Williams's summoning of fellow critical thinkers to attend to 'a specific planet' has gone largely unanswered. And that's unfortunate, given that these literally 'earth-shattering' shifts in the scientific understanding of planetary dynamics do the groundwork for the major geophysical challenges of recent years; the abrupt climate change thesis and the more generalized idea of human-induced earth system change – shorthanded in the notion of the Anthropocene.

The Anthropocene idea may foreground human agency, but it depends on an understanding of an earth bursting with instabilities of its own. Bringing together an older stratigraphic geology with a newer earth system science, the thesis hinges on a novel understanding of the way that the planet's relatively slow moving lithic crust articulates with the more mobile spheres of water, air, ice and life. It is the interaction of these subsystems that give rise to an earth system with multiple possible operating states – with the disturbing possibility of being able to flip rapidly from one regime to another. And with this folding together of the temporalities and dynamics of the geophysical earth and time-spaces of social life, the question of what planet we are on erupts into social thought.

In interesting ways, the Anthropocene reveals the currency of Williams's call both to relinquish human/nature dichotomies and to acknowledge the deep planetary prehistory of the human. But so too does it throw into relief the tension between these two imperatives. Over the intervening years, it is the demand to discompose the society/nature opposition that has prevailed in critical social thought – most notably in a range of 'relational materialisms' that attribute agency to all manner of things and insist on the co-enactment of the social and the natural (Clark 2011: 30–4). Such ontological privileging of mutual or co-constitutive modes of relating often appears to be taken as the very condition of possibility of political change in the complex, messy realities we inhabit. In other words, it is potentially within our grasp to collectively recompose the worlds we share with other beings or entities precisely because we are always already in relations with them.

The idea of a specific universe, planet and evolution as the origin of our social being has very different implications – for it draws us into domains that are before, beneath or beyond the human presence. In these regions or worlds there may well be all manner of entanglements and co-productions – but they do not involve 'us'. To put it crudely, there is 'nature' but not what we would recognize as 'culture' or 'society'.

The tension between nature–society co-enactment and fully inhuman worlds or forces, I want to suggest, is not only to be found in Williams's work or in recent critical engagements with the Anthropocene. It has roots reaching deep into the European Enlightenment, and especially into the emergent geological imaginaries of the latter eighteenth century. For here, in early encounters with the deep temporal rumbling of the earth, are profound premonitions of the geological anxieties of our own era.

Enlightenment geotrauma

When Williams or any of our contemporaries speak of human–nature co-production, they are channelling a lengthy tradition of critical concern with the social transformation of the natural world and the self – or societal transformation seen to be its corollary. As Marx and Engels observed in the *German Ideology*: 'the nature that preceded human history [...] is nature which today no longer exists anywhere (except perhaps on a few Australian coral-islands of recent origin)' ([1845] 2004: 63). If Marx carries forward the Enlightenment vision of the human capacity to improve upon the natural world, so too does he inherit the eighteenth-century concern with the planet's inhuman origins. At high school, the young Marx had been tutored by geologist Johann Steininger – a follower of the geoscience pioneer Abraham Gottlob Werner (Laudan 1987: 94–5). It is from Werner that we get the basic stratigraphic notion of successive 'rock formations' distinguished by the time and mode by which they were formed – the most likely inspiration for Marx's own notion of social formations.

But when Marx later observes that 'the processes by which the earth made the transition from a liquid sea of fire and vapour to its present form now lie beyond its life as finished earth' ([1857] 1973: 460), he seems a little hasty to consign the formative action to the past. This seems to reflect the influence of Hegel. Like many contemporary *philosophes* Hegel was a keen follower of developments in the study of the earth. Which meant, like Kant before him, that he had to grapple with the experience of deep time, the dramatic opening up of earth history from a biblically sanctioned few millennia to a yawning hundreds of millions of years (see Irvine 2014a). As palaeontologist Stephen Jay Gould aptly observes, when Freud recounted the successive 'humiliating' decentrings of a self-important humanity, he neglected perhaps the greatest: the eighteenth-century discovery of a protracted earth history largely devoid of human presence (1987: 1–3). The deepest shock, however, may not have been the expanding time span nor even the radical absence of humans but the perturbing manner in which the earth had come to attain its present state.

Support for an extended geohistory came from increasing evidence that layers of the earth's crust contained fossilized remnants of life forms no longer present in the world. The sense that transitions between geological epochs were marked by events catastrophic enough to expunge entire populations of living creatures found expression in the idea of 'revolutions of the Earth' – a notion Kant and Hegel shared with many late eighteenth- and early nineteenth-century geological thinkers. Kant seems to be one of the first to glimpse the shocking implications of such upheavals. If the earth has annihilated its own living creations many times before, what then is the prospect for the future, the outlook for humankind? For as Kant agonized, if the universe lost its one and only thinking being, then 'the whole creation would be a mere waste, in vain, and without final purpose' ([1790] 2005: 219).

Kant's response was to construct an entire edifice of thought in which humankind and cosmos were so conceptually bound together that it was next to impossible to imagine one without the other: a system in which gazing at a convulsing nature served as a stimulus to strengthen man's steely will and self-responsibility. Hegel too, with a later and even darker comprehension of the earth's susceptibility to 'tremendous revolutions' went a step further. So world-transforming was humankind's ascent, he decided, that by definition the earth's formative tumult must be confined to a long-superseded past. As Hegel announced in the 1817 *Jena Encyclopedia*, revolutions of the earth must now be considered ancient history and thus of mere academic interest. 'This temporal succession of the strata, does not explain anything at all', Hegel insisted:

> One can have interesting thoughts about the long intervals between such revolutions, about the profounder revolutions caused by alterations of the earth's axis, and also those caused by the sea. They are, however, hypotheses in the historical field, and this point of view of a mere succession in time has no philosophical significance whatever. ([1817] 1970: 283)

Henceforth it is humankind that makes history, not the earth. Marx seems to have bought into this. And so, it seems, has nearly all subsequent social thought. Substitute *no social* or *no political* significance for *no philosophical significance* and this seems pretty much where the social sciences and humanities have been for the intervening two centuries.

Much has been said about both the achievements and the pathologies of the European Enlightenment. But perhaps not enough has been made of the era's deep-seated geological anxieties, and the enduring ramifications of strategies to keep 'geotrauma' at bay. In their efforts to improve, to accumulate and to power their progressive advance, modernizing Europeans burrowed deep into the earth's crust. The deeper they dug, the more evidence they unearthed of the planet's proclivity for life-annihilating upheaval – with its accompanying low, rumbling intimation of a future earth bereft of human presence (Clark 2016).

Finding ways to defuse the planet's cataclysmic tendencies may well have been one of the master strokes of modern European thought. Effectively what Kant and Hegel each managed to do was to find a way to neutralize the fearsome potentiality of a dynamic earth, to contain and disarm the threat that inhuman nature posed to the ascendance of our species. As philosopher Quentin Meillassoux (2008) has recently argued, the much mulled-over culture/nature duality may well have functioned as a smokescreen – an alibi for avoiding the bigger, scarier confrontation with the autonomy and indifference of extra-human nature. What Kant succeeded in doing, Meillassoux insists, was not sundering society from nature, not partitioning the human from the non-human, but binding them into a 'correlation'. And this is our inheritance, he argues, for Western social and philosophical thought has continued to disavow the idea of a natural world that is in and for itself ever since Kant.

If we run with Meillassoux's framing of correlationism – and my geological excavations suggest we should – then questions are raised about commitment to the co-enactment of the natural and the social as the best way forward, about prevailing assumptions that the messy reality of nature-culture entanglement is where our full attention ought to be focused. Then again, isn't co-constitution of humankind and the earth – our labour and its forces inextricably mixed – precisely what the Anthropocene thesis is all about? And what might it mean for our thinking about 'nature' and 'culture' if we ceased to imagine that the fate of the planet and the cosmos was bundled up with our own?

The cosmos after nature/culture

Treated cautiously, the conceptual framework of society–nature co-constitution seems to me to be useful for approaching certain kinds of issue: sociotechnical risk, ecological problems, human–animal relations, to name a few. But geophysical events – with their largely inhuman forces and timeframes – grate against assumptions of mutuality and co-presence. Which may help explain why, until very recently, most research in a relational materialist key has been oriented towards technological and biological processes.

If the Anthropocene thesis resuscitates the eighteenth-century thematic of life threatening 'revolutions of the Earth', its novel positing of a human trigger for geophysical threshold events seems to invite a relational (we might say correlational) reading. But it is important to recall that just as human-induced climate change makes little sense without considering the broad sweep of past planetary climatic regimes, so too does an epoch counter-signed by *Anthropos* draw its significance from the context of a great succession of decisively inhuman geological periods. Meanwhile, beyond the anthropic flourish, the sun continues to power the planetary surface and the earth's inner heat incessantly drives convection currents in the viscous rock of the mantle and the movement of tectonic plates.

So, we might say that the Anthropocene predicament simultaneously intensifies both sides of Williams's equation: it foregrounds the zone of social-natural interplay while reminding us that this slender province exists only by consent of the vast, pressing inhuman forces all around it (Clark and Gunaratnam 2016). And in this regard, our late eighteenth- to early nineteenth-century predecessors had every justification for constructing thought systems to salve our geotrauma and boost our confidence. It is just that averting our gaze from potential paroxysms of the earth and seeking to construct our own impregnable worlds turns out to have greatly exacerbated our vulnerability – as repressive strategies are wont to do.

But where else might our deconstructive urges lead us if we recognize that effacing nature/society antinomies is not the first or last word – and if we face the fact that this is not a cosmos organized for our comfort or our continuity? Here I want to return to Vicki Kirby's work, and in particular her reflection on whether there is 'another way to think the order of the nature/culture problematic that doesn't rush to answer it by repeating the very terms that presume it' (1999: 24). What Kirby prompts us to ask is the extent to which evoking a non-human nature that precedes or exceeds the complications of culture is enough to dismantle the society/nature binary – or to avoid erecting it in the first place. For even if we attribute the most momentous powers and agencies to the inhuman, have we necessarily freed ourselves from imagining that culture – if and when it arrives – brings to the world something unique and unprecedented, something unconscionable in 'raw' nature?

Beyond simply repeating that nature does things even in our absence, Kirby inquires what exactly it is about culture or language or subjectivity that we assume belongs to us alone – and what it is that stops us from perceiving these qualities in the world at large. Which brings her to consider whether 'what we conventionally call Nature is as actively literate, numerate, and inventive as anything we might include within Culture' (2011: 66). Moreover, Kirby queries, what if nature not only communicates with itself, but questions itself? And what if our own probings and interrogations of our planet were to be viewed as somehow continuous with 'the Earth's own scientific investigations of itself' (2011: 34). Finally, and coming back to our initial provocation concerning binaries, Kirby then raises the possibility that it is not only ourselves who make distinctions, draw lines, impose divisions, but that biological phenomena (or geological phenomena, it might be added) make their own cuts, their own 'operational differentiations' (2011: 66).

And so, we might wonder, if nature breaches its own integrity – as in the case of an earth that breaks with its own previous operating state – does it also seek to span these divides, to reach across its own rifts? For as poet and writer Anne Michaels muses in the novel *Fugitive Pieces*:

> It is no metaphor to witness the astonishing fidelity of minerals magnetized, after hundreds of millions of years, pointing to the magnetic pole, minerals that have never forgotten magma whose cooling off has left then forever desirous […] Perhaps the electron is neither particle nor wave but something else instead, much less simple – a dissonance – like grief, whose pain is love. (1997: 53, 211)

We have wandered some way from the theme of mixing of our labour with the forces of the earth – but once the culture/nature couplet is prised open, there is no telling where it might lead. At the very least, we have begun to part company with Kant's insistence that without us 'the whole creation would be a mere waste … without final purpose'. If the idea that the earth and cosmos might spiral on without us – sensate, desirous, self-questioning – is not exactly a consolation, it may well offer timely provocations as we face the revolutions of the earth now gathering on the horizon.

Part two (Rupert Stasch)

Which nature/culture distinction for anthropology in Anthropocene time?

In the historical context of the Anthropocene as both a material crisis and a condition of consciousness, is the nature/culture distinction obsolete, or helpful? Addressing this question requires recognizing that there are many different understandings available of 'nature', of 'culture' and of the idea of a 'distinction' between them. The differences between these understandings ought to be clarified as part of any argument affirming or denying a nature/culture distinction. In what follows, I will advocate the heuristic anthropological value of just one limited version of the nature/culture distinction, before then turning to the question of the Anthropocene and how it is illuminated by this specific distinction.

Critiques of nature and culture

Since at least the mid-1970s, there has been a trend in anthropology and allied fields of rejecting the nature/culture distinction. One set of important contributions has opened the question of cultural variability in whether 'nature' is even a widely recognized category in world societies. Strathern (1980), Wagner ([1975] 1981), Viveiros de Castro (1998) and Descola (2013) are among those who have explored this issue. With deep conceptual insight as well as extensive ethnographic support, they have concluded that the Enlightenment's nature/culture distinction is peculiar and not a sound basis for comparative anthropological understanding. In my own broader research I see myself as a student and fellow-traveller of these authors' ideas (for example, Stasch 2009), and a student and partisan of the provincialization of the self-styled universalisms of Enlightenment 'Man' that these anthropologists' work advances (compare Tsing 2016). I view the specific distinction between nature and culture that I propose to rehabilitate here, and the way I propose to use it, as an homage to these authors' contributions, consistent with what they have done, and an attempt at further clarification of issues they raise.

Latour (1993) carries these anthropologists' train of reasoning and forms of evidence back to the Enlightenment formation itself, to argue that while naturalism is the ideology of this formation, it is not even a description of its actual character. Our worlds do not consist of nature and culture but of hybrid nature/cultures. And the non-human is as laden with forms of agency as the human. He takes ecological crises of the Anthropocene as the very model of a network or collective, the understanding of which is not helped by the concept of nature (Latour 2009).

Additionally, a large variety of anthropologists have sought to privilege materiality over idea, sign and category as a site of the cultural (e.g. Gell 1998), or to develop understandings of signification and representation that have an internal relation to materiality rather than being exogenous to materiality (e.g. Keane 2003; Manning 2012; Hull 2012; Ochs 2012). Another specific movement has been interest in 'affect', conceptualized as a domain of monistic unity between human experience and a wider material cosmos, following Spinoza by way of Deleuze, Guattari and Massumi.

In the world or in anthropological research about it, we have also seen the growth in prominence of a variety of phenomena that trouble a nature/culture division, such as technologically assisted reproduction; study of biopolitics, or the making of social orders centrally through the regulation of biology and population; study of infrastructure; projects of non-anthropocentric or post-humanistic study of human-animal and human-machine relations; a proportional shift from fieldsites where land features are not overwhelmingly anthropogenic in all respects, to fieldsites where they are; study of virtualized or mediatized nature, or of locations where the framing of earth features *as* spectacular nature is plainly entangled with human histories; the increasing ambition of kinship studies to unify conception, pregnancy, birth, bodiliness and feeling with issues of kinship as categorial and moral order; and the deepened quality of ethnographic knowledge of many Amerindian people's understandings of their porous social and subjective interchanges with plants, animals, landforms and divinities.

What kind of distinction would we want?

Any nature/culture distinction an anthropologist today might want to utilize would need to take on lessons of this work. And so behind the question 'Can we have our nature/culture distinction back?' is another one: '*Which* nature/culture distinction would we wish to reclaim, in light of what we have learned?'

'Nature' means many different things. The element that critics of the nature/culture distinction most commonly reject as ethnocentric and ideological, rather than a helpful heuristic category in comparative work, is nature as an entity or a place; nature as a system, a unity, a field of laws, and a stable hierarchical order; and nature as a resource base externally given to human dominion (compare Valeri 1990: 264–9). Yet there is a problem of possible slippage between rejecting the 'straw man' of these most Enlightenment-specific layers of what 'nature' can mean, and rejecting other layers of what 'nature' can mean that might better be kept in consideration.

It is long-standing anthropological practice to refine our comparative concepts to mean what we need them to mean and, thereby, to work toward a helpful metalanguage for describing and translating how worlds are organized. One of Latour's own methodological concepts is 'infra-language', by which he means analytic language of minimal semantic specificity (1995: 30). The ultimate purpose of such language, on his account, is to facilitate making the different frames of reference that are being translated between show forth in their specificity. I will borrow his concept of 'infra-language' for my own purposes below.

In veering away from nature as an unitary system and as an entity that is localized in specific places and objects, one could also move away from taking the nature/culture distinction to entail that there are natural things and there are cultural things. Rather, the prototype case could be that there are natural aspects and cultural aspects in the same things, and that in many situations any presence of the natural is also a presence of the cultural. The distinction could describe a border-zone or a threshold of inter-implication more than a separating line between two kingdoms. And yet the distinction could still be worth drawing.

As is also common in anthropological work, we can distinguish the categories informing thought of people whose lives we are seeking to understand, from the categories specific anthropologists wish to inform their own thought. There could be a nature/culture distinction in the thought of people we are in dialogue with (or a range of nature/culture distinctions), that is not exactly the same as a nature/culture distinction in a researcher's thought. Research subjects' judgements of what is natural or cultural should not always be expected to closely track researchers' own. The relation between these levels is always complex. This is another sense in which 'nature' means many things and there are many nature/culture distinctions that could be differently rejected or accepted. Nor should we expect research subjects' concepts to be expressed primarily in the mode of explicit single words or propositions. Those concepts' more consequential life may take oblique forms and require very active but epistemologically problematic work of interpretive inference for an anthropological observer to make them out. Further, specific anthropologists' own thought may be opaque to themselves: just because a researcher affirms or rejects a nature/culture distinction in explicit propositional discourse does not mean this overt discourse closely matches the researcher's own actual practices of thinking and analysis.

In my remaining comments, I will consider directly only the issue of nature/culture distinctions as they might inform the thought of people whose lives we are seeking to understand.

The table below lists at least a few distinctions that the language of 'nature versus culture' sometimes shifts across in different contexts of its use.

It is the last distinction in this list that I would propose retaining, as candidate meanings of 'nature' and 'culture' for a comparative infra-language. This distinction perhaps repeats the prior one of 'determination' versus 'freedom', and bears partial

biology	vs	culture
genes, hard-wiring;		nurture, socialization;
animal;		human;
earth, physics;		human;
things;		humans;
objects;		subjects;
matter;		mind;
raw material of matter, energy, life;		human appropriation and reorganization of matter, energy, life;
extrahuman biophysical environment;		human society;
fact;		value;
primary qualities, things as they are		secondary qualities, things as experienced;
real;		symbolic;
transhistorically universal;		historically particular;
necessary;		contingent;
heteronomy, determination;		autonomy, freedom;
processes and conditions understood to unfold independently of subjects' intentional, mind-mediated control.		processes and conditions subjects are understood to intentionally control.

ties to many of the other distinctions. But it can be separated from presuppositions of 'nature' as environment, as a system of laws, as universal, as singular or as unitary.

One could argue that determination versus freedom is specific to European Enlightenment thought, and not relevant to comparative knowledge. Or one could argue the same about an opposition between human intentional mind and what is outside the mediation of human intention. But there are many areas of ethnography and language where there is evidence of people being oriented by *some* kind of problematic of what can be controlled via the mediation of mental intention, and what is given, constraining or presupposed from sources independent of human mental intention. Enlightenment ideology might promote peculiar understandings of 'freedom' that are ill-suited to understanding people's lives in all times and places. But perhaps a relatively open or semantically reduced understanding of 'freedom' of a different order is relevant beyond Enlightenment-shaped worlds?

Cross-societal phenomena of mourning are one of many possible illustrations of this. Death is organized variably in different social settings, and responses or non-responses to it are also diverse. But in many contexts, death events are a major social disruption and emotional trauma, and there are elaborate processes by which people adjust to those events. This suggests in those contexts a basic problematic of humans having something done to them that they do not intend, control or fully comprehend, and they are reckoning with the actuality of what they did not control and intend. Phenomena of killing, of political use and regulation of death, and of biomedical creation or prolongation of life complicate these dialectics of human autonomy and heteronomy around the life/death threshold, but do not involve the complete elimination of such dialectics.[1]

This proposal posits that all people are likely to have a reflexive understanding of human action as lodged in a dialectical inter-space of the given, the enabling, the constraining on the one hand, and the intentionally performed or mediated-by-consciousness on the other. Yet we can also expect the distinction between intentional control and what unfolds independently of human intention to map onto different areas of experience across societies or contexts. People change the location of this threshold or have multiple thresholds operating at once. And this threshold is likely to be present in most areas of life not in the form of there being natural things and cultural things, but in the form of there being natural or naturalized levels to all objects, activities and states of being, and cultural or culturalized aspects to them.

I am thus suggesting that nature/culture could be a comparative infra-language for talking about people's own cultural sensibilities about agency and its conditions, especially in relation to biophysical levels of being. The nature/culture distinction as understood here would be a heuristic path toward perceiving and thinking about people's reflexive understandings about intentional control versus that which is other to such control. An idea of tension between what humans control and what are uncontrolled or less controlled conditions of their actions is a potentially helpful starting point for comparative work on variation in how that tension is constituted in different societies or institutional settings, and variation in the location of people's understood thresholds between natural and cultural (in this specific sense).

My suggestion implies that the category 'subject' or 'human' itself is a needed infra-language, against the current of contemporary academic post-humanism. It is likely that virtually all humans have concepts of 'human', and that these concepts partly involve a close (but non-exclusive) relation of prototypy between 'human' and 'intentionality' or 'consciousness'. 'Human' could be defined and distributed in all kinds of culturally variable ways. Part of the point of this infra-language would be to open up to the extreme variability in understandings and relationalities of 'human' or 'subject' cross-societally and cross-institutionally, while also registering that categories akin to 'human' or 'subject' are *central* to most people's worlds, whether lexically named or only tacitly entailed in discourse and practice. In other words, rejecting European 'humanism' leads not to post-humanism but to comparative inquiry into the understandings of 'human' or 'subject' and its relationalities that are historically particular to different people and social contexts, something the best critics of the nature/culture distinction have pioneered. Correlatively, 'intentionality' or 'consciousness' are likely to be defined and distributed in all kinds of ways, in different systems of thought and practice. Across this variability, I am suggesting that most people are likely to understand 'human' as being centrally lodged in an ambiguous border-zone of intentionality and conditions independent of human intention, and that studying their theories and practices of the organization of such a border-zone is a core anthropological task.

Some critics of the nature/culture distinction retain distinctions cognate to the one I am making, while eschewing 'nature' as too badly compromised a term to be useful for naming one pole of the distinction.[2] The nature they reject again tends to be most focally the Enlightenment one of a unitary hierarchical system of laws. Perhaps the more limited, intentionality-focused distinction should be drawn using more neutral labels, even merely algebraic ones like 'A' versus 'B'. Additionally, it would be possible to accept a heuristic nature/culture distinction without expecting A or B themselves each to be unitary. Each could be further subdivided, and the A/B distinction itself could be crosscut by other distinctions that are equally important or more important. But in the midst of those needed additional directions of inquiry, retaining for a little while a language of 'nature' versus 'culture' might foster valuable recognition of continuities between the current task and an older anthropological project.

The Anthropocene and the nature/culture distinction: A crisis of 'human'

The current emergence of humans – or rather, of those humans participating in the most energy-intensive tiers of industrial economic systems – into the status of a geophysical force might at first seem to weigh on the side of discarding the nature/culture distinction. For example, at an early moment of popular awareness of climate change some years before the term Anthropocene entered circulation, environmentalist and journalist Bill McKibben argued in *The End of Nature* (1989) that the human and the natural can no longer be distinguished, because the human has overwhelmed the natural. Crutzen, one early coiner of the term 'Anthropocene', co-authored a more recent statement that 'The long-held barriers between nature and culture are breaking down. It's no longer us against "Nature." Instead, it's we who decide what nature is and what it will be' (see Crutzen and Schwägerl 2011).

But this is 'nature' in the popular and historically recent sense of a unitary human-external system. What I will do briefly now is use the different nature/culture distinction I have proposed to try to parse cultural and historical consciousness in the Anthropocene era. I suggest that the Anthropocene is not only a crisis of ecological destruction, but correlatively a crisis and destructive reorganization of the category 'human' and its relationalities. It is a crisis of dominant understandings of human agency.

Enlightenment as destruction and unfreedom

The broadest pattern I wish to track is the Faustian narrative of an Enlightenment project of self-styled rationality and freedom that turns out to cause the destruction of our own lives. The project of heightened realization of culture as control turns out to lead to its opposite, an increased heteronomy in relation to forces humans do not entirely control (compare Boyer and Morton 2016). These include forces humans create or disrupt, but without controlling or rationally understanding them. Even when humans do understand them, we are not able to act intentionally in changed ways in light of what we know about those forces.

Horkheimer and Adorno wrote in 1944 that 'Enlightenment, understood in the widest sense as the advance of thought, has always aimed at liberating human beings from fear and installing them as masters. Yet the wholly enlightened earth is radiant with triumphant calamity' (2002: 1). They were referring to totalitarian regimes and the fast, deliberate technological apocalypse of death camps and industrial warfare, but their model also fits the slow apocalypse of anthropogenic climate change.

Specifically, the Anthropocene exposes the incoherence of modern societies' value commitment to economic growth, and the incoherence of their lack of social will to change that value commitment. Modern societies are centred on the embodied conviction that a good way to realize the Enlightenment value of human freedom is the increase in personal consumption that can be won through ever-accelerating burning of fossil fuels. But planetary finitude increasingly haunts this conviction about growth. It is no longer only fringe critics who have to at least *think* about the idea that growth and cheap carbon-burning leads toward collapse and unfreedom.

Additionally, the Anthropocene thematizes human mental and social self-opacity. Unlike processes of industrial warfare and genocide, anthropogenic climate change does not involve people deliberately using Enlightenment principles to destroy freedom. Instead destruction of freedom is unfolding largely as an uncontrolled – or at least, wilfully ignored or denied – effect of what actors more deliberately intend. To an understanding of culture as consciousness-mediated control, the Anthropocene is extra-shocking. It consists of unintended, freedom-destroying consequences of what are ideologized as freedom-realizing actions.

In this way, the Anthropocene undermines the Enlightenment formation's idea of humans as triumphantly realizing an accelerating proportion of free control over conditions of life. Enlightenment-heritage humans do not even control the processes of their own purported control. We think that in succeeding at economic growth or other modes of progress, we are realizing our high values of freedom, triumphing over exogenous constraint. Then we learn that we have entered our own Faustian trap of vast unfreedom.

This pattern could be described as a historical process that is repudiating the very same concept of 'nature' that Latour and others are at pains to reject, and reinstalling a different dialectics of human intentional control and uncontrolled processes of growth and destruction. Enlightenment was the myth of nature as mere objectivity and as an external, controllable system. Enlightenment tried to claim that everything can be commensurated with human rationality and control, and the problem of givens and foundations can be handled by a nature that is an external objective unitary system. The belief and practice of that myth is at least slightly imploding, as culture on the extractivist model destroys the basis of its own existence, and we are presented with a more troubled internal relation between an exercise of free control and its unfree conditions.

Physical and temporal scale: The thought-defying otherness of geological humanity

Another widely remarked face of the Anthropocene's delivery of these troubling rebuttals of Enlightenment ideologies of intentionality and freedom concerns the physical and temporal scale of what one has to think about in order to posit the Anthropocene.

The shock of the Anthropocene category is the shock that humans could cause changes to world structure on a geological scale, and humans could themselves be a geophysical force. Thinking about geological history involves engagement with a vast scale of time in excess of intentionality. Then the Anthropocene mixes human intentionality and its uncontrolled, impersonal consequences right into the latest temporal phases of that vast scale.

This scale-collapse of the difference between human history and planetary history is also a new challenge of otherness for thought. It is a challenge of stabilizing how to think about close relations between human intentionality and scales of uncontrolled physical process that are too big to think on a human intentional scale. And it is a challenge to stabilize how to think about human intentional action's relations to its presupposed conditions in less anthropocentric ways than the Enlightenment promoted.

Alongside those challenges of physical and temporal scale, there is the equally difficult idea of collective human suffering and mass death, in defiance of most people's habituated understandings of growth and progress as the story of their historical position. Millenarianism is not a mainstream Enlightenment historical model, but ecological millenarianism is now a mainstream spectre.

Thinking the Anthropocene and thinking human social divisions

The last perturbation I will allude to is the Anthropocene's intersections with human social divisions. Under the old nature/culture dispensation in anthropology, one brass ring was to work out how the natural operates as a figural field mediating the constitution of human society. This problematic intersects with something I have barely touched on so far, namely that intentionality and consciousness are not either/or matters. Humans' self-knowing in personal subjectivity and across social networks is ambiguous and multilayered. The nature/culture field I am advocating, as a distinction between what people understand to be intentionally controlled and what they understand to unfold independently of human intentionality, is also a site through which people take on or hide away forms of self-knowledge, and a site through which they organize power-laden aspects of social life. A common anthropological intuition is that inside what people naturalize, such as a landscape or a bodily feeling or condition, are many social and historical commitments. At stake in nature/culture distinctions could be models of intrahuman social otherness and of what a self owes to others.

In the present moment, the Anthropocene intersects with human social divisions in a variety of well-known forms. First, it raises issues of the discrepancy between who causes the ecological crises through massive fossil fuel burning, and who suffers its consequences (Chakrabarty 2009; Hornborg 2014: 9; Haraway 2016). Humans are entering a relatively unitary planetary crisis, but like many other crises this one is created from deep divisions of wealth and political interest, its effects unfold differently across those divisions, and people's perceptual and political responses to it are refracted through those divisions again.

The Anthropocene also intersects with human social divisions by highlighting incapacity for collective social mobilization to do anything substantial about the crisis.

Societies are divided in views or admissions about whether the crisis exists, who needs to do anything about it and what to do.

This is where I would circle back finally to my choice to discuss a nature/culture distinction relevant to comparative understanding of research subjects' own thought: nature versus culture as a 'folk' distinction or ethnotheory, immanent to lives of people in their historical particularity.

Since the Anthropocene is an ecological crisis, one might reasonably argue that the first task is to assess the nature/culture distinction as it applies to understanding the crisis in its ecological dimensions, such as understanding humans *as* geophysical actors. We do not need a cultural analysis of the Anthropocene, centred on a model of human agency organizing the thought of actors. We need the actual nature/culture distinction that is organizing the world and human presence in it.

But the contrary hypothesis that has motivated my discussion here is that it is exactly the ideological commitments in people's models of intentional, mind-mediated control and independently given processes that, in the first place, structure their arguments over what the Anthropocene is and whether it exists. And it is those models that are structuring our ongoing actions of throwing more fuel on the fire.

Notes

1   I once wrote an essay on hunting symbolism that falls squarely within the terms of the nature/culture framework I am elaborating here (Stasch 1996).

2   For example, Descola (2013) posits a distinction between physicality and interiority, and builds his fourfold typology of different ontologies of the human versus non-human field of relations on the universality of a physicality versus interiority split. Latour (1993) advocates the recognition and analysis of nature-culture hybrids, which implies a plural constitution out of distinguishable and mutually irreducible (as well as mutually entangled, mutually produced and mutually interdependent) aspects (compare Hornborg 2009: 95). Later he juxtaposes to the 'collectivity' a 'pluriverse' that is its 'outside', comprising 'new nonhumans' that have not been brought into it (Latour 2009). Wagner ([1975] 1981) retains a distinction between what is taken as innate and what is taken as requiring effort and attention, while drawing attention to cross-societal variation in where these dialectical poles of attention and inattention or masking are located.

References

Boyer, D. and Morton, T. 2016. 'Hyposubjects: Theorizing the Contemporary', *Cultural Anthropology*, 21 January. Available online: https://culanth.org/fieldsights/798-hyposubjects (accessed 14 November 2016).

Brooke, J. 2014. *Climate Change and the Course of Global History: A Rough Journey*. New York: Cambridge University Press.

Chakrabarty, D. 2009. 'The Climate of History: Four Theses'. *Critical Inquiry* 35(2): 197–222.

Clark, N. 2011. *Inhuman Nature: Sociable Life on a Dynamic Planet*. London: Sage.

Clark, N. 2016. 'Politics of Strata'. *Theory, Culture & Society* 34(2–3): 211–31.

Clark, N. and Gunaratnam Y. 2016. 'Earthing the Anthropos? From "Socializing the Anthropocene" to Geologizing the Social'. *European Journal of Social Theory* 20(1): 146–63.

Crutzen, P. J. and Schwägerl, C. 2011. 'Living in the Anthropocene: Toward a New Global Ethos'. *Yale Environment 360*, 24 January. Available online: http://e360.yale.edu/feature/living_in_the_anthropocene_toward_a_new_global_ethos/2363/ (accessed 7 November 2016).

Descola, P. 2013. *Beyond Nature and Culture*. Chicago: University of Chicago Press.

Gell, A. 1998. *Art and Agency: An Anthropological Theory*. Oxford: Oxford University Press.

Gould, S. J. 1987. *Time's Arrow, Time's Cycle*. Cambridge, MA: Harvard University Press.

Haraway, D. J. 2016. *Staying with the Trouble: Making Kin in the Chthulucene*. Durham, NC: Duke University Press.

Hegel, G. [1817] 1970. *Philosophy of Nature*. Oxford: Oxford University Press.

Horkheimer, M. and Adorno, T. W. 2002. *Dialectic of Enlightenment*. Stanford, CA: Stanford University Press.

Hornborg, A. 2009. 'In Defence of the Nature/Culture Distinction: Why Anthropology can Neither Dispense With, nor Be Reduced to, Semiotics'. *Cognitive Semiotics* (4): 92–115.

Hornborg, A. 2014. 'Does the Anthropocene Really Imply the End of Culture/Nature and Subject/Object Distinctions?'. *The Thousand Names of Gaia: From the Anthropocene to the Age of the Earth*. Rio De Janeiro. Available online: https://osmilnomesdegaia.eco.br/textos-dos-palestrantes/ (accessed 14 November 2016).

Hull, M. 2012. *Government of Paper: The Materiality of Bureaucracy in Urban Pakistan*. Berkeley: University of California Press.

Hutton, J. 1788. 'A Theory of the Earth'. In *Transactions of the Royal Society of Edinburgh*, Edinburgh: Royal Society of Edinburgh, vol. 1, part 2, pp. 209–304.

Irvine R. 2014a. 'Deep Time: An Anthropological Problem'. *Social Anthropology/Anthropologie Sociale* 22(2): 157–72.

Irvine R. 2014b. 'The Happisburgh Footprints in Time: Environmental Change and Human Adaptation on the East Anglian Coast'. *Anthropology Today* 30(2): 3–6.

Kant, I. [1790] 2005 *Critique of Judgement*. Mineola, NY: Dover Publications.

Keane, W. 2003. 'Semiotics and the Social Analysis of Material Things'. *Language & Communication* 23(2–3): 409–25.

Kirby, V. 1999. 'Human Nature'. *Australian Feminist Studies* 14(29): 19–29.

Kirby, V. 2011. *Quantum Anthropologies: Life at Large*. Durham, NC, and London: Duke University Press.

Latour, B. 1993. *We Have Never Been Modern*. Cambridge, MA: Harvard University Press.

Latour, B. 1995. *Reassembling the Social: An Introduction to Actor-Network Theory*. Oxford: Oxford University Press.

Latour, B. 2009. *Politics of Nature: How to Bring the Sciences into Democracy*. Cambridge, MA: Harvard University Press.

Laudan R, 1987. *From Mineralogy to Geology: The Foundations of a Science, 1650-1830*. Chicago and London: University of Chicago Press.

Lyell, C. 1830–33. *Principles of Geology*, 3 vols. 1st edition. London: John Murray.

Manning, P. 2012. *The Semiotics of Drink and Drinking*. London: Continuum.

Marx, K. [1857] 1973. *Grundrisse*. London: Penguin.

Marx, K. and Engels, F. [1845] 2004. *The German Ideology Part 1*. New York: International Publishers.

McKibben, B. 1989. *The End of Nature*. New York: Random House.

Meillassoux, Q. 2008. *After Finitude: An Essay on the Necessity of Contingency*. London: Continuum.

Michaels, A. 1997. *Fugitive Pieces*. London: Bloomsbury.

Ochs, E. 2012. 'Experiencing Language'. *Anthropological Theory* 12(2): 142–60.

Stasch, R. 1996. 'Killing as Reproductive Agency: Dugong, Pigs, and Humanity among the Kiwai, circa 1900'. *Anthropos* 91: 359–79.

Stasch, R. 2009. *Society of Others: Kinship and Mourning in a West Papuan Place*. Berkeley: University of California Press.

Strathern, M. 1980. 'No Nature, No Culture: The Hagen Case'. In *Nature, Culture and Gender*, C. P. MacCormack and M. Strathern (eds). Cambridge: Cambridge University Press, pp. 174–222.

Thacker, E. 2011. *In the Dust of This Planet*. Winchester: Zero Books.

Tsing, A. 2016. 'Earth Stalked by Man'. *The Cambridge Journal of Anthropology* 34(1): 2–16.

Valeri, V. 1990. 'Both Nature and Culture: Reflections on Menstrual and Parturitional Taboos in Huaulu (Seram)'. In *Power and Difference: Gender in Island Southeast Asia*, J. Atkinson and S. Errington (eds). Stanford, CA: Stanford University Press, pp. 235–72.

Viveiros de Castro, E. 1998. 'Cosmological Deixis and Amazonian Perspectivism'. *Journal of the Royal Anthropological Institute* 4: 469–88.

Wagner, R. [1975] 1981. *The Invention of Culture*. Chicago: University of Chicago Press.

Williams, R. 1980. *Problems in Materialism and Culture*. London: Verso.

7

Who Are We to Judge? Two Metalogues on Morality

Ronald Stade

One metalogue after the other

The anthropology of morality and the morality of anthropology (and anthropologists) are separate yet inextricable issues. They can be considered separate in a narrowly defined methodological sense; and they are inextricable in a theoretical and practical sense. It is from a methodological perspective that anthropologists tend to offer their students the rather crude idea that they, as observers, should suspend judgement in order to understand and make sense of other people's morality. This is called methodological relativism and it is usually distinguished from moral relativism. The latter, anthropologists tell their students, they would not have to subscribe to or accept. Students should suspend their judgement and keep it, so to speak. How would this work in practice, though? How is the anthropologist who is, for instance, invited to witness the extensive circumcision of a young girl supposed to react? With genuine indifference? With glee, because she (the anthropologist) has been given the rare opportunity to observe the ritual? With curbed outrage and feigned appreciation? Whatever the reaction, it would appear to say something about the moral impulse and inclination of the anthropologist. With some exceptions, human beings are moral beings by nature and culture.[1] Most human beings find it exceptionally challenging, to say the least, to shut off feelings like moral outrage and repulsion. But that, it seems, is exactly what we expect from budding (as well as seasoned) anthropologists.

Is it possible – should we even try – to reconcile the two sides of moral anthropology: the suspension of judgement for the sake of methodological relativism on the one hand, and staying true to one's own sense of morality on the other? Can – should – the perpetual conflict between cultural relativism and generally applicable ethical principles be resolved? In considering these questions, I find myself coming up with two distinct answers. Each answer resembles what Gregory Bateson called a 'metalogue', which he defined as:

> a conversation about some problematic subject. This conversation should be such that not only do the participants discuss the problem but the structure of the conversation as a whole is also relevant to the same subject. (1972: 1)

I will present two metalogues on moral anthropology. One is called 'Three perspectives on morality and the absurdity of their coexistence'; the other, 'Wobbly universalism'.

The first metalogue distinguishes between three types of philosophical-methodological-anthropological perspectives on morality and concludes that the tension between them cannot – and should not – be resolved. This conclusion, and everything leading up to it, is, of course, itself a particular moral argument and, in this sense, a metalogue. The second metalogue argues that relativism, moral and otherwise, is a desert that anthropologists, as well as non-anthropologists in search of open-mindedness, need to cross. Depending on the disposition of the wanderer, the desert of relativism might at first provide rays of clarity, a sudden realization of the randomness of it all; or it might send chills of anxiety and confusion down the spine of someone who is overwhelmed by a loss of direction. The conclusion of the second metalogue, in any case, is that the desert is a good place to shed and bury one's certainties, but that it should not be one's final destination. The argument is its own example.

Metalogue I: Three perspectives on morality and the absurdity of their coexistence

Three perspectives

We can differentiate between three perspectives on moral issues: the first is prescriptive, the second descriptive and the third ascriptive. In a prescriptive perspective, morality is a matter of how human beings ought to act. The descriptive perspective is used to record moral views, past and present. The ascriptive perspective attributes a virtuous nature, or its absence, to individuals and to human beings in general.

The three perspectives focus on different aspects of morality: the prescriptive perspective on norms, the descriptive perspective on practices (including the actual production and reproduction of norms), and the ascriptive perspective on individual character and human nature more generally. The study of each of these three perspectives on morality requires a specific methodology. The scholarly analysis and development of moral norms does not require empirical research. It can be, and usually is, conducted using only general concepts (for examples, see Williams 1985; Singer 1993; Held 2006, etc.). To research moral practice, on the other hand, it is necessary to carry out some form of empirical investigation, for example, by talking and interacting with people or through the study of historical records. The ascriptive approach, that is, defining ethics in terms of individual moral character and human nature, was the preferred philosophical method in antiquity. It has been kept alive for us, for example, by Friedrich Nietzsche and in the late lectures and writings of Michel Foucault. An entirely different take on the same issue has been developed in the natural sciences. Neuroscience, evolutionary biology, moral psychology, etc. study the organic and evolutionary origins of moral intuitions. This approach considers morality to be a matter of neural processes that evolved over millennia and that guide moral attitudes, decisions and actions.

The three perspectives are not easily kept apart. Confucius, for example, prescribed the supreme virtue of filial piety by describing how people behave; that is, he used description for the sake of prescription. The relevant passage in the *Analects* reads as follows:

> The Lord of Yè instructed Confucius, saying, 'There is an upright man in my district. His father stole a sheep, and he testified against him.' Confucius said, 'The upright men in my district are different. Fathers cover up for their sons and sons cover up for their fathers. Uprightness lies therein.' (13.18)

By describing how the men of his district behave, Confucius wanted to educate the Lord of Yè on how people everywhere *ought* to behave. It is common to couch moral admonitions in the language of actual behaviour, as when people say, 'because this is how we have always done it'. David Hume condemned this confusion of *is* and *ought*, ethos and ethics, practice and norm, description and prescription, etc., arguing that prescriptions never can be deduced from descriptions. This is known as 'Hume's Guillotine'.

In classical ethnography there often occurred an inverted type of confusion: moral norms were taken for actual practice; moral prescriptions were presented as if they were descriptions of moral behaviour. The result was that local communities were portrayed as integrated, homogeneous, moral communities. Jomo Kenyatta's diploma thesis can serve as an example.

The illusion of moral community

Kenyatta, personal student of Bronisław Malinowski at the London School of Economics and later first prime minister and first president of Kenya, wrote his diploma thesis in the 1930s. The thesis, subsequently published as *Facing Mount Kenya: The Tribal Life of the Gikuyu* (Kenyatta 1938), was filled with moral tales of 'tribal customs', the most notorious of which was the custom of cutting off the visible part of the clitoris, as well as parts of the labia – a practice known as clitoridectomy. Kenyatta defended this practice as custom. But what is custom? According to Pindar, the ancient Greek poet, 'custom is lord of all' ('νόμος ὁ πάντων βασιλεύς'; fragment 169a). But if custom indeed were the lord of all, morality – and norms more generally – would serve no purpose. Moral norms are needed because custom is *not* lord of all. When Kenyatta, in his thesis, makes a case for the moral benefits and key function in Kikuyu society and culture of clitoridectomy, he defends the custom against attacks not just from 'a number of influential European agencies – missionary, sentimental pro-African, government, educational and medical authorities' (Kenyatta 1938: 125), who demanded the immediate suspension of the practice, but also from fellow Kikuyu who, according to Kenyatta, were 'detribalised' because they had been 'away from home for some years' and now thought fit 'to denounce the custom and to marry uncircumcised girls, especially from coastal tribes' (1938: 127). These are bold words coming from a man who had himself been accused of detribalization because of his Western education, his many years in Europe, his amorous affairs with European women, his Leninist publications and so on.

Resistance to clitoridectomy did not just come from European agencies like the Church of Scotland Mission and from Kikuyu critics, as Kenyatta claimed. It also came from girls about to be cut. A fact that Kenyatta tried his best to mask. He wrote that the girl, who sits with her legs wide open while she is being cut, 'is not supposed to show any fear or make any audible sign of emotion or even to blink' (1938: 140). The key phrase is 'supposed to': the difference between morality and practice lies in these words. *Moral norms exist because people do not follow them.* If everyone always were to act in accordance with moral norms, they would be neither moral nor norms; they would simply be unreflective human behaviour. The defining feature of moral norms is their violation.

Kenyatta reported that girls who do not comply with the moral norm of suffering quietly during clitoridectomy are punished. To blink, wince or whimper 'would be considered cowardice (*kerogi*)' and make the girl 'the butt of ridicule among her companions' (1938). If the natural reaction of each and every girl having her clitoris cut off were to remain unmoved and poised – if it were the equivalent of, say, the gentle braiding of hair – such social sanctions would be wholly unnecessary. Kenyatta added that an uncut Kikuyu girl could not get married. He himself, however, married and had a child with a white British schoolteacher, who, as far as is known, was not required to remove her clitoris before marriage.

Presenting moral norms as social practice served both Kenyatta's political purpose of nationalism and Malinowski's functionalist cause.[2] What unites nationalism and functionalism is their reliance on models of – and for – homogeneous, integrated moral communities. Paying attention to, and describing in detail, trembling bodies and suppressed moans of agony, as sharp instruments cut through flesh, shatters this callous illusion.[3]

Moral relativism and its negation

The historical and ethnographic record abounds with different moral norms concerning right and wrong: 'Slaves should honour their master'/'Slavery should be abolished'; 'Wives should exhibit deference to their husbands'/'Men and women should treat each other as equals'; 'Boys need to be inseminated by adult men or they will not grow up to become men themselves'/'Paedophilia is a crime'; 'Same-sex couples should be allowed to marry each other'/'Homosexuals should be slain'; 'Blasphemy should be a capital offence'/'Freedom of expression must be comprehensive'; and so on.

The wide range and great diversity of moral prescriptions that is empirically observable across space and time might cast doubt on one's own moral commitments. On what grounds should my own moral intuitions and convictions be judged superior to the moral sentiments and ethical systems of others? A logical conclusion could be to adopt a position of moral relativism. But, while most human beings nowadays understand that not everyone on the planet shares their moral feelings, there is little evidence that moral relativism has become a universally held view. On the contrary, judging from the flow of opinions and comments transmitted through old and new media on a daily basis, strong moral convictions seem to persist.[4]

Anthropologists exhibit the same trait of, on one hand, being aware of moral relativity and, on the other, holding moral convictions of their own. Rationally, anthropologists are likely to argue against judging other people's morality on ethnocentric grounds. Yet, the same anthropologists will probably object to being described as people who are indifferent to the suffering of others. To avoid discussing this contradiction, anthropologists tend to resort to lecturing on the difference between methodological relativism and private morality: when studying the norms and behaviour of other people, the anthropologist must suspend her judgement in order to properly understand the meaning and logic of these norms and behaviours; the moral views that the anthropologist herself holds are to be kept separate from her interaction with the people she studies. But what are anthropologists supposed to do when, in the course of their research, they witness child abuse, wife beating, hate crimes, mutilations and so on? This question becomes even more troublesome when we take into consideration that more and more anthropologists conduct field research 'at home'. Is morality in anthropology simply an issue of which role – researcher versus private citizen – the anthropologist assumes in a particular situation?

Robert Redford once wrote:

> It was easy to look with equal benevolence upon all sorts of value systems so long as the values were those of unimportant little people remote from our own concerns. But the equal benevolence is harder to maintain when one is asked to anthropologize the Nazis. (1953: 145)

This is an intriguing statement on at least two accounts. On the one hand, it was possible to write it in the 1950s but hardly in the 2010s. Not because of the suggestion that it might be problematic to 'anthropologize' Nazis, but because Redford calls some people little, unimportant and remote from our own concerns. These days, this formulation would be considered morally problematic because it assumes a 'we' that excludes most inhabitants of the planet, which says something about the changeability of moral norms. On the other hand, Redford's point – that it is harder to hold on to moral relativism when something offends or affects us deeply – reveals the kind of persisting moral dilemma that anthropologists try to cover up by distinguishing between methodological relativism and private morality. Anthropologists have indeed studied neo-Nazis (e.g. Blee 2002), *génocidaires* (e.g. Hedlund 2014), paedophiles (e.g. Lowenkron 2015) and other people usually considered morally questionable. Anthropologists have done this in order to document and better understand the subjectivities of people who commit hate crimes, mass murder, sexual abuse, etc. These anthropologists are left in the undesirable position of having to explain behaviour that most people are likely to find reprehensible without appearing to defend it.

Another question is how anthropologists themselves deal with the contrast between their own moral intuitions and their taking a detached view of violent transgressions. This inner conflict is reminiscent of that experienced by therapists. In psychological research, this is referred to as the problem of countertransference, which, broadly speaking, is how the therapist reacts emotionally towards the patient. In the United States, particular attention has been paid to how therapists are impacted by their work with sexual offenders (see, e.g. Farrenkopf 1992; Mitchell and Melikian 1995; Bird Edmunds 1997; Kadambi and Truscott 2003, etc.). These therapists exhibit increased levels of depersonalization – feelings of losing one's personal identity and of unreality – and burnout. Often they express a loss of trust and safety. No comparable study has been conducted of anthropologists who have lived among, or otherwise closely engaged with, perpetrators of cruelty. If it is hazardous to talk to violent offenders in the safety of clinical settings, one can wonder what the consequences are for the anthropologist who, say, lived for months among people who at one point had hacked and bludgeoned neighbours and their children to death?[5] A coping mechanism might be to take on the role of advocate for 'misunderstood people and practices' (e.g. terrorists and racists, infanticide and genital cutting).[6]

The conflation of detachment and intuition, or countertransference, makes sense in ascriptive perspective. It is a basic assumption in moral psychology, the neuroscience of morality and evolutionary biology that human beings tend to react intuitively to suggestions and acts they find morally offensive. A preferred example in this context is that of how people react to what they perceive to be unfair treatment. Case studies, psychological experiments and the use of functional magnetic resonance imaging suggest that human beings with intact brains react negatively to unfairness. This research also indicates that moral judgements issue from unconscious processes, not from conscious decision-making and that explanations for why an individual made a certain moral choice are rationalizations after the fact.

In her comparative work, the anthropologist/political scientist Alison Dundes Renteln suggests that a transcultural moral feature might be the notion of proportionality of retribution (2013: 71–114). She acknowledges that what is considered to be a proportionate retribution varies – an eye for an eye and a tooth for a tooth in one case, financial compensation and imprisonment in another. But what seems to be rejected universally is arbitrary and unfair forms of retribution. It is not surprising, then, that humanity's first written codes (that we know of) specify proportionate retributions for various infractions. The code of Ur-Nammu, for example, lays down the following laws:

'If a man violates the rights of another and deflowers the virgin wife of a young man, they shall kill that male' – 'If a man acts in violation of the rights of another and deflowers the virgin slave woman of a man, he shall weigh and deliver 5 shekels of silver.' (Roth 1995: 18)

According to the king of Ur these were proportionate retributions. Their proportionality was derived from the social and legal status of the woman in question, who, however, was not seen as the one whose rights had been violated. It was the husband or owner of the woman who had suffered injury, according to the code. While this, as well as the death penalty, might seem morally unacceptable in contemporary human rights perspective, we continue to define the proportionality of retributions in accordance with the status of the involved perpetrators and victims, for example, in terms of their age and position of dependency. Moral intuitions are shaped by such distinctions.

Does the hypothesis of proportionate retribution tell us something about human nature? While many, if not most, people have more or less vague notions about human nature – 'Man is born in sin'; 'Humans are selfish by nature'; 'Human beings come into the world as pure souls', and so on – they are easily dismissed by anthropologists because they do not hold up to the standards of empirical research. Scientific hypotheses, which ascribe moral intuitions such as an innate fairness instinct to human beings and thereby point into the direction of human nature, are more difficult to shrug off, however.[7] At the same time, such hypotheses raise at least two questions: can human history's many elaborate normative systems of morality be deduced from a fairness instinct or some other innate faculty? And why does the supposed fairness instinct not inhibit unfair treatment? Put differently, if everyone is equipped with the moral instinct for fairness, why is there a need for moral norms to ensure fair treatment in the first place? Without being able to address these questions at this point, they are mentioned here to caution against uncritically adopting the explanatory model provided by the ascriptive perspective of moral psychology, the neuroscience of morality and evolutionary biology.[8]

Conclusion of Metalogue I

Three perspectives on moral issues have been considered. The biologically derived ascriptive perspective attributes a fairness instinct to human beings, and seems to demonstrate that moral judgements are made in the shadows of the unconscious, not in the bright light of conscious, rational choice. The descriptive perspective registers moral diversity and lends itself to moral relativism. The prescriptive perspective generates norms and codes for morality, and defines more or less clearly what constitutes their violation. In ascriptive and prescriptive perspectives, morality tends to be viewed as a pan-human phenomenon – either in terms of instincts or capacities common to all human beings or as norms and principles to which everyone ought to conform. Few anthropologists would object to the idea that human beings have a capacity for morality (as well as for moral transgressions). They might, however, disagree with the idea that there is such a thing as universal, unchanging moral principles. A properly devised comparative description of various moral norms and codes testifies to the fact of moral diversity. The descriptive perspective resembles what Thomas Nagel (1986) calls a 'view from nowhere', that is, a view which feigns a nebula's-eye view. This refers to the human capacity to see ourselves 'as arbitrary, idiosyncratic, highly specific occupants of the world, one of countless possible forms of life' (Nagel 1971: 725). Nagel elaborates:

> Humans have the special capacity to step back and survey themselves, and the lives to which they are committed, with that detached amazement which comes from watching an ant struggle up a heap of sand [...] the view is at once sobering and comical. (1971: 720)

Albert Camus believed that this type of sobering and comical view originates in the collision between the human search for meaning and the silence and meaninglessness of the universe (a universe in which 'we find no vestige of a beginning, no prospect of an end', to quote the Scottish Enlightenment figure, James Hutton). The result of this collision, according to Camus, is absurdity. Nagel locates absurdity somewhere else:

> when we take this view and recognise what we do as arbitrary, it does not disengage us from life, and there lies our absurdity: not in the fact that such an external view can be taken of us, but in the fact that we ourselves can take it, without ceasing to be the persons whose ultimate concerns are so coolly regarded. (1971: 720)

We can apply this definition of absurdity to our own predicament as anthropologists: on the one hand, we can adopt a detached view of the moral intuitions that drive us and other people; on the other, we do not cease to be the persons whose morality we so coolly regard. *The absurdity of our condition lies in the fact that we both are and are not moral relativists.* We are moral relativists as soon as we acknowledge the contingency of our moral intuitions and principles. The accident of our birth determines the range of moral choices available to us. At the same time, we are moral beings and cannot help being moral. So, I find myself siding with Nagel when he writes that, 'the human duality of perspectives is too deep for us reasonably to hope to overcome it' (1986: 185). Under these circumstances, finding anthropology's moral voice and vision – and here I part ways with Nagel's view on morality – is not a matter of moving beyond the human duality of perspectives by developing a philosophy in syllogistic steps (if A and B, then C). It is an uneasy, dissatisfying acknowledgement of our absurd dilemma and its consequences, the most important of which is that we simply know too much to speak with fervour and devotion about morality. Living with the absurdity of this realization – and this is the 'meta' of the 'metalogue' – ought to be the fate of anthropologists.

Metalogue II: Wobbly universalism

Relativism and universalism

It is with the idea of relativism that anthropology 'has most disturbed the general intellectual peace' (Geertz 1984: 264). Relativism – or, more precisely, cultural relativism, which can be traced back to, at least, Herodotus – became part of the anthropological canon when the systematic collection of data, and the growing impact of structural thought on anthropology, made it increasingly difficult to relegate people to the savage slot. Relativism also served moral and political purposes in that it was used to battle racism and invalidate notions of primitive mentality (see Spiro 1978: 336). According to Clifford Geertz (1984), anthropologists (and human beings in general) have to guard themselves against two perils: provincialism and nihilism. Be ethnocentric, narrow-minded and incurious, and you have fallen victim to provincialism. You may be convinced that your way of life, beliefs and convictions are right and good and that other ways of life, beliefs and convictions are wrong and bad, or at least inferior to your own. Commit fully to relativism, however, and you are in immediate danger of turning into a nihilist. Because you are convinced that truth and morality depend on historical and cultural contingencies, you conclude that nothing is better than anything else and that, therefore, anything goes. And yet:

> The image of vast numbers of anthropology readers running around in so cosmopolitan a frame of mind as to have no views as to what is and isn't true, or good, or beautiful, seems to me largely a fantasy. (Geertz 1984: 265)

Thus, it can be assumed that anthropologists, just like other folks, are likely to have views as to what is true, good and beautiful. As discussed in the previous metalogue, anthropologists, in this sense, are all too human.

While Geertz denies that anthropologists are more disposed to be nihilist than other people, he wishes to defend relativism against its detractors. Geertz's defence consists of downplaying the actual scale of, and potential threat from, relativism. At the same time, he insists that relativism has been valuable, as it has repositioned horizons and decentred perspectives. 'If we wanted home truths, we should have stayed at home', he concludes (Geertz 1984: 276).

Geertz's argument is flawed on two accounts. To begin with, he fails to provide an explanation for why the idea that anthropologists run around 'in so cosmopolitan a frame of mind as to have no views as to what is and isn't true, or good, or beautiful' is 'largely a fantasy'. While his observation that anthropologists in this respect, by and large, resemble regular human beings might or might not be correct – in the absence of a global survey we simply do not know – Geertz offers no explanation for what might prevent relativist anthropologists from going over the edge of knowledge and morality, and tumbling into the abyss of nihilism. In the previous metalogue I argued that it is nearly impossible for anthropologists to rid themselves of moral impulses and that this is a good thing. Could this serve as an explanation for why the fear of relativism is largely unfounded? The reason for Geertz not arguing along those, or similar, lines is that he was suspicious of what goes under the name of 'essentialism'. An idea like countertransference, for example, is essentialist because it presupposes an innate make-up of the human psyche.

The second weakness of Geertz' argument is that he does not add a social or temporal dimension to his discussion of relativism. Accepting for a moment Geertz's defence of relativism against its most fervent critics, we are still stuck with a binary conceptual scheme, in which relativism is nothing more than the antithesis of universalism. The American philosopher Richard Rorty engaged in a debate with Geertz on the merits of cultural relativism as against universal justice. Rorty (1986) argued that liberal society, for its proper functioning, needs two kinds of agents: agents of love and agents of social justice. Agents of love are anthropologists, historians, novelists and other connoisseurs of human diversity. They empathize with, and develop a deep understanding of, marginalized and excluded people. The agents of love humanize them by making sense of their beliefs and ways of being. Agents of love insist that the marginalized and excluded be empowered and included. Once this is accomplished, however, the agents of social justice – policemen, judges, medical professionals, teachers and so on – must treat them with total impartiality. Relativism is a private matter of aesthetics. It should be kept separate from the universal values of social justice that ought to drive the polis, according to Rorty (1989). The agents of love bring the lot of the marginalized and excluded to the attention of the agents of justice, who, hopefully, grant full and inclusive citizenship to the deprived. This separation of social roles notwithstanding, relativism and universalism are in Rorty's view not just antithetical, they are complementary; both social roles, agents of love and agents of justice, are needed for a liberal society of the kind envisioned by Rorty, to function and develop properly. In the following section, it is precisely this processual aspect of relativism and universalism that will be discussed and elaborated further.

The desert of relativism

The separation of social roles that Rorty proposes is, of course, an 'ought', not an 'is'. It is a meta-value. In practical terms, relativism and universalism are rarely kept apart in a manner that resembles Rorty's model. Empirical research shows that agents of justice like judges are not the kind of impartial practitioners that Rorty has in mind (see, e.g. Philips 1998; Wacquant 2009 and Breda 2016). Proving that there is a difference between ought and is, however, hardly constitutes a major achievement. As argued in the first metalogue, Hume's Guillotine should, but does not necessarily, prevent us from conflating is and ought. A particular type of conflation might even amount to a universal principle of human history: laws (ought) are supposed to dictate actual behaviour (is). But consider this example:

> 199. If anyone have intercourse with a pig or a dog, he shall die. If a man have intercourse with a horse or a mule, there is no punishment. But he shall not approach the king, and shall not become a priest. If an ox spring upon a man for intercourse, the ox shall die but the man shall not die. One sheep shall be fetched as a substitute for the man, and they shall kill it. If a pig spring upon a man for intercourse, there is no punishment. If any man have intercourse with a foreign woman and pick up this one, now that one, there is no punishment. (*The Code of the Nesilim, c.* 1650–1500 BC, quoted in Halsall 1998)

While the practices described, and punishments stipulated, in this Hittite law might appear curious in contemporary perspective, it is still possible to make sense of the words and sentences. With further research, it is even possible to make sense of the norms and normativities expressed through the law. But the very act of translation is indicative of difference; in this case of legal diversity in human history. There is also legal diversity in space, as becomes obvious when we consider Section 251 in Cameroon's penal code, which outlaws 'any act of witchcraft, magic or divination liable to disturb public order or tranquility, or to harm another in his person, property or substance'. I use the example of legal diversity to make clear that cultural diversity is not just a matter of what Arnold Gehlen called 'institutions', and José Ortega y Gasset '*creencias*', and what Pierre Bourdieu (1977: 164 and 168) referred to as '*doxa*', that is, those things that are outside the universe of the discussed and disputed. Legal codes, like the Cameroonian law against witchcraft, are carefully deliberated and worded; they are definitely within the universe of the discussed and disputed. Legal codes are rationally and reflexively produced testimonies to cultural diversity. The existence of legal diversity, therefore, strengthens the relativist argument in that it demonstrates that the desert of relativism contains not just a background of unexamined suppositions but also a foreground of deliberation, reflection and critique.

Thus, the wanderer who rambles through the desert of relativism is stripped not just of what can be taken for granted, but also of that which was believed to be well considered and systematically explored. The *is* of diversity dissolves the *ought* of universal validity. The emptiness of the desert is matched by the nakedness of the wanderer.

Conclusion of Metalogue II

It is possible, however, to exit the desert of relativism in the opposite direction from where one entered. A sense of moral direction can be regained. Except that life knows no reversal, and so any kind of newfound universalism will be 'wobbly' in the same sense that restored health is not the same as original health: someone who has survived a cancer treatment is likely to never feel healthy in the same way as she did before she was diagnosed with the disease. A new sort of awareness and attention has been inserted into the relationship between body and mind. In similar fashion, only a one-way trail leads through the desert of relativism. To surrender to relativism is to leave the enchanted version of universalism behind. A *disenchanted* version of universalism might now be assembled from available materials and blueprints.

One such blueprint might be the Hegelian thesis that history moves inexorably and unidirectionally towards the fulfilment of humanity's potential.[9] According to Hegel, one of the signs of this evolution is the emergence and development of the modern state. The self-imposed regulation of social life in the form of laws and their enforcement, Hegel considered the greatest human achievement. (Nowadays, one could add the struggle for human rights and environmental protection to the catalogue of human progress, in Hegel's sense.) Another blueprint could be Emanuel Levinas's argument for ethics as first philosophy: Because the Other is always already there to take care of us when we are born and to call on us throughout our life, and because the Other is endless, anything we do is per definition moral. Yet another blueprint might be that of Aristotelian essentialism: it is in the nature of human beings to be born with a range of capabilities, such as attachment, development and individuality, which a good social order will nurture. And so on.

Whatever the blueprint, adopting it requires a leap of faith. Anyone who has dwelled in the desert of relativism and is disenchanted with universalism might understandably hesitate to take such a leap. The reluctance also has to do with the nature of the faith towards which one is expected to leap. There can be little doubt that the new faith will be erected on the shaky ground of relativity. A restored, disenchanted universalism will remain wobbly.

So, just as in the conclusion to the first metalogue, the message is once again that a contradiction, in this case between relativism and universalism, is insoluble. The argument of both metalogues is that certain fundamental inconsistencies, like those between 'is' and 'ought', between the particular and the universal, and between doubt and conviction, must be treated as aporia. Descriptively and analytically one may choose to consider these aporia in terms of dialectical processes – ought determines is, and is determines ought; the universal is particular, and the particular is shaped by what is considered universal; doubt is the negation of conviction and this negation can, in turn, give rise to new convictions and so on – but, in my view, the basic contradictions remain without ever being sublated (without ever being *aufgehoben* in Hegel's and Marx's sense). I have argued elsewhere that for human beings, the most consequential aporia is that of meaning and meaninglessness.[10] But that is another discussion.

Notes

1. The exceptions I have in mind, for example, exhibit symptoms that correspond to dissocial personality disorder.
2. See Berman 1996.
3. Worse than Kenyatta's functionalist tale of clitoridectomy – which, after all, was written in the 1930s – are contemporary advocates of female genital amputation such as Carla Obermeyer (2003) and Richard Shweder (2000), who use aggregate statistical data to denounce opponents of the practice. The individual girl who is not 'brave' enough to undergo clitoridectomy – or is left traumatized by the procedure – is likely to be statistically insignificant from their point of view because (a) 'most' girls and women are in favour of continuing the custom, and (b) aggregate data (when interpreted by Obermeyer and Shweder) indicate that the effects of clitoridectomy on the health and sexuality of women are not as bad as anti-female-genital-mutilation activists claim. For an analytically sophisticated critique of Obermeyer and Shweder, see Mackie 2003.
4. In a more dialectical vein, it could be argued that the contemporary situation is characterized by people shielding themselves from the loss of certainty, which might be brought on by moral and cultural relativism, by resorting to increasingly radical forms of 'political incorrectness'.
5. See the special section on anthropological engagements with perpetrators in the journal *Conflict and Society* 1(1) (2015): 4–124.
6. Another possibility is that self-opinionated anthropologists seek out cases that allow them to battle 'political correctness' and 'virtue ethics' more generally in an attempt to 'transvalue all values'.
7. A repeatedly used instrument for measuring people's reactions to unfair treatment is the Ultimatum Game: one player proposes how to divide a sum of money; the second player can accept or reject the offer; if she rejects the offer, neither player receives any money; if she accepts the offer the money is divided according to the first player's proposal. Second players tend to reject offers they consider too unfair, even if this means that they walk away empty-handed.
8. For examples, see Greene 2003; Haidt and Joseph 2004; Hauser 2006 and Haidt 2007. For a more comprehensive review of social decision-making in neuroscientific perspective, see Rilling and Sanfey 2011.
9. The works by Hegel that are most relevant for the discussion of the 'Hegelian blueprint' are Hegel 1980 and 2009.
10. See Rapport and Stade 2014, and Stade 2014.

References

Bateson, G. 1972. *Steps to an Ecology of Mind: Collected Essays in Anthropology, Psychiatry, Evolution, and Epistemology*. Chicago: University of Chicago Press.

Berman, B. 1996. 'Ethnography as Politics, Politics as Ethnography: Kenyatta, Malinowski, and the Making of Facing Mount Kenya'. *Canadian Journal of African Studies* 30(3): 313–44.

Bird Edmunds, S. (ed.). 1997. *Impact: Working with Sexual Abusers*. Brandon, VT: Safer Society Press.

Blee, K. 2002. *Inside Organized Racism: Women in the Hate Movement*. Berkeley: University of California Press.

Bourdieu, P. 1977. *Outline of a Theory of Practice*. Cambridge: Cambridge University Press.

Breda, V. 2016. 'The Grammar of Bias: Judicial Impartiality in European Legal Systems'. *International Journal for the Semiotics of Law* 30(2): 245–60.

Farrenkopf, T. 1992. 'What Happens to Therapists Who Work with Sex Offenders?' *Journal of Offender Rehabilitation* 18: 217–23.

Geertz, C. 1984. 'Distinguished Lecture: Anti Anti-relativism'. *American Anthropologist* 86(2): 263–78.

Greene, J. 2003. 'From Neural "Is" to Moral "Ought": What Are the Moral Implications of Neuroscientific Moral Psychology?' *Nature Reviews Neuroscience* 4(10): 847–50.

Haidt, J. 2007. 'The New Synthesis in Moral Psychology'. *Science* 316(5827): 998–1002.

Haidt, J. and Joseph, C. 2004. 'Intuitive Ethics: How Innately Prepared Intuitions Generate Culturally Variable Virtues'. *Daedalus* 133(4): 55–66.

Halsall, P. 1998. 'Ancient History Sourcebook: The Code of the Nesilim'. Fordham University, August. Available online: https://sourcebooks.fordham.edu/ancient/1650nesilim.asp (accessed 15 July 2018).

Hauser, M. 2006. *Moral Minds: How Nature Designed Our Universal Sense of Right and Wrong*. New York: Ecco.

Hedlund, A. 2014. *Exile Warriors: Violence and Community among Hutu Rebels in the Eastern Congo*. Lund: Department of Sociology, Lund University.

Hegel, G. W. F. 1980. *Phänomenologie des Geistes*, W. Bonsiepen and R. Heede (eds). Hamburg: Meiner.

Hegel, G. W. F. 2009. *Grundlinien der Philosophie des Rechts*, K. Grotsch and E. Weisser-Lohmann (eds). Hamburg: Meiner.

Held, V. 2006. *The Ethics of Care: Personal, Political, and Global*. Oxford: Oxford University Press.

Kadambi, M. and Truscott, D. 2003. 'Vicarious Traumatization and Burnout among Therapists Working with Sex Offenders'. *Traumatology* 9(4): 216–30.

Kenyatta, J. 1938. *Facing Mount Kenya: The Tribal Life of the Gikuyu*. London: Secker & Warburg.

Lowenkron, L. 2015. *O monstro contemporâneo: a construção social da pedofilia em múltiplos planos*. Rio de Janeiro: Editora da Universidade do Estado do Rio de Janeiro.

Mackie, G. 2003. 'Female Genital Cutting: A Harmless Practice?' *Medical Anthropology Quarterly* 17(2): 135–58.

Mitchell, C. and Melikian, K. 1995. 'The Treatment of Male Sexual Offenders: Countertransference Reactions'. *Journal of Child Sexual Abuse* 4: 87–93.

Nagel, T. 1971. 'The Absurd'. *Journal of Philosophy* 68(20): 716–27.

Nagel, T. 1986. *The View from Nowhere*. Oxford: Oxford University Press.

Obermeyer, C. M. 2003. 'The Health Consequences of Female Circumcision: Science, Advocacy, and Standards of Evidence'. *Medical Anthropology Quarterly* 17(3): 394–412.

Philips, S. 1998. *Ideology in the Language of Judges: How Judges Practice Law, Politics, and Courtroom Control*. New York: Oxford University Press.

Rapport, N. and Stade, R. 2014. 'Debating Irony and the Ironic as a Social Phenomenon and a Human Capacity'. *Social Anthropology* 22(4): 443–78.

Redford, R. 1953. *The Primitive World and Its Transformation*. Ithaca, NY: Cornell University Press.

Renteln, A. D. 2013. *International Human Rights: Universalism versus Relativism*. New Orleans, LA: Quid Pro.

Rilling, J. and Sanfey, A. 2011. 'The Neuroscience of Social Decision-making'. *Annual Review of Psychology* 62: 23–48.

Rorty, R. 1986. 'On Ethnocentrism: A Reply to Clifford Geertz'. *Michigan Quarterly Review* 25(3): 525–34.

Rorty, R. 1989. *Contingency, Irony, and Solidarity*. Cambridge: Cambridge University Press.

Roth, M. T. 1995. *Law Collections from Mesopotamia and Asia Minor*. Atlanta, GA: Scholars Press.

Shweder, R. 2000. 'What about Female Genital Mutilation? And Why Understanding Culture Matters in the First Place'. *Daedalus* 129: 209–32.

Singer, P. 1993 *Practical Ethics*. 2nd edition. Cambridge: Cambridge University Press.

Spiro, M. 1978. 'Culture and Human Nature'. In *The Making of Psychological Anthropology*, G. Spindler (ed.). Berkeley: University of California Press, pp. 330–60.

Stade, R. 2014. 'Citizens of Everything: The Aporetics of Cosmopolitanism'. In *We the Cosmopolitans* L. Josephides and A. Hall (eds). Oxford and New York: Berghahn, pp. 29–47.

Wacquant, L. 2009. *Punishing the Poor: The Neoliberal Government of Social Insecurity*. Durham, NC: Duke University Press.

Williams, B. 1985. *Ethics and the Limits of Philosophy*. London: Fontana Press.

8

'We Are All Human':
Cosmopolitanism as a Radically Political, Moral Project

Elisabeth Kirtsoglou

When you see these people coming out of the boats, it feels like a thousand eyes are looking at you. Their eyes, the eyes of your dead grandparents who were refugees too – who carried the identity of the refugee for their entire lives, the eyes of your children, the eyes of the unborn who will be reading about these events one day in their history books. A thousand eyes, a million eyes, looking at you, asking you: 'What are you going to do?' How can I go on with my life as if nothing happens, knowing that so many human beings are tortured in this way? The sea has a thousand eyes and they all stare at us with a question: 'What are you going to do?'

Maria, Athens, 2015, original emphasis

In 2015 and 2016 more than one million refugees, predominantly from Syria, but also from Afghanistan and Iraq, arrived in Greece, through Turkey, in flimsy overcrowded boats. The precarious journey by sea cost the lives of more than a thousand persons.[1] Greek people, an otherwise predominantly xenophobic and openly nationalist public, demonstrated en masse their support to the refugees. The same social actors that conventionally articulate a strong resistance to the ideals of multiculturalism and cosmopolitanism (cf. Kirtsoglou and Theodossopoulos 2010a) manifested their solidarity to the displaced in a variety of discursive and practical ways. Ordinary people expressed their identification with the 'refugees' (*prosfyges*), a term thus far reserved almost exclusively for the Greek-speaking, Christian Orthodox populations that have been forcibly displaced from Asia Minor and Anatolia as a result of the Greco-Turkish War in 1920–22 (cf. Hirschon 1989).[2]

The predicament of the forcibly displaced in 2015 to 2016 was indeed experienced by many as a condition of 'multitemporality' (cf. Knight 2013, 2015; Kirtsoglou and Tsimouris 2016). Refugeeness as collective narrative and transgenerational trauma (cf. Anastasiadis 2012), as well as memories of economic migration to Europe, the United State or Australia, became for a large part of Greek society mechanisms of substitution (Levinas [1974] 1981) through which a number of people identified with the displaced.

The cultural framework through which this identification was expressed was the concept of humanity, as a quality and an ethos that binds all human beings in a universal and timeless manner. A careful examination of what it means to be human in Greece and of the ways in which intimacy, inclusion and exclusion are understood and negotiated reveals the recognition of our common humanity to be an explicitly political expression of the cosmopolitan project. At the heart of the Greek conceptualization of humanity as a state of being we all share, lies empathy as an affirmative political praxis and an affective ethical technology. My contribution here aims to discuss empathy as a cognitive, experiential and affective faculty that is distinct from sympathy, compassion and pity. While I share reservations against humanitarian reason and governance, I maintain that hegemonic understandings of what it means to be human obscure the importance of local, vernacular visions of cosmopolitanism as a moral and yet radically political project.

What is wrong with emotions?

Terms such as sympathy, compassion, philanthropy and charity have received considerable attention in anthropological literature (cf. Rozaldo 1989; Viveiros de Castro 1992; Throop 2008; Bornstein 2009, 2011). Different authors have launched pointed critiques against compassionate volunteering as the basis of humanitarian 'anti-politics' (Fassin 2005, 2007, 2011a, 2011b; Wilson and Brown 2009; Ticktin 2011, 2014; Muehlebach 2012; Trundle 2014). Emotion-based, spontaneous desire to end the misery and suffering of others (cf. Bornstein 2009: 632) on the basis of a common humanity (Ticktin 2006: 39) is seen as creating a hierarchical field of relations at more than one level. Muehlebach stresses the relationship between volunteering and new forms of neo-liberal citizenship (2012; cf also Pedwell 2012, 2014). Fassin highlights the complex ontologies of inequality between humanitarian actors and those who receive their assistance (2007). Locked in an aesthetic of eligibility (cf. Cabot 2014) the sufferer must often prove their innocence through plausible stories, and they must demonstrate a certain alignment to local ideals (cf. Berlant 2004; Ticktin 2006: 43; Giordano 2008; Wilson and Brown 2009: 23; Crowhurst 2012: 497; Cabot 2014; Trundle 2014: 144).

I agree and side with these critiques. Indeed, neo-liberal governance literally depends on shifting welfare-related responsibilities onto the third sector and ordinary citizens. The fragmentary and episodic character of all forms of aid (organized or informal) disputes the unquestionable character of basic political and human rights. Ordinary citizens are asked to alleviate the effects of the deep and painful asymmetries created by integrated world capitalism (Guattari 2000) in ways that are themselves imbued with asymmetry and inequality.

Two particular issues however, deserve further attention and discussion. First, we need to reflect on perceptions of the role of emotion vis-à-vis our vision of the political. If the 'anti-political' character of humanitarianism is established in the affective, spontaneous responses of actors, what is then the primary principle that organizes the 'political' field of citizenship and equal rights? My aim is not to offer an apology for humanitarianism and philanthropy. I can ethnographically ascertain their deeply hierarchical effects. My point here is to problematize the manner in which emotion emerges as hitherto anti-political and as juxtaposed to a certain – I would say modernist – vision of the political that appears to have no legitimate and credible space for the affective and relational components of subjectivity. The notion of this rather masculinist understanding of citizenship does much more than promote an atomistic and bounded concept of the self (cf. Mahmood [2005] 2012: 12). It creates a paradox, especially relevant in the discussion of forced displacement: namely, where is *the right to have rights* established (Arendt 1968: 177; cf Benhabib 2004: 51)? For the rights of others to be enforceable norms (i.e. laws), there must be a sovereign power with the ultimate authority of enforcement (Benhabib 2004: 29). 'The will of the democratic sovereign', however, 'can extend only over the territory under its jurisdiction; democracies require borders. Empires have frontiers, while democracies have borders' (Benhabib 2004: 45). Sovereign bodies, Benhabib rightly observes, depend on this distinction between 'full members' and 'those who fall under the sovereign's protection' (2004: 45). Therefore, there is something inherently paradoxical in regarding nation-states as the guarantors of the rights to inclusive forms of citizenship. While I am not arguing in favour of philanthropy and charity as a solution to this paradox, I call for a reconsideration of our vision of 'the political' that seems far too connected to the ideals of a sovereign nation-state bestowed with the power to enforce rights and obligations according to a contractarian ethos of equality (cf. Kirtsoglou 2006). While I agree that the apolitical sentimentality that humanitarian sympathy entails is deeply problematic, I claim that we need to find legitimate space and role for the shared, affective component within the political.

The second point that arises from current literature on charity, volunteering and philanthropy is our assumptions regarding the meaning of 'human'. It has been argued that belief in 'our common humanity' as the origin of our sympathy towards others can be based on a concept of the human that is too general, anonymous, decontextualized and ahistorical to be socially and politically meaningful (cf. Malkki 1996). Yet, a closer examination of the ethnographic specificity of different works (e.g. Muehlebach 2012; Trundle 2014; Ticktin 2006; Fassin 2007, 2012) reveals that the humanitarian ethos exhibited by the protagonists in each case is very much socially, culturally and historically specific. Ideas about who qualifies as a 'human being in need' are born in a neo-liberal context and remain underwritten by an ethos of confession which establishes the 'truth' about the Other, her innocence, the legitimacy of her suffering and the plausibility of her case. Confession, as the main ritualistic (Catholic) technology for the production of truth in the West was established (as Foucault evidences) in the Middle Ages (1978: 58, 59). The deeply hierarchical nature of philanthropy, sympathy and compassion is, therefore, to be found not necessarily in the relationship between giver and receiver per se but in the fact that confession becomes the foundation of such a relation. The 'gift' of charity is so poisonous, troubling and ambivalent (cf. Derrida 1992; Bornstein 2009; Trundle 2014: 3), because the receiver needs – by means of confessing his or her truth – to prove that he or she is human and, therefore, worthy of it. Charity and philanthropy are technologies of (re)humanization based on a notion of the human that needs to be proven, spelt out and justified. In the process of becoming knowable, the recipient of charity becomes also governable (cf. Tazzioli 2013; Vaughn-Williams 2015). The nature of the relationship that can be established on the basis of such a perception of humanity is of course hierarchical. For, the giver always and finally establishes herself as the ultimate 'judge' of the recipient's confessed truth.

In what follows I will investigate Greek conceptualizations of intimacy, inclusion, exclusion, hierarchy and obligation. I will show that perceptions of what it means to be human form a powerful vernacular of explicitly political manifestations of solidarity mediated by·empathy as an affective and transformative technology.

The poetics of sociality: Intimacy and common humanity

Dhikos/Xenos

The distinction between *dhikos* (one of us, insider, intimate) and *xenos* (foreign, stranger, unknown, outsider) has been discussed in Greek ethnography (cf. Panourgia 1995: 17; Danforth 1989: 171; Herzfeld 2003). The distinction between the two terms that are notoriously difficult to translate accurately, for reasons that will become evident in the following paragraphs, 'demarcates all the boundaries of intimacy from a person to a nation [and] provides the framework for moving from one level to the other and back again' (Herzfeld 2003: 142). In relation to its opposite (*dhikos*), a *xenos* can mean anyone beyond the kin-group, the neighbourhood, a circle of friends, a village/town/city/country/ethnos. *Dhikos* and *xenos* should be seen not as two clear and absolute opposites, which can exist independently of each other, but as a system that constitutes intimacy, belonging and proximity, relative, fluid and contextual processes. Thus, the fellow-supporter of a political party is definitely a *dhikos* in terms of political affiliations but surely *a xenos* when compared to members of one's own family. Even within the extended family, a distant cousin (otherwise a *dhikos* vis-à-vis non-kin) can be seen as *a xenos* in relation to one's siblings. To complicate matters even more, the *dhikos/xenos* schema is not just a reference to belonging but also to emotional attachment and/or trust. A person who is a *xenos* is not only distant but also – by virtue of being unknown – potentially (although not necessarily) hostile and thus mistrusted. In its polysemic character the *dhikos/xenos* identification system creates multiple and sometimes overlapping circles of inclusion and exclusion. The many different qualities of proximity, affinity, intimacy and distance of *dhikos/xenos* (genealogical, emotional, political, national, related to trust and mistrust), and the fact that unavoidably all individuals occupy several of these categories at once, means that one is always at some level a *dhikos* and simultaneously (at another level) a *xenos*.

Apart from being conventionally used as a term of reference for national others,[3] *xenos* in recent years, is being deployed (commonly by ordinary people but also strategically by ultra-right wing and fascist political circles) as a shorthand for the category 'immigrant'. *Xenos* in this sense, often acquires racialized connotations and can denote different degrees of resentment or even hostility towards foreigners, irrespectively of their legal and political status.

The relative and provisional character of intimacy categories, however, means that an individual *xenos* can always become a *dhikos* (despite the fact that in terms of categorical grouping they may remain classed as *xenos*). The generic category of the stranger/foreigner, almost always excludes some particular *xenos* who is perceived as being 'different' (cf. Herzfeld 2005: 85). Either through employment, or through neighbourliness, or in other contexts, the (foreigner) *xenos* becomes known (cf. Herzfeld 2003; 2005: 92) and can be gradually converted from a stranger into an intimate and trusted figure.

The transformation of a *xenos* (in all its different meanings) into a known and trusted *dhikos* happens through sociality that ranges from everyday mundane exchanges to exceptional acts of sheep-stealing (cf. Herzfeld 2003: 141). Sociality-induced relatedness is expressed in Greek with the term 'familiarity' (*oikeiotita*).[4] Like *dhikos*/xenos, familiarity is a provisional and performatively established quality. Social exchanges render a person familiar in varying degrees and provide the chance to establish trust and loyalty allowing strangers to become intimate.[5] Two siblings can grow into strangers (*xenoi* – plural) while complete strangers can become 'close like family', where family here is to be understood not in its genealogical sense but as a metaphor of intimacy and trust.

The synthetic and polysemic system of relatedness instituted through the performative categories of *dhikos/xenos*, familiarity, trust and mistrust, is underwritten by equally complex processes of creating, accepting and avoiding responsibilities and obligations. In an eloquent discussion of presents and promises and through the examination of name-day gift-receiving etiquette, Hirschon (2008) explains the politics of obligation. In the Greek cultural context where people 'abhor' status differences and hierarchical relations 'the notion of obligation is a nexus which generates ongoing exchanges in which the actors seesaw between superior and inferior positions depending at which point in the chain of exchanges they are' (2008: 193). Social actors become trapped in this seesaw as they alternate between the positions of gift-giver and gift receiver (2008: 193). The hierarchical relations between givers and receivers are at the heart of all patron-client relationships (cf. Campbell 1964), regulate the provision and acceptance of hospitality (cf. Candea 2012; Herzfeld 2012), and generally pervade all aspects of everyday sociality (cf. Papataxiarhis 1991). As Hirschon observes, obligation literally means in Greek to be 'under debt', and Greeks visibly detest being indebted and in relations permeated by a sense of obligation (1992, 2008: 193).

Obligation – as the visible sign of dependency – is indeed a worrisome social burden but one that comes as part and parcel of sociality. The burden of indebtedness is alleviated by the responsibility to reciprocate which is an opportunity to find oneself moved from the position of a receiver to that of a giver. Because responsibility implies obligation (and vice versa), ultimately neither condition is comfortable. For, the superiority established through giving is fleeting, provisional and self-subversive, insofar as the moment of giving prefigures the moment of receiving.

Obligation and responsibility become particularly interesting technologies of sociality when examined vis-à-vis *dhikos/xenos*, trust, intimacy, emotional proximity and familiarity. One way of transforming a *xenos*, from a distant outsider to a more intimate insider (*dhikos*) is through initiating cycles of reciprocity that operate as spaces for exhibiting loyalty which gradually dissolves feelings of mistrust. Thus, the seesaw of obligation and responsibility (cf. Hirschon 2008) is a way of 'knowing' the Other and of creating intimacy, which has the power of eroding indebtedness. Within a family – as the primary metaphor for social and genealogical relatedness – indebtedness between individuals is ideally absent as members are *ex officio* obliged to cater to each other's needs.

At this point, and before I proceed to examine another important category that mediates relations of inclusion, exclusion, intimacy, trust and hierarchy, I must say that the aforementioned cultural analysis of *dhikos/xenos*, obligation and responsibility is not a rigid and predictable structural schema. On the contrary, it is filled with ambiguity, misunderstandings, ambivalence and even hyperbole, and it is perpetually caught in the politics of successful and failed social performance (cf. Herzfeld 1985; Kirtsoglou 2004). The inchoate quality of intimacy anticipates its own subversion. Intimacy and relatedness, in their performative character, contain within them the seeds of their own negation.

Anthropos

The term 'human' is used in Greek far more often than it is used in English, in the place of the generic English word 'man', to mean a human being and a person. 'The man needs his privacy' is translated, for instance, as 'the human needs his privacy' (*o anthropos thelei tin isihia tou*). 'Have you got someone to take care of you?' translates in Greek as 'have you got a human?' (*exeis anthropo?*), and a common expression for 'being alone' is 'I don't even have a single human' (*den eho oute enan anthropo*). To ask someone 'what sort of human are you' (*ti soi anthropos eisai*) directly questions their moral ground, while wondering 'aren't I human?' (*ego den eimai anthropos?*) is a rhetorical way of ascertaining one's rights in a social context.

A 'human being', beyond having their basic needs covered, is seen as deserving respect, fair treatment, being considered and taken into account. To be a 'human', *anthropos*, means to belong to a category of existence by 'birthright' and as a matter of ontology (cf. Rapport 2012). It follows that everyone – both *dhikos* and *xenos* – is a human being. Humans are conceived in Greek culture as sharing a number of common predicaments and a fundamental bond with each other, as they endure the difficulties of life as struggle (*agonas*) (cf. Theodossopoulos 2008).

Human beings are known and defined by their humanity (*anthropia*), which stands for all emotions, habits, attitudes and behaviours appropriate for and towards human persons. Much like all other qualities, humanity in the Greek context is performatively established. To be human (*anthropos*) and to have humanity (*anthropia*) means to be willing to see the world from the Other's point of view, to engage others in their capacity as human beings and not as members of any other category (including gender, race, religion or nationality).

To relate to others as humans also means to consciously and significantly play down the hierarchies associated with giving and receiving. All human beings are seen as being by default vulnerable and, therefore, potentially in need. This is encapsulated in the common, almost stereotypical phrase, 'We are all human: today it is you, tomorrow [in the future] it will be me.'[6] Reciprocity, as the element that alleviates and subverts the burden of obligations, is taken in such cases for granted within the time frame of human kind, a kind of timeless, primal time within which we all end up owing to each other and being collectively indebted to the supernatural (represented as God, life or the universe).

The opposite – refusing to transcend the level of categorical groupings or to inappropriately enforce hierarchical relations of indebtedness – can earn someone the accusation of not being human (*dhen eisai anthropos esy*). While success or failure to honour one's obligations within the *dhikos/xenos* system is sanctioned at the level of society (*koinonia, kosmos* cf. Just 2000), failure to respond properly to other human beings is ultimately judged by the supernatural (cf. Herzfeld 2005: 160–70). On more than one occasion during the 2015 to 2016 refugee arrivals, and particularly upon learning about shipwrecks or dramatic landings, I have heard different Greek people (not necessarily religious) exclaiming that 'God will burn us to the ground', or 'God will punish us' (*tha mas kapsei o Theos, tha mas timorisei o Theos*), or simply that 'We will pay for these things' (*tha plirosoume gia auta ta pragmata*). 'Us' and 'we' referred in this case to the human collectivity, to 'humankind' which failed so dramatically to uphold its primary responsibility of protecting all of its members.

The meaning of human (*anthropos*) and of being imbued with a sense of respect towards other humans (*anthropia*), becomes especially relevant against the Aristotelian distinction between *zoe* and *bios* as theorized by Hannah Arendt (1958). According to Arendt, *zoe* is the kind of unqualified, bare life which becomes meaningful only when it is transformed to *bios*, social life embedded in the body politic. Developing Arendt's thought further, Agamben (1998) discusses *homo sacer* as a special category of the Roman law, within which a human being remains the subject of the law but only in terms of bare life. As *homo sacer*'s rights as a citizen are suspended, her or his *bios* is reduced to *zoe* and as a result has no political value; thus, her death can remain without retribution. Arendt's and Agamben's analyses seek to theoretically grasp the phenomenon of the Holocaust and subsequently of all concentration camps as contexts where political existence is reduced, via a process of violent depoliticization to bare life.

What it means to be 'human' in the Greek context questions this radical distinction between *zoe* and *bios* (cf. Panourgia 2009: 113), sometimes turning it on its head. Attempts to reduce a human being into a *homo sacer* can have the opposite effect, that is, to trigger a process of 'recognition' of the humanity of the other. This basic-level recognition compels social actors to redeem a fellow human from the status of 'naked existence' and reinstate her to the position of having a *bios*, thereby granting her the right to a dignified and socially recognized life. Thus, an idiosyncratic version of cosmopolitanism is accomplished through the refusal to sustain the distinction between *zoe* and *bios* (cf. Rapport 2012), and through a deep-seated belief in their ideal unity.

According to my Greek informants, 'Everyone deserves to live like a human being.'[7] The spectrum of rights credited to every human is wide (and in some ways outside the scope of this chapter), but amongst the most fundamental rights is the right to sociality and to being treated by others with humanity. Humanity in this case fits very much the Kantian representation of a moral limit to what one is and is not permitted to do to other humans. While for Kant every person deserves respect independently of their deeds, in the Greek case, however, humanity is performatively established.

Greek people tend to feel responsible for what they do and for what they *let happen* to others. Failure to exhibit humanity can earn someone the characterization of inhuman (*apanthropos*), or animal (*zoon*) (cf. Herzfeld 2005: 76). Inhumanity or animality stems from failing to acknowledge the bundle of rights credited to all human kind. If one goes beyond this point, and starts actively hurting others, he or she then transforms into a beast (*ktinos*), and finally into a monster (*teras*), a freak of nature that emerges out of disobeying the most fundamental rules of the cosmos.[8]

What I have tried to accomplish in this section is to demonstrate the complexity and fluidity of local systems of intimacy, belonging, hierarchy and obligation. While it is true that acts of giving and receiving are generally hierarchical and establish asymmetrical relationships, in the Greek context they are also means and ways of assuming responsibility and of transforming a distrusted stranger into an intimate insider. At the level of *dhikos/xenos*, every act of giving pre-empts the act of receiving rendering the ensuing hierarchies provisional and self-negating. Intimacy, granted or gained through genealogical and social relatedness, erodes significantly the sense of indebtedness associated with giving and receiving. Even if one is stripped of all social networks of intimacy and trust (as in the case of refugees), or when these networks have no power to cast their protective shade onto her or him (cf. Loizos 1975), he or she still remains a human being who deserves the support and fellowship of other human beings around her or him. The manner in which vulnerability and need are envisaged in Greece as common predicaments of all humans destabilizes hierarchical relations between givers and receivers through the belief that at a fundamental level we are all indebted to each other.

As much as I side with the critics of humanitarianism, charity and compassionate volunteering, I claim that hierarchical relations between givers and receivers are not uniformly understood and constructed in all contexts. In some cases, these relations are envisaged as far less rigid and they remain mediated by local understandings of what it means to be human, insider/outsider and by culturally informed notions of need, responsibility and obligation. References to our common humanity therefore, far from being abstract, general and ahistorical, are established in culturally and historically specific ways of understanding and enacting what it means to be human.

Where is the right to have rights established?

One of the main issues at heart in the critique launched against the deeply unequal character of humanitarian reason (cf. Fassin 2012) is that the receiver depends on the goodwill of the benefactor. This hierarchical relationship precludes the establishment of political rights within stable and permanent frameworks and leaves large numbers of people at the mercy of their fellow human beings, trapped at the receiving end of gifts that 'call for no counter gift' (Fassin 2012: 3). I agree with this observation that calls for careful examination of alternatives. If one's rights are not established in the will (good or not) of other social actors, two options remain. These rights are either guaranteed by sovereign nation-states, or, they come as part and parcel with one's humanity (cf. Rapport 2012). The very existence of sovereign nation-states, however, depends on borders (cf. Benhabib 2004) and aggressive politics of exclusion. When it comes to certain rights (such as those of mobility), the nation-state is certainly not a suitable guarantor. In this sense, I find myself in profound agreement with Rapport's position that 'the cosmopolitan project is to know Anyone in terms of a universal human nature', where Anyone is a 'human actor who is to be recognized as at once universal and individual' (2012: 2). The recognition and respect of one another's common humanity promote a kind of cosmopolitan project that is at once political and moral.

The moral aspect of social relations has been central to a number of Enlightenment scholars such as Kant, Hume and Adam Smith. For Kant morality is connected to reason and the autonomy of individual agents who enforce moral obligations upon themselves (cf. Timmerman 2010). Kant's thought is useful in our understanding of how and why social actors force themselves to obey moral codes even at the absence of witnesses. However, his decisive exclusion of sentiments, as it becomes apparent in the *Groundwork of the Metaphysics of Morals*, makes it difficult to account for the role of the affective component in moral social relations (Timmerman 2010).

In contrast to Kant, Hume is an explicit anti-rationalist. He maintains that morality cannot be derived from reason alone, or from the combination of reasoning knowledge and belief (Mackie 1980: 52); the seat of morality is to be found in sentiments. In Hume we also find an interesting formulation of 'sympathy' – not as compassion or pity – but as an inclination to share the feelings of Others (Mackie 1980: 5). Hume's concept of 'sympathy' inspires Adam Smith. In *The Theory of Moral Sentiments* ([1759] 1853) Adam Smith envisages 'sympathy' to be the effect of a process of mirroring through which we understand how others feel in a given situation.

Smith's concept of sympathy opens up a very interesting window in our understanding of moral sentiments and of what could possibly motivate us to become each other's keepers of rights. In the previous section, while discussing Greek conceptualizations of 'what it means to be human', I have claimed that one of the basic dimensions of humanity is the ideal unity between *zoe* (bare life) and *bios* (social life) that all human beings are seen as hitherto deserving in the Greek context. I have also maintained that profound ruptures in this unity tend to trigger the conscious efforts of other social actors who feel compelled to relieve the suffering of their fellow humans (cf. Bornstein 2009), restoring them to sociality. What Bornstein calls *philanthropy* (Bornstein 2009) is in this case an urge to safeguard a person's right 'to live like a human being'. The motivation behind this urge appears to be established in our capacity to recognize and identify with the feelings of others in a way that transcends (in the Greek case) categorical identifications predicated by the scheme of *dhikos/xenos*. The leap from viewing someone as *dhikos/xenos* (intimate/stranger or insider/outsider) to engaging them simply as human beings is mediated – as I have claimed – by the quality, feeling and attitude of humanity (*anthropia*). As a feeling, humanity (*anthropia*) depends on empathy, the recognition of the position of the other and the ability to imagine oneself as another in order to appreciate their current problems and conditions. As a quality, humanity (*anthropia*) is the capacity to recognize ruptures in the fundamental unity between *zoe* and *bios*, and as an attitude it is the actions one takes in order to repair the aforementioned ruptures.

My use of the term 'empathy' here is similar to the 'essence' of Adam Smith's sympathy. However, the term 'sympathy' is almost impossible to reclaim due to its close semantic association with compassion and pity (as largely established in the work of Nietzsche). In Nietzsche (*Human All too Human, Beyond Good and Evil*, but more so in *Thus Said Zarathustra* [1978]) we see an understanding of compassion as deeply hierarchical, profoundly self-driven and condescending. The Nietzschean term *Mitleid* (cf. Frazer 2006) inspired a genealogy of critiques of compassion, pity and sympathy that marked the meaning of all of these terms in an irreversible manner.

As opposed to sympathy, pity and compassion in the Nietzschean sense, empathy needs to be understood as a cognitive and affective mechanism related to responsibility and, as Levinas claims, to accountability ([1981] 2013). For Levinas, identification with the Other holds the Self 'hostage' and 'accountable for what [he or she] did not do, accountable for the others before the others' (Lingis 2013: xxix). Empathy as the feeling that mediates the manifestation of humanity presupposes an embodied being who reacts to the face of the Other in a visceral manner (cf. Levinas [1981] 2013: 88, 89). The ideal unity of *zoe* and *bios* is then enacted in the human being who is at once a body and a person, and can partake in the symbolism and physicality of the feelings of Others.

The ability to empathize with others, in conjunction with the culturally specific understanding of vulnerability and need as a common predicament of all human beings (as I have already discussed) has tremendous political potential. The idea that weakness, vulnerability and need – as much as one tries to avoid them – are associated with human existence, challenges perceptions and representations of stable hierarchies of powerful and weak persons. The saying, 'Today it is you, tomorrow it could be me; we are human beings,' encapsulates a vernacular understanding of power that is almost Foucauldian in character, since power is not understood here as something that is acquired or possessed by any one in particular but is seen as exercised from 'innumerable points' (Foucault 1978: 94). In order better to understand the fundamental difference between perceiving subjective positions (and thus hierarchies) as stable and viewing them as provisional, unpredictable and in a state of flux I will juxtapose two quotations. The first, is from Didier Fassin:

> Humanitarian reason governs precarious lives: the lives of the unemployed and the asylum seekers, the lives of sick immigrants [...] threaten and forgotten lives that humanitarian government brings into existence by protecting and revealing them. When compassion is exercised in the public space, it is therefore always directed from above to below, from the more powerful to the weaker [...] The concept of precarious lives therefore needs to be taken in the strongest sense of its Latin etymology: lives that are not guaranteed but bestowed in answer to prayer, or in other words are defined [...] in the relation to those that have power over them. (2012: 4)

I follow this with an extract from my fieldnotes that refers to the 2015 to 2016 arrival of refugees in Greece:

More than six thousand people live in the makeshift camp of Piraeus in small, flimsy tents and some – very few – in larger UNHCR ones. The few showers and bathrooms are insufficient as the weather is getting hotter. Eleni, a woman in her fifties comes every day in the camp; two and sometimes three and four times. Each time she takes people back to her house to have a bath and do their laundry. Eleni carries big IKEA bags with the dry clothes to the camp, where they get emptied and filled back again with more clothes to be washed. Randa [Syrian refugee woman] tells me that the smell of clothes, washed in Eleni's house, remind her of her mother. Eleni also talks about her own mother who came as a refugee from Asia Minor in 1922.[9] 'You see?' she contemplates, 'this is the fate of human beings' (auti einai h moira ton anthropon). Back then, it was my mother, today it is those people and tomorrow … who knows? It could be me or my children. How can you stay indifferent to what happens here? How can you go to your house and eat, and have a bath and relax when you know that there are human beings forced to live in these conditions? Human beings like me and you. I am not rich, but I have a bathroom and a washing machine. Life? Fate? God? – name it as you want – allowed me to have a bathroom and a washing machine. This is what I have. This is what I share.[10]

From reading these two excerpts, it becomes evident that while Fassin refers to a stable hierarchy of lives instituted and sustained by the violence of governance, Eleni does not view herself as a powerful benefactor, or as a 'moral neoliberal' (cf. Muehlebach 2012). Quite the contrary, she views plenty of common political ground between herself and the refugees in the makeshift camp. Their condition is something that can happen to anyone. It follows then that Anyone is 'a human actor who is to be recongised as at once universal and individual' (Rapport 2012: 2): capable of practising 'a particular localised life […] and yet [one who] continually embodies global entitlements and continues to be recognized as bearing universal capacities' (Rapport 2012: 6). Such 'entitlements' and 'capacities' may not always be positive in the manner that Rapport's jouissance-imbued concept of the 'life project' entails (cf. Rapport 2003). More often than not in the historically formed Greek consciousness they are not entitlements at all, but (similarly global) misfortunes, disasters and calamities that test the (similarly universal) capacities of people to endure and survive them.

Other minds

Through the example of Greek perceptions of what it means to be human, I have tried to show how culturally nuanced moral visions can destabilize and subvert neo-liberal sensibilities. All human beings are locally seen as being flimsy, vulnerable and at the mercy of wars, famines, natural disasters and a capricious supernatural that is constantly criticized in Greece for looking the other way (cf. Knight 2015). While God's gaze (*vlepei o Theos*) is frequently evoked by Greek people as an admonition against wrongdoing, far too often the opposite also holds true. The exclamation, 'God, can't you see?' (*De vlepeis Thee?*), serves to remind everyone that God, much like the state (cf. Herzfeld 1992) and every other source of power, is in fact indifferent to human suffering. The quality and ethos of humanity as *anthropia* possessed and exhibited by fellow beings is in many ways the ultimate guarantor of one's rights when all else fails.

Humanity as *anthropia* cannot be confused with humanitarian governance, charity, pity or compassion. It constitutes a vernacular cosmopolitan ethos that is at once a specific kind of morality, a social condition and an orientation (cf. Rapport 2012: 27, 30–31), but also an aesthetic, and a radically transformative affective, political technology (Rapport 2012: 40–1). One's humanity as *anthropia* is mediated by her capacity to empathize with the feelings and predicaments of others to become mobilized and responsible in the face of the Other. *Empathy in this case promotes an understanding of the human condition that is at once timeless and universal.* The tragedies, misfortunes and afflictions suffered by one's grandparents as refugees in the past (for instance), are similar to the ones suffered by refugees in the present (cf. Kirtsoglou and Tsimouris 2016). The calamities of life here (whatever this 'here' might be) are seen in Greece as essentially similar to the ones suffered 'over there' as human beings are 'the same everywhere and always'.[11]

The culturally specific belief that we are all 'fundamentally the same' in our common humanity allows one to empathize with the feelings of others. Does this mean, however, that they *actually know* how other people feel? Does this kind of empathy as affective technology and political praxis collapse the Other onto the Self, thereby obliterating the differences between them? How is empathy as affective recognition achieved in conditions where the difference of the Other can be safeguarded and respected?

In order to appreciate what 'the same' refers to in the Greek case, we need to remember the anxiety and ambivalence that a stranger (*xenos*) causes. The definitional quality of the 'stranger', 'outsider' (and potentially mistrusted) *xenos* is lack of knowledge about them. Knowing someone, in turn, is not a matter of knowing their story (cf. Fassin 2012), or their soul (cf. Foucault 1978). As Herzfeld observes: 'for most Greek villagers, moral evaluations are not assessments of innate character – which they deny being able to read even as they try to do so– but rather of social inclusion' (2005: 86). The 'truth' of or about the Other is in Greece a kind of unattainable knowledge epitomized in the saying 'abyss is the soul of human beings'.[12] Confession, is similarly seen as an unreliable technology for the production of truth (cf. Foucault 1978), since Greek people casually urge each other to not reveal things in confessions.[13] Sociality (that gradually transforms a person from a stranger into 'one of us') is actually the only way of knowing *something* about others. This is especially evident in local beliefs about children and young people who have not yet had the time to prove themselves through socialization. Knowledge about them comes from what one knows about their parents and family. The manner in which one's family and social milieu operates as a proxy becomes apparent in the saying, 'A shoe from your own place even if it is patched / but where you know the craftsman who made it', phrased as an admonition against marrying an undecipherable outsider or a non-Greek (cf. Herzfeld 2005: 87, 232).

Given that knowledge about the Other is always provisional and established in social relations, and given than a stranger/outsider/*xenos* is seen as an impenetrable and obscure entity, how can empathy operate and how can Greek people claim that 'all human beings are the same'? The quality of sameness refers here to the *consequences* of our common humanity, rather than to our 'essence'. The Other is hitherto different in very many ways that include conventional categorical ascriptions but also feelings, thoughts and intentions. Her membership in the timeless and placeless community of humans, however, grants her similar strengths and vulnerabilities in the face of adversity, comparable options and a certain repertoire of reactions to happy and joyful events. And yet, sameness at the level of the consequences of humanity does not fully explain how we can claim to empathize with the feelings of Others, given that it is virtually impossible to know how others feel. The question then remains: does empathy need sameness in order to be accomplished?

In a creative reading of the *Ode to Man* in Sophocles' tragedy *Antigone*, Castoriadis (2007) observes the paradoxical capacities credited by Sophocles to human beings, Man, Sophocles says, 'has developed language and learned to build cities' (353–360). Man is all-resourceful, and although he or she does not know the future, he or she manages to 'make herself a path through everything', and he or she 'advances toward nothing of what is to come without having some resource' (360–1). How, Castoriadis asks, do human beings 'learn' if no one teaches them? How do they manage to carve paths into the unknown, being prepared (always having some resource), while not knowing what to prepare for? The paradox is solved, Castoriadis argues when we understand the power of human beings to self-create and to become autodidacts (2007: 33). Human beings invent through their radical power of imagination that is (compare with Rapport 2012) at once individual and collective. The 'radical imagination', Castoriadis argues 'does not exist only at the level of the individual psyche, but also at the social-historical, collective level qua *radical imaginary*' (Castoriadis 2007: 372, original emphasis).

Taking my cue from Castoriadis's analysis, I claim that *the possibility to empathize with other human beings and to understand their feelings relies on the power of the radical imagination*. At some fundamental level, we all 'know each other', while 'knowing nothing about each other' and this is possible, because despite our differences we are made of the same qualities. My Greek informants who empathized with the predicament of the refugees in 2015 to 2016 and declared their solidarity in discursive and practical forms did not profess to 'know' the Others. They employed their knowledge of past catastrophes learnt through the stories of their own grandparents (cf. Hirschon 1989), their knowledge of what it means to be a foreigner and a migrant in Germany, Australia, Belgium or the United States, and their socially acquired knowledge of what the ethos of humanity as *anthropia* commands one to do in such cases. Using this kind of knowledge as a basis, they went on to become *autodidacts* in other people's feelings and experiences.

In sum, the process of *autodidaxis* facilitates human-to-human relationships in the absence of knowledge about non-intimate Others. The experiential ('I can see'), cognitive ('I can understand') and affective ('I co-feel') components of empathy, are instituted in an autodidactic manner and they make relatedness with strangers possible without forcing the Other to become one with the Self. As a transformative technology empathy remains an elusive process that depends on conjectures. We believe we can see, we assume we understand and we infer the feelings of Others. The 'intersubjective space' is indeed 'not symmetrical' (Levinas 1991: 84). 'Things', Levinas points out 'are never known in their totality; an essential character of our perception of them is that of being inadequate' ([1981] 1995: 22). The face of the Other can be a mirror that aids processes of recognition, substitution and identification, but mirroring is itself nothing but an *antanaclasis*.[14] In literary theory, 'antanaclasis' refers to 'the repetition of a word with a different meaning in each time' (Childers and Hentzi 1995: xiii). Our experiential, cognitive and affective perception of the Other is a hermeneutic effort. The intersubjective space of our 'common humanity' is filled with the asymmetries and asynchronicities of this hermeneutic effort. It is in this sense intertextual, and allows for misunderstandings, for the existence of different meanings and for slight (or bigger) misinterpretations and misconstructions of each other. Human beings as social actors manage to reach a common-ground without necessarily, fully and finally sharing each others' views, beliefs, perceptions and understandings of each other or of a given situation. Our common humanity is possible not despite but *because* of *antanaclasis*: because we are capable of imagining oneself in the position of the Other, while knowing that we are still separate entities, entitled to the differences between us.

To be human is a deeply political thing

Rather than being understood as a bounded entity, the self emerges as an assemblage of forces, composed through history, culture and relatedness. Not despite cultural specificity but because of it Greek subjects can grant moral recognition to others. Through ideas about what it means to be human and what our common humanity compels us to do, Greek people appear to be capable of placing themselves in the position of the Other, in the full knowledge that each and every one remains a separate entity, entitled to her difference.

The modern Greek vision of humanity, as an unmediated category of belonging, allows actors to supersede all other categories of identification (kinship, gender, race, religion, ethnicity) which, thus prove to be provisional. The recognition of a common humanity gives rise to empathy as a moral sentiment and initiates spirals of responsibility and obligation, through which we attempt to bridge the gap between *zoe* and *bios* around us. The culturally and historically specific content and form of moral sentiments such as empathy cannot be always and fully appreciated through an analysis of large historical forces – such as neo-liberalism – or through other culturally and historically specific models of confession-based beneficiary-benefactor relations.

This does not mean that concerns over what constitutes humanitarian reason are not valid, widespread and hegemonically present in Greece and around the world. It is the task of anthropology, however (and dare I say of a postcolonial anthropology), to mine for alternative understandings and visions of cosmopolitan morality. For such visions can operate as fields for the development of new, grassroots, 'open ecologies' of solidarity that will form viable alternatives to humanitarian governmentality models.

'We are all human' means in the Greek context that we are all vulnerable, precarious, fleeting and provisional, and as such the thing we 'owe' to each other is a break from indebtedness and hierarchical, asymmetrical relations of power. In this sense to be human is a deeply and explicitly moral and political position, intimately connected to the cosmopolitan order.

Notes

1 I refer here to the Eastern Mediterranean route (Aegean Sea). Overall, more than 4,000 people lost their lives trying to cross the Mediterranean in the same period.

2 The displacement of Greek-speaking, Christian Orthodox populations was confirmed by the ensuing Treaty of Lausanne that commanded the exchange of populations between Greece and Turkey in favour of the ethnic homogenization of the respective nation-states.

3 The term foreign powers (*xenes dynameis*) and the role of Americans and Europeans as *xenoi* have been discussed in detail by Kirtsoglou and Theodossopoulos (2010b).

4 Please note that the term *oikeiotita* is etymologically traced to *oikos* (house – household)

5 And vice versa. The absence of social exchange or breaking trust leads to estrangement.

6 *Anthropoi eimaste; simera esy, aurio ego.*

7 *Na zei san anthropos.*

8 The Nazis, for instance, are frequently characterized as beasts and when it comes to the Holocaust as monsters. The term monster is typically used for perpetrators of especially heinous crimes such as physical or sexual abuse of children or infanticide.

9 A large number of Greek people experienced the predicament of the refugees who came in 2015 to 2016 as a condition of multitemporality (cf. Knight 2013, 2015; Kirtsoglou and Tsimouris 2016). Both Piraeus and the islands where the present refugees landed are primarily inhabited by the descendants of the Greek-speaking Christian Orthodox populations that have been forcibly displaced from Asia Minor and Anatolia as a result of the Greco-Turkish War in 1920–22 and the ensuing Treaty of Lausanne that commanded the exchange of populations between Greece and Turkey in favour of the ethnic homogenization of the respective nation-states (cf. Hirschon 1989). Refugeeness as collective narrative and transgenerational trauma (cf. Anastasiadis 2012), as well as memories of economic migration to Europe, the United States or Australia became for a large part of Greek society mechanisms of *substitution* (Levinas [1974] 1981) through which a number of people treated the 'stranger' as another human being in need, similar to the self.

10 *H zoe, h moira, o Theos? Pes to opos thes, dosane ki eho ena mpanio kai ena plyntirio. Ayta exo, ayta.*

11 *Oloi oi anthropoi to idio einai,* or *panta oi anthropoi einai idioi,* or *ola gia tous anthropous einai.*

12 *Avyssos h psyche tou anthropou.*

13 As epitomized in the saying 'don't even tell the priest about this' (*min to peis oute tou papa*).

14 Interestingly *antanaclasis* literally means in Greek 'reflection' (as one's reflection in the mirror).

References

Agamben, G. 1998. *Homo Sacer: Sovereign Power and Bare Life*. Stanford, CA: Stanford University Press.

Anastasiadis, A. 2012. 'Transgenerational Communication of Traumatic Experiences: Narrating the Past from a Postmemorial Position'. *Journal of Literary Theory* 6(1): 1–24.

Arendt, H. 1958. *The Human Condition*. Chicago: University of Chicago Press.

Arendt, H. 1968. *The Origins of Totalitarianism*. New York: Harcourt, Brace and Jovanovich.

Benhabib, S. 2004. *The Rights of Others: Aliens, Residents and Citizens*. Cambridge: Cambridge University Press.

Bornstein, E. 2009. 'The Impulse of Philanthropy'. *Cultural Anthropology* 24(4): 622–51.

Bornstein E. and P. Redfield 2011. 'An Introduction to the Anthropology of Humanitarianism.' In *Forces of Compassion*, E. Bornstein and P. Redfield (eds.). Santa Fe: School for Advanced Research Press, pp. 3–30.

Berlant, L. G. 2004. 'Introduction: Compassion (and Withholding)'. In *Compassion: The Culture and Politics of an Emotion*, L. G. Berlant (ed.). London: Routledge, pp. 1–14.

Cabot, H. 2014. *On the Doorstep of Europe*. Philadelphia: University of Pennsylvania Press.

Campbell, J. 1964. *Honour Family and Patronage*. Oxford: Clarendon.

Candea, M. 2012. 'Derrida en Corse: Hospitality as Scale-free Abstraction'. *Journal of Royal Anthropological Institute* 18: S34–48.

Castoriadis, C. 2007. *Figures of the Thinkable*. Stanford, CA: Stanford University Press.

Childers, J. and Hentzi, G. 1995. 'Antanaclasis'. *The Columbia Dictionary of Modern Literary and Cultural Criticism*. New York: Columbia University Press.

Crowhurst, I. 2012. 'Caught in the Victim/Criminal Paradigm: Female Migrant Prostitution in Contemporary Italy'. *Modern Italy* 17(4): 493–506.

Danforth, L. 1989. *Firewalking and Religious Healing: The Anastenaria of Greece and the American Firewalking Movement*. Princeton, NJ: Princeton University Press.

Derrida, J. 1992. *Given Time: 1. Counterfeit Money*. Chicago: University of Chicago Press.

Fassin, D. 2005. 'Compassion and Repression: The Moral Economy of Immigration Policies in France'. *Cultural Anthropology* 20(3): 362–87.

Fassin, D. 2007. 'Humanitarianism as Politics of Life'. *Public Culture* 19(3): 499–520.

Fassin, D. 2011a. *Humanitarian Reason*. Berkeley: University of California Press.

Fassin, D. 2011b. 'A Contribution to the Critique of Moral Reason'. *Anthropological Theory* 11(4): 481–91.

Fassin, D. 2012. *Humanitarian Reason: A Moral History of the Present*. Berkeley: University of California Press.

Foucault, M. 1978. *The History of Sexuality*, Vol. 1. London: Penguin.

Frazer, M. 2006. 'The compassion of Zarathustra: Nietzsche on Sympathy and Strength'. *Review of Politics* 68(1): 49–78.

Giordano, C. 2008. 'Practices of Translation and the Making of Migrant Subjectivities in Contemporary Italy'. *American Ethnologist* 35(4): 588–606.

Guattari, F. 2000. *The Three Ecologies*. London: Athlone.

Herzfeld, M. 1985. *The Poetics of Manhood: Contest and Identity in a Cretan Mountain Cillage*. Princeton, NJ: Princeton University Press.

Herzfeld, M. 1992. *The Social Production of Indifference*. Chicago: University of Chicago Press.

Herzfeld, M. 2003. 'It Takes One to Know One: Cultural Resentment and Mutual Recognition among Greeks in Local and Global Contexts'. In *Counterworks: Managing the Diversity of Knowledge*, R. Fardon (ed.). London: Routledge, pp. 124–42.

Herzfeld, M. 2005. *Cultural Intimacy: Social Poetics in the Nation-State*. London: Routledge.

Herzfeld, M. 2012. 'Afterword: Reciprocating the Hospitality of these Pages'. *Journal of Royal Anthropological Institute* 18: S 210–17.

Hirschon, R. 1989. *Heirs of the Greek Catastrophe: The Social Life of Asia Minor Refugees in Piraeus*. Oxford: Clarendon.

Hirschon, R. 1992. 'Greek Adults' Verbal Play, or, How to Train for Caution'. *Journal of Modern Greek Studies* 10: 35–56.

Hirschon, R. 2008. 'Presents, Promises and Punctuality: Accountability and Obligation in Greek Social Life'. In *Networks of Power in Modern Greece: Essays in Honour of John Campbell*, M. Mazower (ed.). London: Hurst, pp. 189–207.

Just, R. 2000. *A Greek Island Cosmos: Kinship and Community on Meganisi*. Santa Fe, NM: School of American Research Press.

Kirtsoglou, E. 2004. *For the Love of Women: Gender, Identity and Same-sex Relationships in a Greek Provincial Town*. London: Routledge.

Kirtsoglou, E. 2006. 'Unspeakable Crimes: Athenian Greek Perceptions of Local and International Terrorism'. In *Terror and Violence: Imagination and the Unimaginable*, A. Strathern, P. Stewart and N. L. Whitehead (eds). London: Pluto, pp. 61–88.

Kirtsoglou, E. and Theodossopoulos, D. 2010a. 'Intimacies of Anti–globalization: Imagining Unhappy Others as Oneself in Greece'. In *United in Discontent: Local Responses to Cosmopolitanism, Multiculturalism and Globalization*, D. Theodossopoulos and E. Kirtsoglou (eds). Oxford: Berghahn, pp. 83–102.

Kirtsoglou, E. and Theodossopoulos, D. 2010b. 'The Poetics of Anti–Americanism in Greece: Rhetoric, Agency and Local Meaning'. *Social Analysis* 54(1): 106–24.

Kirtsoglou, E. and Tsimouris, G. 2016. '"Il était un petit navire": The "Refugee Crisis", Neo-orientalism, and the Production of Radical Alterity'. *Journal of Modern Greek Studies, Occasional Paper Series*, 9: 1–14.

Knight, D. M. 2013. 'The Greek Economic Crisis as Trope'. *Focaal: Journal of Global and Historical Anthropology* 65: 147–9.

Knight, D. M. 2015. *History Time and Economic Crisis in Central Greece*. New York: Palgrave Macmillan.

Levinas, E. [1974] 1981. *Otherwise than Being, or Beyond Essence*. Pittsburgh, PA: Duquesne University Press.

Levinas, E. [1981] 1995. *The Theory of Intuition in Husserl's Phenomenology*, A. Orianne (trans.). Evanston, IL: Northwestern University Press.

Levinas, E. 1991. *Totality and Infinity*. Netherlands: Kluwer Academic Publishers.

Lingis, Alfonso. 2013. Translator's introduction in Levinas Emmanuel *Otherwise than Being: Beyond Essence* 2013 Springer.

Loizos, Peter. *The Greek gift: politics in a Cypriot village*. Oxford: Blackwell.

Mackie, J. L. 1980. *Hume's Moral Theory*. London: Routledge.

Malkki, L. 1996. 'Speechless Emissaries: Refugees, Humanitarianism and Dehistorisation'. *Cultural Anthropology* 11(3): 377–404.

Muehlebach, A. 2012. *The Moral Neoliberal Welfare and Citizenship in Italy*. Chicago: University of Chicago Press.

Nietzsche, F. 1978. *Thus Spake Zarathustra*. New York: Penguin.

Nietzsche, F. 1986. *Human All too Human*. Cambridge University Press; Nietzsche, F. 2002. *Beyond Good and Evil: Prelude to a Philosophy of the Future (Cambridge Texts in the History of Philosophy)* Cambridge University Press.

Panourgia, Neni. 1995. *Fragments of Death, Fables of Identity: An Athenian Anthropography*. University of Wisconsin Press.

Panourgia, Neni. 2009. *Dangerous Citizens: The Greek Left and the Terror of the State*. New York: Fordham University Press.

Papataxiarhis, E. 1991. 'Friends of the Heart: Male Commensal Solidarity, Gender and Kinship in Aegean Greece'. In P. Loizos and E. Papataxiarhis (eds). *Contested Identities: Gender and Kinship in Modern Greece*. Princeton: Princeton University Press.

Pedwell, C. 2012. 'Economies of Empathy: Obama, Neoliberalism and Social Justice'. *Environment and Planning D: Society and Space* 30(2): 280–97.

Pedwell, C. 2014. *Affective Relations: The Transnational Politics of Empathy*. Basingstoke: Palgrave.

Rapport, N. 2003. '*I am Dynamite*': *An Alternative Anthropology of Power*. London: Routledge.

Rapport, N. 2012. *Anyone: The Cosmopolitan Subject of Anthropology*. Oxford: Berghahn.

Rosaldo, R. 1989. *Culture and Truth: The Remaking of Social Analysis*. London: Routledge.

Mahmood, S. [2005] 2012. *The Politics of Piety: Islamic Revival and the Feminist Subject*. Princeton, NJ: Princeton University Press.

Smith, A. [1759] 1853. *The Theory of Moral Sentiments*. London: Bohn's Standard Library.

Tazzioli, M. 2013. 'Which Europe? Migrants' Uneven Geographies and Counter-mapping at the Limits of Representation'. *Movements. Journal für kritische Migrations- und Grenzregimeforschung* 1(2): 1–20.

Theodossopoulos, D. 2008. *Troubles with Turtles: Cultural Understandings of the Environment on a Greek Island*. Oxford: Berghahn.

Throop, J. 2008. 'On the Problem of Empathy: The Case of Yap, Federated States of Micronesia'. *Ethos* 36(4): 402–26.

Ticktin, M. 2006. 'When Ethics and Politics Meet: The Violence of Humanitarianism in France'. *American Ethnologist* 33(1): 33–49.

Ticktin, M. 2011. *Casualties of Care: Immigration and the Politics of Humanitarianism in France*. Berkeley: University of California Press.

Ticktin, M. 2014. 'Transnational Humanitarianism'. *Annual Review of Anthropology* 43: 273–89.

Timmerman, J. 2010. *Kant's Groundwork of the Metaphysics of Morals: A Commentary*. Cambridge: Cambridge University Press.

Trundle, C. 2014. *Americans in Tuscany: Charity, Compassion and Belonging*. Oxford: Berghahn.

Vaughan-Williams, N. 2015. '"We Are *Not* Animals!" Humanitarian Border Security and Zoopolitical Spaces in Europe'. *Political Geography* 45: 1–10.

Viveiros de Castro, E. 1992. *From the Enemy's Point of View: Humanity and Divinity in an Amazonian Society*. Chicago: University of Chicago Press.

Wilson, A. R. and Brown, R. (eds). 2009. *Humanitarianism and Suffering: The Mobilisation of Empathy*. Cambridge: Cambridge University Press.

9

Transference and Cosmopolitan Politesse: Coming to Terms with the Distorted, 'Tragic' Quality of Social Relations between Individual Human Beings

Nigel Rapport

There is a distinctiveness to anthropological research methodology. The fieldworker locates herself or himself in a physical space or in a frame of mind that is new and takes up the task of making 'sense'. What is entering her or his bodily senses? What are its regularities, if any, and what does it mean? What do the sensations convey about what other human beings in the immediate environment might themselves be sensing and about what they might be experiencing? The consciousness, the bodily awareness of the fieldworker, is the only certainty: the instrument of both data-gathering and of sense-making, of interpretation and analysis.

Enormous weight is thereby placed on the fieldworker. What a datum, a piece of local information, is and how that datum properly connects with another and another to form a stream of data – a text, a discourse, a practice – is dependent on the experiencing and the interpreting of the anthropologist in the field. He or she invents a 'social' reality in which there are units of information out there beyond her or his body and those units conventionally, normally coalesce into patterned shapes of habitual 'cultural' life. The aim, moreover, is a holistic one. All the fieldworkers' senses are to be brought into play and given space to fulfil themselves; all data are to be deemed worthy of inclusion, their significance only apparent in the context of the whole collection: what is said by 'A' and by 'B', and what is done, and how and when; what it feels like to be with 'A' or 'B', to hear, and see, and touch and even taste them, now and then.

But then does this distinctive methodology not mimic in an insightful way the mundane experience of social life as this is practised by the cultural 'members' that the anthropologist has set out to examine? Is not their existence as members who 'belong' to social relations within a life-world – a locale, a community, a movement – equally dependent on the individual sense-making they make from their particular bodily perspectives? Here, too, social life is made out from particular points of consciousness: centres of bodily energy that gather data, collate, interpret and analyse it, and so make 'the social'. And here, too, there is no certainty of understanding, no knowledge that what is interpreted in one consciousness is not a distortion of the senses made by conscious others. 'Social' life is an arbitrary affair, an existential domain characterized by likely misapprehension. To borrow a Freudian term, social life concerns 'transference': an uneasy truce between individuals' personal systems of interpretation that are likely to remain solitary and phantastical. We invent the world around us according to blueprints that derive from personal ontogenies of individual development, as Freud concludes. Or in Janet Malcolm's assessment:

> The concept of transference [how we invent the social other] at once destroys faith in personal relations and explains why they are tragic. We cannot know each other. We must grope around for each other through a dense thicket of absent others. We cannot see each other plain. (1982: 6)

For Simmel (1971a, 1971b), too, there was a 'tragic' dimension to social life, when considering 'the problem of society' and estimating 'How is society possible?' – asking himself to what extent social relations entailed knowledge of the individual Other. In this chapter, after reprising the way in which 'transference', even if by other names, accords with the ethnographic record and how anthropology has already seen fit to give account of the routine distortions and miscommunications of social life and exchange, the emphasis is a moral one. In a situation of ignorance and likely misapprehension concerning the sense being made by an individual's human fellows, what is a 'moral' vision of social engagement? What are the forms of social exchange that an anthropologist might propose that best accommodate transference as an existential condition, so that the 'uneasy truce' between a diversity of world-views is, nevertheless, mutually gratifying?

The everyday distortion of social life

The 'social relation' of connecting one aspect of one's experience – one datum – to others, as if they possessed a natural or necessary relationship of their own, and so building up a sense of the ordered and patterned nature of the environment beyond oneself, is a practice, I have argued, that characterizes alike the anthropological fieldworker and the societal and cultural 'member'. The difference being that the member is more likely to take the practice for granted; when not being especially self-conscious and ironic, he or she makes sense (and discerns orderliness) as an unremarked mundane undertaking.

Not only does the societal and cultural 'member' make sense in an environment – human, practical, physical, temporal – that gives to her or his interpretative practice a sense of routine, of ordinariness and second nature, but he or she has probably developed a place in a kind of social choreography whereby the member and her or his fellow-members move round one another and relative to one another in a habitual and expectable way. Each makes his or her own kind of sense but they do so in a kind of dance whose steps have achieved the regularity of normativity. Social life often has the settled quality of a kind of role-play. Anthony Wallace famously described social life as an 'organized diversity' (1961). Individual 'A' knows that as he does 'x', individual 'B' is likely to respond with 'y'; then he does 'z' at which point individual 'C' arrives and does 'n'; and so on.

This point has been regularly observed in anthropological description and analysis, not least my own (Rapport 1993, 1997, 2016). I do not mean it to become a central focus in this article but it is necessary, nevertheless, to rehearse it in outline. It is the context or ground upon which the central moral questions of the article offer vantage. Returning to Simmel's insights is a good place to begin.

Society is a symbolic reality: society is made possible, Simmel observes (1971a), by virtue of systems of symbols, languages, shared by its members that serve to 'synthesise' their diverse beings, their individual consciousnesses, natures and intentions. This is effected through symbols' intrinsic ambiguity. Symbols provide a form within which a diversity of contents or meanings can be carried in such a way that that diversity need not become apparent. Members of a society learn to exchange common systems of symbols – a 'culture' – in routine, habitual and conventional ways, sharing in the 'choreography' of social life, all the time having their individual differences of being and awareness expressed and yet disguised by the common forms. Simmel described this as the tragedy of social life: the means by which human beings endeavour most deliberately to communicate is insufficient to the task. For how may a common form convey an uncommon sense, the world view from a particular, indeed unique, perspective? The denotations of the forms may be relatively apparent and translatable – 'cat', 'table', 'sour', 'silent', 'sharp', even 'unfair', 'taboo', and 'death' and 'freedom' – but their connotations, what they mean to their individual users and how it feels to use them, are far more difficult to discern, if at all. Indeed, is it not the case, Simmel concludes, that the more widely the symbolic forms travel the less likely what they are intended to connote will be conveyed: that at the very time human beings are most engaged with others they are least communicative? Simmel's conclusion itself echoes an earlier one of Wilhelm von Humboldt (from 1836) who expressed the insights as well as anyone:

> Language assumes its final distinctiveness in the individual. Upon hearing a word, no one thinks precisely what the other does, and even the smallest difference trembles, like a circle in the water, on through the whole language. All understanding is therefore simultaneously a non-understanding, all mutual agreement a moving apart in thought and feeling. The way in which language is modified in every individual shows man's power over it. [...] The influence exercised on him (on man) reflects the rule-relatedness of language [...], and his response reveals a principle of freedom. (Von Humboldt 1995: 59)

For Edward Sapir, too, the insight is fundamental to any description and understanding of human social and cultural life that must always assume a certain shape or texture: a formal sharing and coming together that hides depths of possible incommensurability and miscommunication such that societal and cultural members remain deeply if not absolutely ignorant of one another. Albeit that Sapir views the outcome more positively than Simmel. He writes:

The true locus of culture is in the interactions of specific individuals, and, on the subjective side, in the world of meanings which each one of these individuals may unconsciously abstract for himself from his participation in these interactions [...] [T]he friendly ambiguities of language conspire to reinterpret for each individual all behaviour which he has under observation in terms of those meanings which are relevant to his own life. (1956: 151,153)

In identifying the so-called 'true locus' of culture in individual interactions I can hear Sapir musing on the same paradox as Simmel. The routine 'economy' of social exchange – its 'friendly ambiguities' – results in members of cultural communities having actual cultures in their heads likely to be as significantly different, as Sapir puts it, as if one were Italian and one Turkish. The surface of apparent exchange belies depths of radical differences in interpretation.

The 'social structure' that anthropology has been at pains to apprehend – the regular and habitual, conventional and normative, patterned and institutional nature of social exchange that members of a collectivity may hope to take for granted as the orderly grounds of life – appears in the above theorization as a surface calm, a synthesizing of radical difference, beneath which are being played out individual lives of particular sensation, interpretation, meaningfulness, intention, gratification, fulfilment and failure. I have thought to describe anthropology as a study of the effects – inadvertent, indirect, unintended, very often – that human beings as individual, energetic things-in-the-world have upon one another as their distinct and often incommensurate world-views and life projects come into contact courtesy of the institutions of social structure such as spoken language (cf. Rapport 2003: 75–6).

Before turning to the possible moral dimension of this understanding of human social relations, let me provide an ethnographic grounding to the theorizing and the moralizing I would undertake.

Social relations among porters in a Scottish hospital

'Constance Hospital' is a large teaching hospital serving the east of Scotland and based in the port-city of 'Easterneuk'. Included in a workforce of thousands are some 250 porters among whom I conducted participant-observation fieldwork (Rapport 2008). All but two of the porters are men, employed largely for their physical abilities to push patients and visitors across the hospital plant (and its many corridors), discerning the most appropriate routes between wards, clinics and operating theatres, and also ferrying body-parts and substances between operating theatres, wards and hospital laboratories. Together with the largely female contingent of cleaners ('domestics'), the porters stand out among the more highly specialized (and educated) hospital staff of doctors and nurses, administrators and managers, and members of ancillary trades (from physiotherapists to joiners and plumbers). Seemingly demeaned by this hierarchy of skills, the porters maintain something of an oppositional communitarian stance among themselves, insisting on their rights, their manliness, their knowledge in acquiring for themselves what they need for a fulfilled local life. Their 'locale' is both the streets, housing estates, football pitches and pubs of Easterneuk, and also the porters' lodge or 'buckie' at the hospital, two small rooms where they are based, away from the wards and operating theatres where they congregate between jobs. The buckie has chairs and tables, a fridge, microwave and radio; it is often crammed with the porters' jostling, male bodies, often the setting for ribald exchanges, raucous laughter and macho posturing.

Steve Coleman is one of the few porters who is not Scottish. He has worked at Constance Hospital for more than five years, having followed his now wife, Tracy, up north. She is a nurse and has herself worked at Constance for approaching twenty years. They met in London where she was on holiday, at a pub, run by a cousin of hers, where Steve regularly drank. 'That was that!', Steve explains: he met Tracy and 'never went back' – not that his first wife was too pleased at the turn of events!

Albert, a Scottish porter, assures me that there is no discrimination at Constance Hospital against non-Scots. All it amounts to is the odd bout of kidding around and teasing. Steve Coleman, for instance, 'sometimes gets it a bit hard', having his accent mimicked; and Albert laughs at the thought. And nor does Steve duck the issue, often enough having recourse to the admission that some idiosyncratic episode or behavioural quirk or failure is "cos I'm a bloody Englishman, I know'.

A key player in this 'kidding around' with Steve is Arthur. Arthur is a 'big man' in a number of respects: big in size, bulky and strong (if overweight), a figure of authority in white shirt and tie – a 'chargehand' or supervisor, responsible for handing out jobs to porters throughout the day – and also somewhat larger than life in personality. Arthur is talkative, witty and opinionated; as the chargehand on duty he sits at a table in the buckie, facing the array of telephones, answering calls for portering assistance, filing them in a book and then looking around to see who is available for work. He commands a view of both the buckie and the corridor outside, a gatekeeper to the porters who come and go on their tasks, and he holds forth:

> **Arthur** (*as Oliver enters the buckie whistling*)   No! And I'm gonna get eight more hours of shite from this fuckwit! (*Then seeing Fred pushing a trolley in the corridor outside the buckie, looking distinctly tired and the worse for wear*) Drunk in charge of a barrow, Fred!
>
> **Fred** (*leaving his trolley and coming into the buckie for a drink of water*)   That's my third glass of water today! I dunno what's wrong with me today.
>
> **Arthur** You probably had that postcard this morning from those three black babies: They're coming over to see you! 'Father!'!
>
> **Fred** Aye! And the monkey, too!

I intend to examine the routine social relations in which Steve finds himself at work in Constance Hospital, and in order to do so I shall describe Arthur's public persona and the exchanges he involves himself in in a little more detail. My argument is that Arthur is influential in affecting how Steve finds himself known and seen among the porters at Constance. The moral ecology of Steve's everyday interactions at work is well instantiated by a description of his talking-relations with Arthur.

Arthur's wittiness most often takes the form of stereotypical assignations: the world as Arthur professes to recognize it in his public statements at work concerns certain collective markers, including race, nationality, gender, work-role, residential neighbourhood, sport team support and bodily physiology, to which people can be inevitably assigned. For Arthur, these assignations seem to define people in significant ways – explain them – but are also worthy of public commentary not only to make sense of the world – make it orderly – but also to make it enjoyable, fateful and funny. Here are some instances of the stereotypical collectivities and affiliations constituted by Arthur, and expressed apparently for the benefit of the others involved as well as himself:

> **Arthur** The Welsh are okay: they're fellow Celts. At least they're not all mixtures like you English, Reg!

> **Arthur** (*Reg farts deliberately close to where Gary is eating his dinner in the buckie*) You English bastard, Reg! (*Laughing.*) You finished your dinner now then, Gary?

> **Arthur** Do I want sugar in my tea, Mick!? Are you fucking English!

> **Ian** [a semi-professional footballer (as well as porter)] My agent is still looking into the possibility of me signing for a Hong Kong team. Lots of Italians go over there now.
> **Arthur** You'd not be short for a Chinky, either, Ian! You'd be tall over there. Be a centre half! And you'd get paid thousands of Yen a week – which would translate into £200, probably! Ha! Mind you, you'd have to take all your [sex] videos with you. You'd have your socks and pants in one hand at the airport and be weighed down in the other hand by films! (*He mimes.*)

> **Arthur** The Germans should shoot all their Argies [Argentinians] like we did. They invaded a part of Britain – even though it was thousands of miles away! – and we showed them!
> **Ian** So what about the Argies in Easterneuk, playing for Easterneuk United?!
> **Arthur** Those are different Argies! The good ones. Those are the ones who were not on the Belgrano [an Argentine warship sunk in the Falklands War]!

> **Arthur** You walk like a cat on a hot tin roof, Jim! You're a typical Fifer [from the Scottish area of Fife, distinct from Easterneuk] right in there, quick quick, doing your night shift straight after your day shift … I heard it's the same in the Theatres: you're right in there, with female patients! My wife's cousin was another Fifer: a mechanic, always up to the elbows in grease and oil. Eight in the morning, there he'd be, in his garage and working till 6.30, went home for tea and then out again for a night shift at Asda! He's from Cupar – where they're not stupid, just daft!! 'Oyyyy', he used to say [not 'Aye']. Mechanics are always coated in grease – they can never remove the oil from under their nails.

> **Arthur** (*jokes*) You A & E cunt! (*As Jim walks to his posting in the 'Accident and Emergency Department'.*)

Arthur The nurses are phoning us up now just to carry patients' luggage to the front door for them! What do they think we are? Fucking darkies in Africa?! Kaffirs!?

Arthur (*as a suntanned ambulance driver whom he knows passes the entrance to the buckie*) You Black bastard! (*Putting on a South African accent.*) When you see me coming down the street you better walk in the road!

Arthur Don't you know, Dave, you live in the slaves' part of Easterneuk?! It's true! Braehead was built for servants.

I do not mean to imply that stereotypical discourses were Arthur's only medium of public engagement. He also spoke seriously about his politics as a Scottish Nationalist, about his apprenticeship as a roofer and slater, graduating to a business with his brother fitting television aerials and satellite dishes – and about how the fearlessness or foolhardiness of youth had now deserted him when it came to roofs and heights. He spoke about his holidays and about his hobbies, cycling and weight-training, and how he would have to lose weight if he wanted to get back to the soccer. He spoke about his family's roots on the Isle of Skye, about how his brothers spoke Gaelic and teased him in it and how he would like to learn himself; and also about how he would like to move out of Easterneuk and live in the country. He spoke about the poor way Constance Hospital was run, about the laziness and superciliousness of the nurses – about the arguments he had had with them about portering tasks – and about the porters' need to assert themselves. And he spoke about his wife, about how she worked in an office; and – in a self-deprecating way – about how she earned more than him and how she bossed him around at home:

Arthur My missus just says 'No' [to sex]. 'Here's a [dirty] mag instead; go away.' That's what she says (*Porters in the buckie laugh.*). 'Here's a book: now Fuck Off.'

Nevertheless, it is certainly the case that Arthur has a real fondness for stereotypical classifications of life at work. Therefore, let me reintroduce Steve Coleman at this point and recount something of the tenor of his and Arthur's interactions.

Steve is also a tall man, and one who makes his physical presence felt among the porters when he can. However, he seems less confident than Arthur, less assured or comfortable in his own skin, Steve's expansive physical gestures and loud voicings come across as more intrusive and aggressive than Arthur's; other porters are more wary of him than appreciative of his announcements and interjections. He seems a more brittle personality, more on edge:

Steve Every job I've done today has been a cock-up, going to the wrong place. And I think I'm gonna be disciplined. Yesterday I told a doctor to 'Fuck Off!' Not the best thing to do. (*He laughs.*) The doctor in Ward 7 said 'Come back' cos his patient wasn't ready to go, and I replied: 'Stick your patient up your arse!' So the doctor asked me my name and said he was gonna report me.

I hate Clinics' days. I remember driving my trolley right through four student doctors once on a Clinics' day: had them on their arses cos they wouldn't budge in time! It was great!

Steve Great holiday: I don't remember most of it! Didn't leave the pub all week! Pat tried to ban me from drinking at The Drivers but Ali wouldn't let him do it! Cos I have £2000 of their money sitting in my bank account – what I owe them! I'll never get banned … And now I'm gonna do what a man does best: a 'Barry White' [shite].

Steve (*reading news of upcoming nuptials in the local newspaper*) That's the Trev who used to work here in Stores … and his wife was sitting on my face three weeks ago, with my tongue up her! (*He laughs.*) You know, what they should ask you when you come here to the hospital for an interviews is: 'Do you smoke?' and 'Are you married?' Because after six months working here you will drink – and you'll be divorced! That reminds me. (*He goes to the chargehand's desk and uses a free telephone to dial his wife's ward number.*) Tracy? Have you got some deodorant with you? No? Fuck! … What? … Am I going to the pub after work?? Do bears shit in the woods?! (*He puts the phone down.*) Ron [a senior manager] picked me up last week for wearing my own T-shirt to work. So I had to remind him that she (*indicating Tracy at the other end of the telephone line*) works too; so there isn't always time to do the laundry. But the real reason is that I can't operate our washing machine! Even after we'd plugged it in I had to phone Tracy and ask her how to rinse! Its cos I'm thick as pigshit! (*Porters laugh.*) I am. Thick as mince. No, but, why should I know about the washing?? I married a dishwasher! A cook!

Steve [*to Dorothy, one of the very few female porters, who comes to the buckie to clock out*] What an ugly man, you are! Why don't you comb your hair next time you come in? Why don't you use deodorant and shower? You smell. When was your last shower? Wednesday!? (*Dorothy beats a retreat as Steve and others laugh.*) I thinks I'm gonna get disciplined cos I told Anne [the portering manager] to 'Fuck Off' – and she's the boss. But she always manages to rile me on a Friday! I think she does it on purpose cos she knows I'll have been out drinking on the Thursday [pay day].

Steve (*standing in the middle of the buckie practicing his golf swing with an imaginary club and making clicking noise as he ostensibly connects with a ball*) I won a golf club last year cos I was the only boy to get the ball onto the green. 'Come to Daddy! Yes!' I knocked it all of 200 yards. Cos it was downhill! (*He laughs.*) And I could hit it 500 yards if I imagined the ball was your head, Phil!
Phil You're a lazy fuck!
Steve Me? Never lazy! … I may be an English bastard but I'm never lazy. Jake there: he's the lazy one. He does absolutely nothing at all!
Jake Cos I'm paid absolutely nothing at all!

Steve … absolutely nothing at all.

Tracy (*in civilian clothes, arrives at the buckie entrance*)   I've come for his dirty washing. I told him to give it me this morning – cos I'm off today – but he wouldn't.

Steve That's right. I'm going to the Easterneuk United match with Wardy and Ewan Rutherford. (*To Tracy.*) You'll go ahead – I'll give you money – and I'll meet you in the pub later.(*Steve returns to practising his golf swing for some minutes and exchanging banter with fellow porters as Tracy patiently waits. Finally he goes to the changing room and returns to the buckie entrance, washed and changed, in civvies and some loud jewellery. Ostentatiously he scratches his testicles through his trousers.*)

Tracy (*smiling*) Your nuts itchy?!

Steve   Yep! Off now then, lads. But back Sunday: I'm working Sunday. Whenever I can for the extra money.

Tracy Are you?! Then I'll be at home stripping the wallpaper in the kitchen.

Steve Saturday's gonna be a golf day out … You can come too if you like: a woman's day out; to carry the clubs! (*He laughs.*)

Tracy Thanks very much!

Steve Well, you have to earn your keep somehow!

Dave Go on, Steve. Away with you: go and buy Tracy a drink. You've got enough money.

Tracy Has Steve money?!

Dave Loads! (*Tracy look surprised and Steve embarrassed.*) Enough to go on holiday to Benidorm, eh!

Steve (*proudly*) And going again next year!

Tracy He is not!

Steve I am! 30 of us from the pub. I'm the group treasurer. We were £30 out, and I couldn't see why. Now I'm £25 up!

Tracy Well, not before I've had a holiday this year! And you owe me £100 this month, and I've not seen it.

Steve It was £55 I owed last time! What interest rate are you using!? (*People laugh.*) Okay: you can have two weeks holiday in the Ferry [a seaside town just outside Easterneuk]! (*He laughs.*)

Dave, in the above exchange, is another chargehand. He appears embarrassed at the way Tracy is being treated, waiting patiently for long minutes in the buckie while her husband seemingly ignores her and continues to chat and posture with his workmates. Tracy seems bullied, and Dave will know that bullying, verbal and physical, is something that Steve commonly does to his portering fellows too, threatening violence when he feels affronted:

Steve Don Smythe was so rude to me. Kept telling him 'Fuck this' and 'Fuck that' and swearing at me. Don can be a rude cunt at times and he goes too far, and I don't like it. I'd have put Don on his arse if he hadn't already been sitting on it. Take him outside and banjo him! (*There is a sucking in of breath a shaking of heads from the other porters at the fighting talk.*)

Steve What are the chances of me smacking Brendan [a portering manager] in the head on Monday!? They're gonna deduct me pay. But if they think I'm gonna have worked a public holiday for nothing … they got another fucking thing coming … I'm being discriminated against by the Management. It's just because I'm an English bastard. (*The porters laugh.*)

The apparent self-deprecations from Steve – 'I'm thick as pigshit', 'I'm an English bastard' – appear more as rhetorical devices to gain public support for further self-centred claims on his part.

However, it is different when it comes to Arthur: Arthur counters Steve's speech-acts by calling his bluff, as it were. First, there is a respect between them:

Arthur I'm surprised you didn't go for the chargehand job being advertised.
Steve I didn't see it. But I wouldn't have anyway. I like my job. And I see the bedlam in Management each morning I come in with Tracy and I wouldn't like to be part of that.
Arthur Trouble is that Peggy [the head portering manager] inherited a fucked department.
Steve She should be down here, not stuck in an office somewhere else.
Arthur Aye, Management should be down here … managing!
Steve Yes, talking. And anyway, I'll never forgive Peggy for what she did to me. I hate her. What she did was bang out of order. Bang out of order.
Arthur Well, here's a nice job for you: Ward 21. And on the way look out for the nice new techie in Back Lab. She does great blow jobs!
Steve She'd better have a great big mouth, then, cos I'm loaded! (*He spreads his thighs wide on his chair before leaving the buckie laughing.*)

But over and above this, Arthur responds to Steve's self-deprecations at face value:

Arthur (*as Steve enters the buckie*) 'Cor blimey'!
Steve No! I say, 'Watch it mush.' I'm not from south London, so don't confuse me with that lot … It's bad enough being from London!
Arthur It's bad enough being from England!
Steve Don't start, now! (*Michael enters and laughs at the repartee.*) Nor you, Spike-Head.
Arthur (*faking a Cockney accent*) You South London wanker! Walthamstow wanker! (*He and Michael leave together for a smoke outside, laughing.*)

Some months later, the jibe is repeated:

Arthur (*as Steve enters the buckie dressed in civvies*) You South London shite!
Steve Not South London!
Arthur Walthamstow?
Steve Yes.
Arthur Walthamstow wanker!

The 'masculinist' or macho nature of these work-exchanges among low-paid British manual labourers, and also the ambiguities involved, is something I have dwelt on previously (Rapport 2008: 157–82). Also the way in which the teasing and posturing can convey a certain solicitude, even gentleness. The teasing is a form of acknowledgement and also inclusion and caring. It is a way legitimately to express emotion; and a way to deal creatively with the tedium of the job; even a way to satirize and scorn the hospital's own discourse of uniforms and uniformity, regimentation and hierarchical discrimination. The teasing allocation of identity, and self-allocation, and the judgements of value and worth, and self-judgements, I have argued, were means by which workmates could pretend to a knowledge of one another while real identities (outside work) might be unknown or could be kept at a safe and discreet distance. 'You A & E cunt'; 'You typical Fifer!'; 'You Black bastard'; 'I'm an English bastard'; 'I'm thick as pigshit'; 'I'm never lazy'; 'I'm like a scared old man'. These were the stereotypical, masculinist and humorous tokens – superficial and yet shared – by which the working community of hospital porters conducted itself, identifying members, integrating them into talking-relations and maintaining boundaries.

But is there another dimension to be broached here, of a moral nature? The boundary between work identity and 'home', between relations within the workspace and beyond, may not be so easy to draw, it seems to me now. That is, I have no evidence that either Steve or Arthur inhabit versions of themselves beyond the hospital site that are so different from those at work: less a matter of role-playing, more true, nuanced and subtle, more idiosyncratic. Steve drinks with his male pals, plays golf with them, goes on holidays abroad with them, and it is the same man that he is there and then that I can see him bringing into the work space of the hospital; here, too, he finds his wife, Tracy, and shares with her domestic issues of laundry, finance and nights out. For Arthur, outside work, there are his frequent nights out 'on the pish', his Scottish family and its traditional pursuits (Gaelic, music), his cycling and weight-training and memories of youthful skills as a worker and sportsman, and there are his relations with his wife who nags him to improve the house, earn more and bother her less for sex; here, too, work appears as a space at which a non-work self is quite fully and accurately presented. To return to the question with which this chapter began, then, is it my judgement that Arthur and Steve, as a case study, 'see each other plain'? Even though 'work' versus 'home' may not represent a radical dichotomy for these lives – between the homely and personal of more authentic selves and the workaday and public of more superficial role-playing – is there, nevertheless, a 'tragic' dimension, still, to the social life of the porters at Constance Hospital, of them talking past one another and never truly recognizing one another? And if so, what as 'their' anthropologist may I offer as a prescription for possible moral advance? I have argued that the social structures that anthropology has sought to uncover – the habitual, normative, institutional pattern of social exchanges among members of a collectivity – represent a synthetic surface beneath which the authentic lives of the members – individual, sensorial, self-conscious, meaningful and intentional – are played out. How precisely does the ethnography of Constance Hospital, and more nearly the speech-acts of Steve and Arthur, bear this out?

The hospital is a hierarchical organization. Different work roles have different statuses, marked by different uniforms worn, different parts of the plant occupied, different hours of work and different scales of pay. The porters find themselves below the hospital administrators, medical staff and even clerical and janitorial staff in terms of status and pay. And even here, hierarchical differences intrude: between portering managers, chargehands and porters proper. Furthermore, porters are divided between different branches of the plant, such as X-Ray, Accident and Emergency, Operating Theatres, ICU, and these too speak to differences in working conditions and responsibility. Much of the daily interaction among porters plays on these formal differences of hospital structuration. To this, then, is added informal differentiation by the porters, on the basis of personality, longevity, physiology and estimations of origin, worth and so on. Another way to consider what I now recognize to be a disinclination on the porters' part to dichotomize or differentiate work spaces and work identities from home ones is as a form of resistance to hospital institutionalism and hierarchy. They are the same men at work as they are beyond: there is much more to life than the claims of Constance Hospital to define them according to (lowly) work statuses. The hospital may know them as porters – as 'chargehands' and 'X-Ray porters' and 'A & E porters', and so on – but they know themselves as 'Scots' and 'English', as 'Fifers' and residents of 'Braehead', as 'golfers' and 'boozers', as 'thick' and 'fat' and 'lazy' and 'men'. There is a wide provenance to these identities – far wider than those that pertain to the narrow confines of workaday worlds at Constance Hospital – and there is a fixity and certainty to them that supervenes upon the temporary contingencies of how and where Constance Hospital allocates them work, jobs, pay and overtime. The following exchange between Steve and another porter, Fergus, is illustrative here:

> **Steve** (*as Fergus nods agreement*)   That bastard Dermot [a manager]! He expects
> you to stand up if he so much as looks through the window at you! I'd like
> him to get a heart-attack in the hospital; cos then I, for one, would rush for
> the job of taking him oxygen: I'd love to rifle through his top pockets and
> get all the money there while he's collapsed! (*He laughs.*) Knowing my luck,
> though, the bastard'd collapse on his front [thus protecting his wallet]!

Supervening upon the hospital employee and well-paid manager who stands on ceremony is Dermot the man, mortal, fallible and potentially dependent. Insisting on the last is a means to see through the masquerade of statuses at work.

In the light of this communal portering strategy, how do Steve and Arthur compare? Arthur seems to combine a measure of formal authority as a chargehand with informal authority as a big man, witty, personable, relaxed, knowledgeable of both hospital workings and history, and also Scottish and local workings and history. His speech-acts are a combination of stereotypical allocations of identity to other porters (and beyond) and assertions of his own selfhood (often self-deprecating in nature). 'You are ABC', Arthur asserts, (canny, quick, dirty, a mongrel, a cunt, servile) 'because you are XYZ' (English, a Londoner, a Fifer, Black, an A & E porter, resident of Braehead). 'I am also ABC' (an ex-slater, overweight, sexually frustrated, a Gael, a Scottish Nationalist, boozy). Steve, meanwhile, does not possess Arthur's formal authority as a chargehand, nor even his informal authority as a relaxed and likeable personality. His assertions are more challenges to fellow-porters' own identities; he bullies his workmates into accession or silence, and only appears self-deprecating when he wishes for others' support in situations where he, too, feels bullied ('discriminated against') or treated without respect ('out of order'). Primarily his speech-acts concern himself: 'I am a golfer, the man of the house, a boozer, a fighter, ill-disciplined, thick, an earner, not lazy, sweaty, English, a north Londoner.' *In extremis*, however, in situations where he feels absolutely in control over a weaker fellow or else fearful of losing all control when a workmate is brazenly demeaning, Steve will also allocate markers of identity to others: 'You are lazy, fat, smelly, rude, at risk of violence.' The discourse of both Steve and Arthur concern *external* criteria and markers of identity, in short, pertaining to demarcations beyond the provenance and purview of the hospital. However, Arthur seems to feel far more comfortable at work: more settled in his own identities, and more generous or even-handed and comical in his assignations of identity to others. (Not that Arthur does not still become heated in his identifications when he feels put upon by those in more senior positions to himself, such as managers or bossy nurses ['I'm no kaffir!'].) For Steve it is regularly a matter of asserting himself in the hospital as the man that he is when much remains uncertain: his pay and overtime allocation and favoured worksite and relations to management at Constance; his being an Englishman and Londoner in Scotland and Easterneuk; his bringing home enough money to be the man of the house, to buy clothes, booze, play golf and holiday abroad. But what strikes me, again, in closing the ethnography, is the extent to which his workmates endeavour to accommodate him: to recognize the markers he sets for himself as a public man. The following exchange takes place on the day of an international football match involving England, when 'tension' surrounding nationalities is always raised. But Steve himself is not present:

> **Albert** Pete is always too mean to buy any beer: but then what do you expect of the English?!
> **Angus** Not all! Look at Steve Coleman. I can walk in to The Drovers and order a pint of mild and a cigar and say: 'And change it to that big tall cunt [i.e. Steve]!', and that's okay. Steve'll take it. 'Bastard', actually I should say, not 'Cunt'. Steve does not like 'Cunt'. 'Call me anything you like – "Bastard", whatever – but never call me "Cunt"', Steve says.
> **Albert** (*laughing*)Is he serious?
> **Angus** It's true! I asked Tracy, and she said the same, 'Oh, its true!', she said, 'Never call him that.'

Not only is the porters' internal discourse as a working community at the hospital a generally generous and kindly one (for its male members), accommodating of non-work identities that are claimed as being more fixed and certain than fortuitous work ones, it is also largely and contrastingly democratic in ethos. A final extract finds Jim, the Accident & Emergency porter, giving some background and overview to Steve's situation:

> **Jim** I got Steve Coleman his job here. Steve asked me cos we knew each other. And I encouraged him, saying he could be a supervisor here in six months. And he was. Cos those supervisors [chargehands] are shite up there. It's a shit job anyway: they have it cos no one else wants it. But then Steve left it soon after cos he wasn't

suited to it. Then he got my old Pharmacy job when I left that for here. And then there's Steve boasting about the great new salary he's on: £600, £700 a week! Blabbing away. So I had to bring him down. Had to. Cos I knew what he was on. And I said to Steve: 'That's shite. Your basic pay is £520 a month'. Cos I knew. And Steve's lip wavered when I said it, but he knew he could say nothing. Cos I knew.

Life at work at Constance Hospital is, for the porters, an uncertain matter. There is relatively high job security (as employees of the UK National Health Service) but there is still much negotiation – on pay, overtime, holidays, job description and work allocation – that is undertaken from positions of relative weakness, both individual and communal. The world outside work, of wives and families, housing and recreation, is not necessarily or always more certain or secure, more a matter of power, authority or control, but here, nevertheless, are to be accrued kinds of identities and evaluations of performance that contrast with those of the hospital and can claim more universal provenance, more fixity and authenticity. The question still to be answered is whether that apparently 'homely' discursive recourse to stereotypes of nationality, domicile, gender and so forth, and to behavioural habits concerning drinking, cycling, golfing, lusting and fighting, actually represents an authentic or optimal presentation, recognition and accommodation of individual identities in public space, or whether something different is morally to be preferred.

Moral social relations

'Cosmopolitan politesse' is the name I have suggested for a certain ethos of politeness or mannerly behaviour and also the code or practical form of such behaviour (Rapport 2012: 174–97). Cosmopolitan politesse is an ethos of recognizing 'Anyone' – any individual human being – and of admitting Anyone into ongoing interactional exchange or public belonging; social inclusion is the due of any human individual. Cosmopolitan politesse is also an attempt to formulate a template for such an ethos – a kind of interactional Esperanto – whereby a set of interactional practices might be imagined as globally operationalized that had the 'good manners' to recognize the individual identity of any human being and admit them to a universal community. (Esperanto was the invention of the ghetto Jew, Ludwig Zamenhof, who anguished over the fact that members of a global species should know themselves only as members of bounded languages of nationality and division.)

Mannerly behaviour as an ethos appears frequently in the ethnographic record: there are many and diverse instances of 'regimes' of formal politeness (e.g. Murphy 1972; Gilsenan 1976; Hughes-Freeland 2001). But how might one imagine instituting such a 'regime' as an ideal: more than a mere form or surface of politeness but one that was anticipatory and capable of admitting anyone and everyone, and that did not translate into versions of hierarchy and exclusivity (only certain people being due politeness or knowing how to be properly polite)?

Cosmopolitan politesse was, I argued, a matter of proportion. On the one hand, one imagined a code that was open to all to learn and participate in or 'belong to': one anticipated the participation of Anyone, any individual human being. On the other hand, this openness and universalism was not a matter of anticipating any specific knowledge concerning individual participants, not a matter of prescribing certain identities for Anyone, beyond her or his humanity and individuality. All a participant had to be in order to be recognized, welcomed and included as a participant was an individual human being, able and willing to learn the form of universal politeness. One did not need to know more than this about one's fellow participants, and one did not presume to know, nor to judge. Who the participant was, beyond her or his individual humanity, who they were to themselves or even to their significant others, was irrelevant to the public domain and the public medium (or 'regime') that recognized and admitted them on the basis of a cosmopolitan politesse.

I have considered cosmopolitan politesse to be a morally optimal way of according recognition and including anyone and everyone – while not basing recognition and inclusion on criteria of identity whose choice, delineation and evaluation remained anything other than matters of personal and individual intentionality. I do not and cannot know my human fellows as they know themselves. (I do not know the meanings they impart to the world and I cannot know these things.) Moreover, I do not expect to know them and do not need to know them in order to interact with them. All they and I need to share in order to partake jointly in an ethos and regimen of cosmopolitan politesse is a mutual recognition or and respect for our common individuality and humanity. 'Here is someone who demonstrates their individual human commitment to a cosmopolitan politesse by their public practising of its mannerliness.' I need and expect to know no more than this.

It can be seen that cosmopolitan politesse is a version of what Emmanuel Levinas has described as an ethics of ignorance (1989; cf. Rapport 2015). One knows the other human being with whom one is faced as a physical event that imposes itself unmistakeably on one's conscious awareness. At the same time, the other is a mystery, absolute and irreducible: there is no more way to know the life as experienced beneath the face of the other than there is to know death. In Levinas's words: 'The face is an irreducible mode in which being can present itself in its identity' (1990: 8). Interaction with that other human being must thus be conducted by way of an ethics of ignorance that both consists of the duty to do justice to the physical event of meeting another living human body and the responsibility not to claim to know more than that human surface. Any epistemology, any publicly shared medium of recognition and classification, must have at its core a moral ignorance in regard to the actual identity of the individual human beings whom it treats; there remains a 'not-knowing' which is fundamental.

But how might cosmopolitan politesse, as the above ideal, throw light on the 'natural' practices and ethos of exchange among the porters at Constance Hospital? Whether the reader is convinced by the moral claims of cosmopolitan politesse as a template for universal social inclusion or not, the differences between it and what routinely transpires at Constance are clear. Habitual discursive modes at the hospital, among porters, involve assertive identifications and claims to identity of highly categorial and typified kinds; they allow no room for individual idiosyncrasy or uniqueness. Habitually, porters at Constance – Arthur and Steve as key witnesses in my exemplification – fit each other into stereotypes, the assertions amounting to kinds of symbolic coercion. Or else they agonistically assert their ownership of certain typical (masculine) identity markers: 'This is me (golfer, drinker, fighter, husband, manual worker), as the apogee of this role in this space at this time, and who is man enough to challenge that, to gainsay or remove me?' The individual appears in the space of public exchange either as a member of a fabricated, homogenized collective – a Walthamstower, Londoner, Englander, A & E-er, Easterneuk United supporter and so on – or else by virtue of aggressively claiming ownership of one of a few recognized masculine roles. Judged by the terms of a cosmopolitan politesse, this entails, on the one hand, an immoral ascribing by an Other of an individual to a specific class, membership of which is claimed to reveal certain essential features of that individual's identity and to delineate certain normative aspects of that individual's proper behaviour. Instead of the ontological realities of Anyone, the individual human being, public exchange becomes a matter of classifying and pigeon-holing on the basis of coercive fabrication: 'You are this kind of being; you can be expected to behave in this kind of way; these are the bases of your public belonging and recognition.' On the other hand, again according to the terms of a cosmopolitan politesse, there is the immorality of having to assert one's individuality only in terms of a fixed set of publicly recognized and valued roles. The alternative to having a stereotypical and homogenizing identity ascribed to one is to claim an individual status according to a narrow range of practises and roles, and challenge others to stake rival claims. 'I practise X or Y or Z; who will deny that, and who will claim to practice X, Y, Z as I do?' This is instead of Anyone being accepted in public exchange not on the basis of any specific doing but merely due to their being (and being capacitated to partake). How they otherwise perform – beyond the minimum requirements, as it were, of the Esperanto of a global template of public communication – and *what* they perform – in what manner they decide personally to put into practise their human capacities – is of no consequence to cosmopolitan politesse. The individual may aspire to be an expert golfer, but he or she may equally aspire to being expert in something that has no public name, no public criteria for evaluation and about which the public has no knowledge. Under cosmopolitan politesse, the only 'ascriptions' are the recognition of the ontological realities of individuality and humanity; and the only necessary achievement is competency in the code: the giving and taking of those mannerly forms that afford other human beings the space to be.

But the 'space to be' is a limited space, the reader may object, and often contested. Moreover, the 'space to be' includes work, the *making* of a living, where resources are limited and unequally distributed and where skilled practices involve divisions of labour and hierarchies of organization of increasingly complex kinds. How do the 'mere human being' and 'irreducible individuality' of cosmopolitan politesse fare here? More immediately, living space in Easterneuk is limited; the housing stock is of highly unequal kinds; work is limited; some work calls for far greater degrees of learned skill than others and commands very different levels of remuneration. Against this background, the routine discourse of the porters at Constance Hospital is (to repeat) to be seen as a way (clever, often fun) to pass time at work that can be tedious; also a way to distinguish themselves and to know themselves as distinct, as a community or subculture with its own symbolic and physical space, within the large-scale institutional culture (regimented, hierarchical) of the workplace; also a way in which male actors who have not had upbringings that have afforded them the best of opportunities remind one another of those ways of being that have enabled them to survive and even proudly to prosper in adversity. 'This is how we as "working-class men" have learnt to labour' (cf. Roy 1960; Handelman 1976; Willis 1978); 'Our "restricted code" of public exchange embodies the disciplines necessarily for our relative prosperity as a disadvantaged group' (Bernstein 1973).

I may not claim cosmopolitan politesse as a panacea. Nonetheless, I can claim it as a template for social interaction that I would have anthropology advocate as a form of global moral relation. Yes, physical space is limited and contested; by contrast, the symbolic space of cosmopolitan politesse would give everyone a place on the basis of their individuality and their humanity. Yes, the division of labour in a world of increasing technological specialization, and perhaps an increasing differentiation between those with specialized skills and those with little skilled specialism or none, manifests itself in large discrepancies in rewards and living standards; by contrast, the inclusiveness of cosmopolitan politesse and the way that Anyone is seen as potentially standing in for Anyone else make manifest the intrinsic equality between any and all human beings. If at the same time as the world's brute realities are inhabited one inhabits, too, an ethos and a code whose foundation is cosmopolitan, then I can hope that the latter will not only throw a moral light on the former but also act as a practical lever. Thinking in terms of the categories that the porters at Constance routinely exchange, and operationalizing them with their characteristic vigour, may show fortitude and be funny and parodic and even communitarian – a 'weapon of the weak' (Scott 1985) – but there is more that anthropology can hope for: recognition of a common humanity beyond categories of symbolic difference.

Coda: The technologized and communitarian in Levinasian perspective

Again I am heartened by Emmanuel Levinas's reflections. Modern technology may be feared for reducing human beings to cogs in highly complex systems of skills and rewards, he writes, but technology is less dangerous than the sentimentalism of place and community that reduce human beings to rootedness in land, language and culture, and splits them into natives and strangers. Technology has the capacity to wrench us out this world of traditional emplacement and differentiation with its irrational ascriptions. 'From this point on, an opportunity appears to us: to perceive men outside the situation in which they are placed, and let the human face shine in all its nudity' (Levinas 1990: 233). More precisely, 'beyond situation' lies the 'demystified and disenchanted world' of absolute, homogeneous, geometric space; technology assists us in rooting our piety not in landscapes and memories but in an abstract universalism and, so, to 'discover man' and his place in the 'economy of the Real'. Contrast this with the kind of 'mythic knowledge' that names and classifies: seizing hold of its object and claiming to possess it in denial of the independence of its being, a kind of violence that denies otherness. Freed from 'the prestige of myths, the discord they introduce into ideas and the cruelty they perpetuate in social customs', A technologized world is one in which we might develop a love for truth beyond a politics of identity (Levinas 1990: 273). 'Reason' might enable us to avoid 'doctrine' in our thought, to mistrust opinion and to aspire to the universal. 'Herald a man freed from myths' and a civilization 'built on justice [that] unfolds in science' (Levinas 1990: 276, 275).

For Levinas, again, such knowledge begins on the path that leads from one individual human being to another. It is the event of meeting otherness – the experience of being external to one's own – that opens up the possibility of fundamental, objective knowledge that is at once ontological and moral. Levinas speaks of the encounter with the other as a kind of 'passion' and 'surplus' and 'anarchy': one's sensibility is affected in spite of itself (1989: 92, 164). Proximity is anarchic inasmuch as it entails 'a relationship with a singularity without the mediation of any principle, any ideality' (Levinas 1989: 90). In other words, one encounters an otherness independent of any *a priori* (mythical, stereotypical, categorial) expectations and incommensurable with such. For the Other cannot be adapted to the scale of *ego*'s existence without violence, war or bureaucracy. 'The face is an irreducible mode in which being can present itself in its identity': 'When I really stare, with a straightforwardness devoid of trickery or evasion, into [the Other's] unguarded, absolutely unprotected eyes', I accede to a kind of knowledge that is not self-knowledge – knowledge from one's own doctrines and qualities – but 'heteronomy through and through' (Levinas 1990: 8,293–4).

A technologized global world is a space in which the experience of the human other, as physically and symbolically proximate, is common. The experience can be valued as 'the first intelligible': an opening to objectivity 'before cultures and their alluvions and allusions' (Levinas 1990: 294–5). One resists mythic possession and welcomes the new dimension in the perception of being that is opened up: a universal dimension and absolute. 'Civilization' is conversation with the other as interlocutor, renouncing any claims to sovereignty of culture: renouncing category thinking (cf. Rapport 2011).

References

Bernstein, B. 1973. *Class, Codes and Control*. St. Albans: Paladin.

Gilsenan, M. 1976. 'Lying, Honour and Contradiction'. In *Transaction and Meaning*, B. Kapferer (ed.). Philadelphia: Institute for the Study of Human Issues, pp. 191–219.

Handelman, D. 1976. 'Rethinking "Banana Time": Symbolic Integration in the Work-Setting'. *Urban Life* 4(4): 433–47.

Hughes-Freeland, F. 2001. 'Dance, Dissimulation and Identity in Indonesia'. In *The Anthropology of Indirect Communication*, J. Hendry and C. W. Watson (eds). ASA Monographs 37. London: Routledge, pp. 145–62.

Levinas, E. 1989. *The Levinas Reader*, S. Hand (ed.). Oxford: Blackwell.

Levinas, E. 1990. *Difficult Freedom: Essays on Judaism*. London: Athlone.

Malcolm, J. 1982. *Psychoanalysis: The Impossible Profession*. New York: Vintage.

Murphy, R. 1972. *The Dialectics of Social Life*. London: Allen & Unwin.

Rapport, N. 1993. *Diverse World-Views in an English Village*. Edinburgh: Edinburgh University Press.

Rapport, N. 1997. *Transcendent Individual: Towards a Literary and Liberal Anthropology*. London: Routledge.

Rapport, N. 2003. *I Am Dynamite: An Alternative Anthropology or Power*. London: Routledge.

Rapport, N. 2008. *Of Orderlies and Men: Hospital Porters Achieving Wellness at Work.* Durham, NC: Carolina Academic Press.

Rapport, N. 2011. 'The Liberal Treatment of Difference: An Untimely Meditation on Culture and Civilization'. *Current Anthropology* 52(5): 687–710.

Rapport, N. 2012. *Anyone, the Cosmopolitan Subject of Anthropology.* Oxford: Berghahn.

Rapport, N. 2015. 'Anthropology through Levinas: Knowing the Uniqueness of Ego and the Mystery of Otherness'. *Current Anthropology* 56(2): 256–76.

Rapport, N. 2016. *Distortion and Love: An Anthropological Reading of the Art and Life of Stanley Spencer.* London: Ashgate.

Roy, D. 1960. 'Banana Time: Job Satisfaction and Informal Interaction'. *Human Organization* 18(4): 156–68.

Sapir, E. 1956. *Culture, Language and Personality*, D. Mandelbaum (ed.). Berkeley: University of California Press.

Scott, J. 1985. *Weapons of the Weak.* New Haven, CT: Yale University Press.

Simmel, G. 1971a. 'How Is Society Possible?' In *On Individuality and Social Forms*, D. Levine (ed.). Chicago: University of Chicago Press, pp. 6–22.

Simmel, G. 1971b. 'The Problem of Sociology'. In *On Individuality and Social Forms*, D. Levine (ed.). Chicago: University of Chicago Press, pp. 23–35.

Von Humboldt, W. 1995. *Schriften zur Sprache*, M. Böhler (ed.). Stuttgart: Reclam.

Wallace, A. F. C. 1961. 'The Psychic Unity of Human Groups'. In *Studying Personality Cross-Culturally*, B. Kaplan (ed.). New York: Harper & Row, pp. 129–58.

Willis, P. 1978. *Learning to Labour.* Farnborough: Saxon House.

10

Afterword: Becoming Enlightened about Relations

Marilyn Strathern

Raymond Firth called the first chapter of his 1951 summative *Elements of Social Organization* 'The meaning of social anthropology'[1] – its value, import, character. A decade later he introduced his third edition at a moment when there was, across the disciplines, more understanding of what anthropologists did than ever before. At the same time, anthropologists' own efforts *at* understanding were not straightforward. How do they know what they know? When he describes how they set about reaching their primary objective, 'correct observation', he at once identifies a problem of method. The problem is acute when it comes to social relations. Social anthropologists might be said to study society, Firth says, but that is not what they observe. 'They do not even observe social relationships; they infer them' ([1951] 1961: 22, emphases omitted). Rather, anthropologists – and he is thinking of them as fieldworkers – abstract types of social relations out of continuous behaviour in which the observer 'is a moving point in a flow of activity' ([1951] 1961: 22). The key term, 'social process', draws attention to the ever changing, ever growing, nature of such activity.

Yet the argument does not really need the observer, let alone fieldworker, to make the point about relations. Relation is in and of itself an abstract concept. It refers to a state of coexistence imagined as a link or tie, entities and entailments unspecified. It is not just that *social* relationships have to be inferred: *any* statement of relation proceeds by inference. This includes logical or epistemic connections, as when Firth writes of 'the relations between economic and moral standards' ([1951] 1961: 138). In English, as he implies, the language of relations is very much part of the language of knowledge-making. Now the issues would not have been unfamiliar to David Hume, and other luminaries of the Scottish Enlightenment, who dwelt on the power of relations in (human) understanding and (scholarly) narrative. This is a thread to pull upon. It leads an antecedent period in the European Enlightenment at large, among other things for its interest in narratives of the known and unknown.

I have my own interest in the unknown. I want to talk about something that didn't happen – in fact by the time it didn't take place it probably could never have. It is a counterfactual that comes from social anthropology largely as the subject has developed since the ASA was founded in 1946, when *Elements* must have already been in Firth's mind. So only in retrospect might we sense its after-effect, the jolt of realizing that something had never been there. The language of what-could-have-been does not entail any specific premonition of it, but perhaps I can eventually convey something of that jolt.

Abstractions and their counterparts

Varieties of abstraction

It is almost in the genre of anthropological arrivals (as Firth began *We the Tikopia*, in 1936) that the historian Natalie Zemon Davis introduces us to a seventeenth-century artist and naturalist, Maria Sibylla Merian, boarding a boat in Amsterdam bound for a Dutch colony in Suriname. It was 1699; she stayed in South America for two years. Already in her fifties (her daughter was with her) and already with a reputation as a skilled painter, 'she was also a knowing observer of the habits of caterpillars, flies, spiders, and other such creatures' (Davis 1995: 140). She had published on the feeding habits and transformation of caterpillars, which she bred as well as painted and engraved, and she was seeking out their tropical counterparts. It was not unusual for naturalists to go to distant places for the sake of the unknown, but it was unusual to have no official sponsorship. Nonetheless, Merian returned home with many specimens and drawings, and her double volume on the insects of Suriname secured her position among Amsterdam's scientists and collectors.

The sugar planters of Suriname could not understand her preoccupation. 'People ridiculed me for seeking anything other than sugar,' said Merian (Davis 1995: 173). But then, as Davis also drily remarks, resident Africans and Amerindians assisted her more than European planters, and Merian drew on the knowledge ('testimony') of both slaves and Arawak/Carib 'Indians'. European naturalists rarely mentioned the servants who assisted them with their research; from Merian we hear of her conversations, her texts 'filled with ethnographic nuggets' (Davis 1995: 187). She did not go on, as did the marine biologist Haddon two hundred years later, and turn from an interest in natural life to an interest in the residents. Nonetheless, Davis emphasizes that 'Merian's scientific style and conversational exchange encouraged ethnographic writing indifferent to the civilized/savage boundary' (1995: 190), a marked divergence from that of the travel literature of the time.

Consider how this painter-naturalist presented the South American insects to people at home. Her 1705 *Metamorphosis of the Insects of Suriname* has been described as belonging to a new form of planetary consciousness on the part of Europeans (Davis 1995: 180–1, quoting Pratt 1992: 31), as one by one plant 'life forms were to be drawn out of the tangled threads of their life surroundings and rewoven into European-based patterns of global unity and order … [and] into the language of the system'. Abstracted, in other words, through observation, naming and classification. At the same time, and this is Davis's own point, Merian's ecological awareness left space for Suriname insects and plants to flourish 'in local terms and relations'. The narrative strategy was one she had deployed before, leading the reader from the familiar to the strange and back again. What she now took to a new level was her interest in the life cycle, in the origin and transformation of insects and the food on which they lived, in short, in 'nature's processes and relationships' (1995: 179). In the preface to her new book Merian stated that what had been missing from the overseas collections of specimens – from the Americas, Africa, the Pacific as they had come to Amsterdam through Dutch traders – were precisely the origins and transformations of the insects. 'The beautiful specimens were stilled, wrenched from context, lacking process'; context, process, these are of course Davis's words (1995: 167), just as Firth might have put it.

Merian wanted to do for South America what she had done earlier when, across copious copperplates, she depicted insects from life. Their immediate environment was present, as in the many pictures organized around a flowering or fruiting plant showing the leaves on which caterpillars fed and where eggs were laid. Davis (1995: 149) says, she was not – like many still-life painters – striving for metaphor or allegory; rather, 'her insects and plants were telling a life story ... to evoke a particular and interconnected process of change'. Her vision was ecological; her subject a set of events (the metamorphoses or transformations). We might say that her concern were the relations involved in the metamorphosis of these living forms. For the illustrations themselves followed no recognized classificatory order; the observer was instead directed to look within each life and appreciate how the process was repeated, insect after insect. The effect insisted, Davis concludes, 'on nature's connections'.

Tearing an individual specimen out of its living habitat is a compelling image of abstraction, rendering information useful to the comparison of general forms. However, what followed was surely another mode of abstraction. If indeed Merian focused on process and context, as modern parlance would put it, this too entailed abstraction of a kind, namely an inference about connections. Or at least this is what she presented to her readers.[2] Had Merian been writing in English (rather than German, Dutch or Latin), she might have used this very term, 'connection', which since the beginning of the seventeenth century had indicated a bond of interdependence or coherence in the linking together of ideas. Well embedded as it came to be in Enlightenment speech, it acquired the status of an abstract principle. Adam Smith's notable observation of 1795 deployed it thus: 'Philosophy is the science of the connecting principles of nature ... ', he wrote, 'by representing the invisible chains which bind together ... disjointed objects' (quoted in Porter 2000: 150).[3]

Perhaps to arrive at this point it was not necessary to introduce Merian; exactly what she is doing in this account will become more apparent by the end.

Abstract or concrete?

Now, in Smith's idiom, in order to introduce order into the 'chaos of jarring and discordant appearances', as one might have taken a creeping caterpillar and a fluttering moth, philosophy must describe the principles of coherence. If in being presented to the imagination an abstraction acquires concrete form, this is the story of Baroque sensibilities in art and science (Corsín Jiménez 2013); it is also the story of the Enlightenment savant concerned with the nature of understanding. To the extent that an abstract principle makes a concrete appearance, then what is abstract and what is concrete fold into each other: that which is inferred from observation comes to have its own 'observable' characteristics. For some mid-twentieth-century anthropologists, for instance, when relations were conceived as parts of a system, 'relations' acquired a concretivity even as 'system' emerged as the new abstraction.

Available at once as a synonym for connection and introducing its own nuances, the concept of 'relation' when used in a logical or epistemic sense is familiar to English-speakers in two registers. It refers both to the connecting of ideas, events and other entities, and to the narration of a story. Let me bring this latter connotation to the imagination. While any story becomes a narrative of connections (relating relations), a philosophical or scientific story puts particular weight on demonstrating – describing – the connections as such. The question of how one knows what one knows, how one verifies an observation, was obviously an issue among Enlightenment thinkers; with scientific experiments, it was solved in part by the counterpart verification of the standing of patrons and witnesses. And here there is an interesting twist to the relation. For a period the term relation was also widely used for a concrete type of story, best understood as a report, one that had a certain status as a narrative that – despite often being about the unfamiliar – was believable. The genre carried something of its own authority.

Known to historians as *relazione* (*relazioni*, from the prototype, Venetian diplomatic reports),[4] a relation in this sense became increasingly common across Europe in the sixteenth and seventeenth centuries, most famously for anthropologists including reports sent back by Jesuit missionaries from New France. It was to a large extent overtaken by subsequent conventions of writing (such as the kinds of reports encouraged in England by the Royal Society in its *Philosophical Transactions*) and fell into disuse. But in their heyday *relazione* served among other things as a device to bridge the known and unknown through the authentication of the author presenting his (and it would have been mainly his) observations. By no means everything that related occurrences counted. According to Cohen and Warkentin (2011: 9), *relazione* were set apart from treatises, meditations and essays in the way that the author cited 'the authority of experience'. They were meant to establish a relation of trust between author and reader. What subsequently overtook this form of relation was the transfer of trust from the teller to the investigation as such; Cohen and Warkentin have called this Descartes's victory: trust the method, not the investigator. That indeed was what experimentation aimed to do. In England the natural philosophers of the seventeenth century had turned their description of the connections by which they knew things along different paths, to put it briefly (Gow 2009: 24), rejecting the acquisition of knowledge through authority in favour of its acquisition through reason. But why bring them in?

There is some interest in the English-speaking corner of Europe at this particular time, in that the intellectual alliances encouraged by natural philosophy – the seventeenth-century scientific revolution so-called – was arguably England's counterpart to the Scottish Enlightenment of the eighteenth, which seemingly yielded nothing comparable to the Scottish 'movement'. In this light we might listen to Peter Gow's (2009: 24) characterization of what distinguished the Scottish Enlightenment from its European cousins, namely the way in which it 'was specifically scientific and contributed to the Age of Improvement'. In any event, English idiom was the medium of Scottish philosophizing. The particular connotations of *relazione* might be fading, but the English 'relation' remained in use as a substantive for narrative, as well as being, broadly speaking, a synonym for connection, or for association in the sense of linkage. If in English the language of relations was very much part of the language of knowledge-making then that included Scotsmen's English too.

Hume's *Treatise of Human Nature* ([1739–40] 2000), subtitled *The Experimental Method and the Science of Human Nature*, begins with what we need to know of the workings of the mind in order to know how we know anything (with understanding understanding). His thesis famously turned on what he took as a self-evident and ubiquitous facility, the connection or association of ideas, with how one may typify different kinds of 'relations' created thereby. Indeed, relations were crucial to Hume's engagement in a long-standing debate about the particularity or individuality of ideas as such. We may well ask how as an idea they (relations) were brought to the imagination – 'figmented' in Tim Ingold's (2013: 737) epithet, where in an earlier Firth lecture he talks of the work that dragons did in medieval knowledge-making.

We may start with Hume's own discussion of abstractions, and the vexed characterization of ideas as abstract, that is, as general rather than particular in character. ''Tis evident, that in forming most of our general ideas ... we abstract from every particular degree of quantity and quality, and that an object ceases not to be of any particular species' ([1739–40] 2000: 1.1.7, p. 17).[5] Evident this process might be, he set it against the impossibility of forming an idea, as in the idea of an object, without also summoning some particular impression of it. Consequently, although it is quite possible for ideas to be general in their representation, they are invariably particular or individual in themselves. Hume instances 'figure' as a general term that is brought to the imagination by circles, squares, triangles and so forth, for indeed the mind may 'run over' several individual examples without resting on any one. It is the capacity to connect ideas that allows the sense of generality. 'A particular idea becomes general by being annex'd to a general term; that is, to a term, which from a customary conjunction has a relation to many other particular ideas, and readily recals them in the imagination' (1.1.7, p. 20).

If Hume is here engaging with the seventeenth-century English philosopher John Locke, who used the idea of a triangle to argue the converse point (namely that it is possible, with some contrivance, to think of a triangle without thinking of it in any particular form) (Hume [1739–40] 2000: p. 432), this point and counterpoint might lead the anthropologist back to the relativity of the epithets abstract and concrete in exposition. We have already had an example. It was to concretize or make a figure of relation as narrative that I drew on the *relazione*. For what might have seemed to us an abstract type of discourse could equally appear as a particular instrument, specifiable through its conventions. As we heard, its authority was to be effaced by later genres of reporting with their own sources of (anti)authority. So relating as storytelling can be brought to the present-day imagination through a historically particular form of it, the *relazione*, a concrete embodiment of what was once widespread reporting practice. It is not something one would ordinarily evoke these days – a dragon, in a manner of speaking, even if rather a tame one. Let me return to how other kinds of relations are brought to the imagination.

Varieties of the concrete

Speaking of social relationships, Firth declared that anthropologists can only infer them from people's activities. From this viewpoint, abstraction is necessary. He opposes the abstract and the concrete: the 'more one thinks of the structure of a society in abstract terms, as a group of relations or of ideal patterns, the more necessary it is to think separately of social organization in terms of concrete activity' (Firth [1951] 1961: 35–6). It could almost have been as a rejoinder to Firth that Meyer Fortes offered a very different observation about relationships to chew on:

> Textbooks always remind us that social relations are abstractions, since they are not directly visible or tangible, as individuals and activities are, but have to be established by inference [...] 'Siblingship' is manifested in kinship words, in eating customs, in incest taboos [...] etc. *But let us turn the matter inside out.* We can then say that in order to be at the disposal of [including, bring to the imagination of] those who engage in them, social relations *must become* discernible, objectified. They must be bodied forth in material objects and places, in words, acts, ideas, attitudes, rules and sanctions [...] Ego knows that he is B's sibling and acts accordingly [...] He signifies his engagement in the relationship by the nomenclature he uses towards and about B, by his attitudes, claims, and conduct [...] It is distinctive custom that makes a social relation signifiable by those who participate in it and cognizable by those who are external to it. (Fortes 1969: 60–1, my emphasis)

It is concretization that is necessary. In other words, if abstraction is one form of objectification, so too are all the ways in which a concept is made to appear, as Fortes suggests is evident in the customs or conventions people observe. His example is the otherwise abstract idea of 'siblingship'. The reader can turn this around even further. After all, in drawing attention to relations between siblings Fortes is himself offering a concrete instance of siblingship, siblingship in turn being offered as a concrete instance of (social) relations.

Given Fortes's interests in kinship,[6] the example is hardly surprising. However, an evocation of kin ties does not have to be restricted to 'social' relations. As I have remarked elsewhere (Strathern 2014), Locke also evoked kin ties in order to illustrate the character of relations in general. When Hume was dilating on the nature of understanding fifty years later, and on the troubled notion of an idea, he made the same move. This is Hume talking of the connections and associations of ideas, and the especially powerful relation of cause and effect, in the way the imagination runs from one idea to another:

> Two objects are connected together in the imagination, not only when the one is immediately resembling, contiguous to, or the cause of the other, but also when

there is interpos'd betwixt them a third object, which bears to both of them any of these relations. [...] Cousins in the fourth degree are connected by causation, if I may be allow'd to use that term; but not so closely as brothers, much less as child and parent. (Hume [1739–40] 2000: 1.1.4, p. 13, emphasis omitted)

Kinship thickens his discourse again when he describes the abstract notions of attraction or resemblance by asserting the affect they carry. He has been writing on how objects or circumstances can arouse emotions and draws easily on interpersonal relations (not his phrase) in this regard:

Whoever is united to us by any connexion is always sure of a share of our love, proportion'd to the connexion, without enquiring into his other qualities. Thus the relation of blood produces the strongest tie the mind is capable of in the love of parents to their children, and a lesser degree of the same affection, as the relation lessens. Nor has consanguinity alone this effect, but any other relation without exception. (Hume [1739–40] 2.2.4, p. 228)

He then runs through varieties of acquaintances, for it is clear that otherwise than by degree he does not differentiate the emotions insofar as they flow towards any person who is an object of attention. At the same time, in the very manner in which he represents this knowledge, the terms connection and relation seem to be concretized by the discussion of persons and particular kinspersons at that. What kinds of persons are they?

Norton and Norton, the editors of Hume's *Treatise* on whom I have been drawing, comment at this point that 'Hume is discussing two kinds of relation: those between individuals who are relatives or closely associated, and those between impressions and ideas. An experience of a person with whom we are closely associated always produces a double relation of impressions and ideas' (Hume [1739–40] 2000: 511). In Hume's illustrative conjunction of relations and persons, we might specifically ask what impression/idea of *kins*person he offers. This brings us to the discussion in which I hope to make good my claim to describe an event that never happened.

Persons and relations

Interpersonal relations

Given the distinction already established in eighteenth-century classifications of knowledge, Hume's general address was to persons as moral agents rather than as physical entities (Demeter 2012: 17). The conditions for, and what counts as, human flourishing included the sensibilities informed by people's inclinations and feelings towards others, and we seem to be in a thoroughly recognizable world. Acquaintances and friends are as significant as kin. And in part what appears recognizable about it is precisely the kinship in this milieu.

Although Hume refers to specific relationships – fourth cousins, for instance – he was using blood ties to illustrate an abstract quality, namely degrees of intensity in relating. (He points out that, contrary to common parlance of the day, distance is itself a relation.) If we infer that he apprehends bilateral kin reckoning in terms of circles of kin at ever more close or remote degrees of distance, that was of course a model Europeans had long encoded in the kind of rules and sanctions Fortes might have had in mind, such as marriage prohibitions concerning consanguines and affines alike. However, what is modern about this rendering is a particular emphasis given to two, interrelated, components. First is the way in which emanations of sentiment and feeling are not just calibrated to proportions of kinship distance, but also find exemplars in connections of acquaintance and friendship. Hume seems to be evoking a general sphere of interpersonal relations of which kinship is a part. Second is the way in which connection itself becomes the calibrator of degree. As he said, whoever is united to one by a connection is loved 'proportion'd to the connexion'. In short a connection in and of itself is sufficient to carry affect, and does not have to be further specified.[7] It is almost as though it had a concrete presence as such. In eighteenth-century English, we might add, 'connection' was used of kin, just as today English-speakers use the term 'relative'.

Hume's narrative has an interesting effect. While examples drawn from kinship may make concrete otherwise abstract notions of relations, thinking of kinship simply in terms of a close or distant connection surely flattens or generalizes the connotations that summoning blood ties might otherwise carry. The same effect is true of the term relation itself. Hume pairs (and sometimes elides) relation and acquaintance. He writes, 'There is another phaenomenon [...] viz, that acquaintance, without any kind of relation [glossed here as "blood relationship"], gives rise to love and kindness [...] These two phaenomena of the effects of relation and acquaintance will give mutual light to each other, and may be both explain'd from the same principle' (Hume [1739–40] 2000: 2.2.4, p. 228; emphasis omitted). In English, the nouns 'relation' and 'acquaintance' can of course refer simultaneously to the idea of a connection between persons, and to those persons so connected, as in reference to one's acquaintances or one's relations. This dual usage of acquaintance was long established; relation as a substantive for persons who are kin was largely a seventeenth-century innovation. Both generic forms allow attachment of moral regard for others without the terms having to specify the nature of the tie involved, or indeed without indicating any further identity of those so connected (Tadmor 2001).

We could almost say that, in *this* light, there is no ontological difference being posited between relations (kinsfolk) and acquaintances. It is against such an anglophone possibility that I would put Janet Carsten's broader rethinking of personhood and kinship, and her resounding call to appreciate people's 'everyday sense of relationality' (2004: 107). The question then, as she makes very clear, is how the world ever made just such a call for appreciation necessary. Was it an outcome of what did not happen as well as what did? Could it possibly flow from, among other channels, the seventeenth-century event that never took place? If that non-event endures as a kind of after-effect, we should be able to record its reverberations. Perhaps we can do so in Hume's writings.

Degrees of the familiar

Hume was not alone among writers of the Scottish Enlightenment to dwell on the power of the relation in (human) understanding and in (philosophical) narrative, although through his interest in the connection of ideas he seems to have displayed something of a scholarly affection for it. Indeed we might add to the trio interpersonal sympathy, taking this last term from Hume himself. The language of attraction that had served the natural philosophers witnessing the effects of materials upon one another could be equally deployed to indicate the morality of interpersonal sentiment in the formation of human nature. When Hume titles a chapter 'Of the Love of Relations', he draws together all the benign principles of association by which people understand familiarity, resemblance or likeness, and the 'sympathy, which always arises betwixt similar characters [qualities]', so that the very conception of such a nexus is *itself* 'peculiarly agreeable, and makes us have an affectionate regard for every thing that produces it, when the proper object of kindness and good-will' ([1739–40] 2000: 2.2.4, p. 229). This is where he is talking about relations of blood, adding that it is not consanguinity alone that has this effect, 'but any other relation without exception. We love our countrymen, our neighbours, those of the same trade [...] [and] [e]very one of these relations is esteem'd some tie, and gives a title to a share of our affection' (2.2.4, p. 228). By relation he has already indicated he means whoever is united to a person by a connection, the recognition of the connection leading to claim or entitlement.

In the same chapter, we also read what could almost be Fortes on the need for concretization, except that when Hume refers to 'custom' he refers to something closer to habituation than convention. Hume is discussing the 'double sympathy', entailing both impression and idea, of the special relationship we have with relatives and acquaintances that comes from durability over time.

> Custom also, or acquaintance [...] strengthens the conception of any object [...] And as reasoning and education concur only in producing a lively and strong idea of any object; so is this [durability] the only particular, which is common to relation and acquaintance. This must, therefore, be the influencing quality, by which they produce all their common effects; and love and kindness being one of these effects, it must be from the force and liveliness of conception [idea formation], that the passion is deriv'd. ([1739–40] 2000: 2.2.4; p. 229)

It is in turn an example of a general proposition, namely 'whatever is related to us is conceiv'd in a lively manner by the easy transition from ourselves to the related object' ([1739–40] 2000: 2.2.4, pp. 228–9).

This is breathtaking – is it not? And I don't think it only has to be anthropologists, with their global knowledge of kinship systems of all kinds, who might admit to that effect. Let us catch our breath in two stages.

First, consider Hume's delineation of non-specific sentiments, of the kind that had by the 1740s been cultivated for some time in public life, to be found expressed in associations and 'societies' of all kinds, consociations formed on the basis of common interests, such as social class, or found in shared pursuits. Hume himself observed that 'people associate together according to their particular tempers and dispositions [...] [and may] remark this resemblance between themselves and others' ([1739–40] 2000: 2.2.4, p. 229). He then draws us back into an epistemological observation: for where, he says, 'they remark the resemblance, it operates after the manner of a relation, by producing a connexion of ideas' (2.2.4, p. 229). In other words, both the ideational formation and the sentiment one has for others are matters of human nature. Reiterated here are all the ingredients of that generalized notion of the person whose alliances and affinities are determined by degrees of similarity to and dissimilarity from others. For all that Hume's subject matter is benign sentiment, this is also the kind of lethal premise that underlines the worst European excesses of what is colloquially called us/them thinking.

Second, consider the very evocation of kinship that had initially provided Hume with a concrete exemplification of relations. Compelling one would think for its specificity, it becomes swept up in this non-specific field of generalized human sentiment, with its differentiations attuned to relative closeness and distance. When his discourse on persons' interactions with one another included talking about kin, it was rarely to introduce an ethics of kinship that retained any kind of distinctiveness, let alone to attend to particular modes of linking or reckoning of connections.[8] We know such distinctiveness from other writings, through genres such as the novel or theatre, or in works on household economics and property relations, but here it was seemingly offstage. Hume refers to ties between father and son because they afford a good illustration of proximate relations. The particular and potentially thick example is applied with the thinness of a generality, at least insofar as all that is implied is that intimacy and fond feelings can be experienced to a greater or lesser degree.

Without making too much of it, we may note that Hume rarely draws on the generic terms 'kin' or 'kindred'. (In my discussion, the usage of 'kin', along with 'kinship' [a much later invention], remains mine.) Yet, he would have found in kin and kindred a description of the kind of human nature he was delineating. Since Anglo-Saxon usage these terms had long been generics not only for family and blood relations but for a 'natural' group of which a being is a member (a 'kind'), or for a class of persons, and thus for persons allied through nature or character. In the sixteenth and seventeenth centuries kindred became a general term for an affinity with respect to resemblance or agreement, as when entities sharing some feature or characteristic may be described as akin to one another. Such a generic idea would seem to have answered so many of his purposes. Maybe Hume simply was not thinking of kinship as a domain of relations to be specifically demarcated. Maybe he wanted to avoid specifying the feelings that kinsmen/women or kinsfolk have towards one another, or at least in any way that presupposed kin were different from close acquaintances. In short, in theorizing on human nature, maybe he did not want to emphasize that there was anything qualitatively distinct about kin in terms of interpersonal connection. For where kin ties *were* thought to be qualitatively unique, they posed a problem in certain kinds of loyalties and bonds his contemporaries were still concerned to shake off.

To those who took the European Enlightenment as continuing the apparently liberating process of freeing public life from patronage and patriarchy, and freeing persons from the bondage of kin ties,[9] making an address to a publicly lived life beyond the sphere of family matters must have seemed unremarkable. And Hume was writing a philosophical treatise, not a novel or personal diary. Concomitantly, the inclusion of references to relatives in the passages I have cited would have been equally unremarkable. English-speaking kinship conventions at the time entertained a certain understanding of interpersonal ties which, on the one hand, valued a generalized or public sympathy for others and, on the other hand, classed diverse relatives (kinsfolk) through their connections – their relations – in terms of consociation, social recognition and permitted or desired familiarity. At certain moments Hume refers to specific kinspersons. Through, for instance, comparing what happens to a relation between child and parent according to whether it is the father or the mother who marries for a second time, he illustrates how the reciprocal flow of relations between objects may or may not be affected by their independent relations with third parties (Hume [1739–40] 2000: 2.2.5, pp. 230–1). But he seemingly has no use for notions of kin or kindred as separate objects of attention. Albeit sometimes qualified by 'blood' (he also talks of 'ties of blood'), he depends upon that then much more up to date and diffuse generic, 'relations'.

What never happened

That Hume was building on the work of Locke is generally acknowledged. Locke's illustration of a point about relations with reference to kinship ties (my phrase) has already been mentioned. For present purposes let me treat him as a predecessor. For it is at his door that I wish to lay what never happened. If Locke was writing at a time when the concept of relation became generally used as a term for kinsfolk, this was an old term with fresh usages. Terms were also coined, and one that ushered in a new concept was that of 'identity'.

Personal identity or the self, Locke declared in 1690, 'is not determined by identity or diversity of substance, which it cannot be sure of, but only by identity of consciousness' or understanding ([1690] 1975: 2.27.23, p. 345).[10] Hardly surprising, others found the same instability in consciousness that Locke did in substance or 'flesh', arguing, for example, that perception was discontinuous and divisible (Porter 2000: 167). While not mincing words over various bizarre aspects of Locke's arguments, one twentieth-century political scientist reflects on Locke's stance at large 'as a new, unprecedentedly radical form of self-objectification [...] [enabling us] to see ourselves as objects of far-reaching reformation [...] To take this stance is to identify oneself with the power to objectify and remake, and by this act to distance oneself from all the particular features which are objects of potential change [...] This power reposes in consciousness' (Taylor 1989: 171–2).

As with Hume, in the 'person' Locke is dealing with a 'thinking, intelligent being' ([1690] 1975: 2.27.9, p. 335). This entity could not be constituted more differently from an individual organism or 'man', what later parlance would call the human being.[11] When he addresses the permanent sameness of the latter, he concludes that the identity of the individual human organism is no different from that of plants or animals.

> For in them the variation of great parcels of matter alters not the identity; an oak, growing from a plant to a great tree, and then lopp'd, is still the same oak [...] [For a] plant which has [...] an organization of parts in one coherent body, partaking of one common life [...] continues to be the same plant as long as it partakes of the same life. ([1690] 1975: 2.27.3-4, p. 330–1)

As far as fixing their identity applies (the objectification to which Taylor refers), a single question is being addressed to plants, animals and 'man' on the one hand and on the other to the 'person'. However, although we 'know that, in the ordinary way of speaking, the same person and the same man stand for one and the same thing' ([1690] 1975: 2.27.15, p. 340), his (philosophical) enquiry into the matter has revealed a radical divergence between the way the identity of persons and the identity of human beings is formed.

Here is the jolt! We are drawn into the discussion about personal identity and living organisms without noticing that there is not a single reference to kinship. Well, why should there be, you may ask. Only because it is present elsewhere. The absence draws attention to where that elsewhere is.[12] Locke drew in kinship freely enough in order to provide concrete examples of an otherwise abstract conception, but it was not of persons and mankind. Rather, it was to provide examples of *relations* and their relativity. Could Locke have taken his argument in a different direction if he had thought about persons and selves as kinspersons, or about the procreation and nurture of human beings? These attributes of kinship could have been the link that brought relations to mind. As it is, and deliberate or not, questions about the identity of persons or man never get to be questions about relations. That is what didn't happen.

So what *is* happening? Locke's text introduced kinship to represent an arena of self-referential relations (though kin relations are by no means his only example). He does not mention kinship in the context of his discussion of identity; neither 'man' nor 'person' is conceived as held in place by their relations with others; instead the former has natural characteristics such as 'life', 'an organization of parts', the latter quasi-theological or moral ones such as 'consciousness'. Otherwise put, relations are concretized through kinship (relatives); men/persons are concretized respectively through life and through consciousness. Each constellation of ideas appears extraneous to the other in this formulation. In the latter, the reader is invited to imagine a being whose relations – including those of kinship – lie outside.[13]

Yet the jolt itself must come from a present-day understanding of 'kinship' in the way specific ties of blood or marriage have been used as illustrations. Standing back, one might instead wish to take the very implication of rendering relations external both to the individual organic being and to the conscious person or self *as* an emergent modelling of kinship. It is intriguing that the notion of an entity with (external) relations attached echoes the way people of the time were apparently coming to think about kin ties. What was to take off in the eighteenth century, and across Europe at large, although admittedly in fits and starts (Sabean and Teuscher 2007: 16), were new kinds of relations. In the words of two historians of Europe, Sabean and Teuscher, 'the structures stressing descent, inheritance, and succession, patrilines, agnatic lineages, and clans, paternal authority, house discipline, and exogamy gradually gave way to patterns centered around alliance, sentiment, interlocking networks of kindred, and social and familial endogamy' (2007: 16). In my mind this is concretized in the image of a being with (external) relations attached, a family (now meaning a conjugal family) looking outwards to its (cultivated, class-laden) 'connections'.

The writings of Locke and Hume were but moments in a cascade and have no particular priority.[14] But they do show us something that did not occur, a link never made and, whether unremarked or deliberately avoided, a dissociation of ideas about human beings and personal identity from ideas about relations. One might comment that treatises on knowledge and human nature were not the place to find anything different. Or, to the contrary, that they were surely the very place! In any event, in these arguments the person's identity or selfhood does not depend on relations but is concretely apprehended in its consciousness; even if not materially concrete in the way man (the human being) is, the effects of consciousness can be particularized. Conversely, it is relations that can come to appear abstract, insofar as they have to be the subject of intellectual work to be visible at all; Locke's concrete references to kinship are seemingly introduced to colour an abstract notion. In such a line of thought, relations become an observer's inferences. What was it Firth said? The more one thinks of a society in abstract terms as a set of relations, the more it is necessary to think of social organization in terms of concrete activity: he glosses 'the idea of organization' as that of people getting things done by conscious (his word is 'planned') action (Firth [1951] 1961: 35–6).

And what was it that Fortes said? That relations have to be bodied forth. How interesting that when Hume concretizes relations it is with generic qualities of association, including the familiarity of resemblance that itself 'operates after the manner of a relation, by producing a connexion of ideas' ([1739–40] 2000: 2.2.4, p. 229).

Conclusion

We might ponder on the diverse ways in which relations are invoked for purposes of exposition, the concept of them abstracted as an object of knowledge and then concretized again. Hume dwells especially on relations of interest in philosophizing, which arise though intellectual work being done on them, as in the comparison of ideas. If that focus was already presupposed in arguments of the day – and I brought in Locke as a notional predecessor – it also looks forward to a contemporary understanding that has been the very devil in English-language attempts to get to grips with some of the materials anthropologists deal with.[15] The absence of any address to interpersonal relations, let alone kinship relations, in discussions of the self and personal identity makes *in*visible, for example, the process of intersubjective self-creation of the kind that Christina Toren (e.g. 2009) has consistently had to bring to our attention.

If in the eighteenth-century milieu to which the Scottish Enlightenment addressed itself one could talk about kinship in a way, and of course not the only way, indistinguishable from general observations of human nature and the conduct of interpersonal relations, perhaps it was precisely because the person could be imagined as separate from its relations to others. A person whose identity is secured through consciousness has relations aplenty, but they seem in the first instance extrinsic. Those external relations become a source of intense ethical reflection, as Hume's writings make abundantly clear, and from this emerges a particular kind of moral person. It is one who reaches outwards towards others, whoever they are, undifferentiated among themselves apart from the discrimination implied in recognizing others like oneself. We may recall the concomitant premise that degrees of similarity and difference indicate closeness and distance, that likeness or similarity is the basis of solidarity and common feeling while difference leads to strangeness and estrangement. Now I am not making particular Enlightenment thinkers responsible for these views – and this is not the place to enlarge on changing conventions of sociability in general – but they did provide a framework of thought for perpetrating them.

As to the painter-naturalist, Merian was at the beginning of this account in part for the ethnographic eye an anthropologist might appreciate about her endeavours. Yet not just for that. And not just as an allusion to the observation sometimes made that the sources of Scottish Enlightenment were as much Dutch as English. Nor, for that matter, simply as an example of the late seventeenth-century era of collecting and recording specimens of natural history that was the harbinger for interest in human curiosities: the most notable English collector of the time placed Merian's two volumes on the insects of Suriname at the top of the stairs in Montagu House, the predecessor of the British Museum, for visitors to look through (Sloan 2003: 19). Initially she was there for the abstractions, for her pictorial description of stages in the lives of caterpillars and moths that we might conceptualize as processual and relational.

Merian was illustrating a series of moments linked by a causal chain, as the philosophers tried so hard to make causal chains out of ideas. At the same time those processes and relations were made concrete in her depictions, and I am not referring to drawing or colouring. Rather, just as *relazione* reported specific occurrences, so observations were verified insofar as they were encoded in recorded events, summoning memorable geographic locales or times of the year. Event is the word: as Davis remarked, Merian's subject was a set of events. Conversely, as well as the transformations/metamorphoses that put temporally distinct moments together, her visual recording of a caterpillar feeding, a plant in flower, made an event of each observational moment. I labour the point insofar as one historian (Dear 2001: 139; cf Shapin: 1994: 197) of the scientific revolution emphasizes the event in the new genre of reporting adopted by the Royal Society, whose purpose was to narrate an occurrence located in place and time. However, this is not quite the end of the story. Merian was also present, for me, with regard to something else.

I hope to have conveyed the jolt I experienced in realizing that philosophical conventions of the day could engage in discussions about personal identity and human beings without any reference to kinship. What was (and seemingly instead) present was a discourse of sociability and the elevation of common/shared feeling that went with it. The old pre-Enlightenment logic of resemblance may have been superseded in classificatory schema by a new emphasis on the systematic comparison of similarity and difference, yet it seems that in some quarters at least 'resemblance' continued to flourish, or flourished all over again, as an ethical value in human affairs. It is there in the brief excerpts from Hume's works, where conventions of sociability became seen as a basis for (to use an anachronism) sociality as such. The assumption that sociality can be described in terms of similarity – along with its negation, dissimilarity – is an Enlightenment legacy I do not find necessarily benign. Indeed, the very possibility of formulating similarity and difference as 'likeness and unlikeness' perpetuates similarity as a key modality of relating.[16] Consider Merian, then, and what she was putting together on one page.

Her illustration of the life cycle of a (Surinamese) frog[17] brings several events together. It depicts a frog releasing eggs, tadpoles at diverse stages, the plants on which they lie or under which they shelter, the watery environment. The life cycle – of a frog – how banal! Or, how very *not* banal. The plants that attract insects, the frog's dinner painted, thus, in one corner: this is a depiction of species interdependence. However, what is striking, in a thoroughly conventional way, is that if you look at each of the animals you see quite distinct forms (and elsewhere she draws the different-looking stages of plants as well). The distinct forms are of course related by the unfolding of life, what Firth called a worldwide system of interlocking concrescent processes, possibly an intimation of development, progress and the discrimination into lower and higher forms of life that other schemas of classification were to bring. But I draw out an altogether more simple point. What Merian has done, concretely in her illustrations, is to show that resemblance and similarity are not the only possible markers of intimate relationships. Quite radically different beings may metamorphose into one another.

Locke had mentioned something like this in talking of the oak tree, his attention being in the identity of an organism over its lifespan regardless of the material form in which it exists. However, it is precisely those material forms themselves that Merian's pictures thrust before the viewer. In the case of frogs and butterflies it may be hard to see beyond a present-day familiarity with the idea, and Merian's juxtapositions of distinct forms do not amount to the kinds of relations of alterity anthropologists are accustomed to pondering upon in some kinship/knowledge systems. Nonetheless, to a latter-day eye, her illustrations draw attention to unlikely manifestations of life, where a premise about degrees of similarity would be supremely inadequate for understanding relations. You could not infer the relations between these forms on the grounds of the likeness and unlikeness of their attributes. She offers an alternative source of illumination, a side-long glance, a present-day comment on the persistence of this particular premise amidst all that we might otherwise value from the Enlightenment impulse.

Acknowledgements

Natalie Zemon Davis has been a powerful presence behind this account and a generous feeder of it. This was for me the happy outcome of a meeting at the University of St Andrews. I owe thanks to the St Andrews student body as well for the RAI undergraduate conference, 'Close Encounters' (April 2013), at which some of these ideas were first tried out, as they were at a panel on 'Multiple nature-cultures and diverse anthropologies', convened by Atsuro Morita and Casper Bruun Jensen, at the JASCA/IUAES conference in Tokyo (May 2014).

Notes

1   Given as the Firth lecture at the ASA Decennial meeting, *Anthropology and Enlightenment,* Edinburgh, 2014.

2   Reproductive process was a common image at the time for representing relations or connections; here, what was based on an observation in a few cases became a source for inference in the many.

3   In drawing on Smith's *Essays on Philosophical Subjects*, Porter notes how reminiscent of Hume the formulation is. In 'An Inquiry Concerning Human Understanding', Hume's section on the association of ideas begins: 'It is evident that there is a principle of connection between the different thoughts and ideas of the mind', and he goes on to introduce 'principles of connection among ideas' (1748 n.d.: 320–1).

4   From Davis's Foreword to a special issue on the subject (see Cohen and Warkentin 2011); I am grateful to her for the reference. One connotation of the Latin *relatio* was a deposition before a judge.

5   References to Hume [1739–40] 2000 are in the format 1.1.7, p. 17 = book 1, chapter 1, section 7, page 17.

6   Here it is particularly in the crucial role played by rules ('customs'), which introduces his own perspective on abstraction. 'The one element that is constant and critical through all these vicissitudes of generic, specific, and optional activities is the relationship as such. It is always [...] identifiable by terminology and by norms, rules and customs', to which he appends a footnote: 'That is why [...] kinship relations, like all social relations, can be referred to and discussed in abstraction from any actual situations in which they emerge' (1969: 62).

7   Hume writes generally: 'The farthest we can go towards a conception of external objects, when suppos'd specifically different from our perceptions, is to form a relative idea of them, without pretending to comprehend the related objects [themselves]. Generally speaking, we do not suppose them specifically different; but only attribute to them different relations, connexions and durations' ([1739–40] 2000: 1.2.6, p. 49, original emphasis omitted). One can conceive of relations affecting things without otherwise knowing the identity of what is related.

8   He, who elsewhere says so clearly that distance is also a relation, has in these passages nothing to say about the categorical valorization of difference. 'Difference' appears as the simple converse of an interest in degrees of similarity or likeness (dissimilarity or unlikeness implied).

9   Primarily male persons; female persons were instead being conjugalized into 'family' life. In the background were changing conventions of kin relations that had once been the source of 'public' alliances, networks and political action, not to speak of women's freedoms. An allusion to this is given towards the end.

10   Subsequently reference to Locke are shortened to the format 2.27.23, p. 345 = book 2, chapter 27, section 23, page 345.

11   Substance as a mass of matter has its own type of identity; here he is talking of the identity of an individual organism that has a typical and distinct form, what he calls 'individual identity' or what we may gloss in the case of man as referring to the 'human individual' (Balibar [1998] 2013: 57). Attending to its textual location and context in arguments of the time, Balibar credits Locke with inventing the concept of consciousness.

12   In the passages with which I have been concerned; in some of his political writings Locke deliberately and polemically separates kinship from politics (see Zengotita 1984), but such a banishment is not at issue here.

13   This is not to overlook the fact that Locke's concept of identity can be construed as 'a relation' (Fausto 2012: 36, after Balibar [1998] 2013). My thanks to Carlos Fausto for drawing Balibar to my attention.

14   Although one should not under-emphasize the popular power of both philosophers, whose works went into numerous editions, especially those for general readers. These two contributed to an agenda concerning the appropriate subjects matters of (philosophical) reflection.

15   For a twenty-first-century example, see Jacob's (2012: 160) observation on the legal and bioethical literature on transplant patients, which attends to *either* the functioning bodily as a 'biomedical whole-parts aggregate' *or* to 'the thinking, reflexive person'. The person that is neglected in her view is the one (relationally) shaped by bureaucratic legitimation, kinship and the market.

16   This was penned before I encountered Raffle's (2010: 165) description of Merian's own afterlife in the ponderings of the nineteenth-century French historian and naturalist Michelet. Refusing the idea that the butterfly is the fulfilment of the caterpillar, Michelet was struck instead by the impermanence of form. I am grateful to Hugh Raffles for this illumination.

17   Merian's paintings are widely reproduced. The one I have in mind, a watercolour made in Suriname 1699–1701, is illustrated in Huxley (2003: 81, plate 68).

References

Balibar, E. [1998] 2013. *Identity and Difference. John Locke and the Invention of Consciousness*, S. Sandford (ed.), W. Montag (trans.). London: Verso.

Carsten, J. 2004. *After Kinship*. Cambridge: Cambridge University Press.

Cohen, T. and Warkentin, G. 2011. 'Things Not Easily Believed: Introducing the Early Modern Relation'. *Renaissance and Reformation/Renaissance et Réforme* 34(1-2): 7–23.

Corsín Jiménez, A. 2013. *An Anthropological Trompe l'Oeil for a Common World: An Essay on the Economy of Knowledge*. Oxford: Berghahn.

Dear, P. 2001. *Revolutionizing the Sciences: European Knowledge and Its Ambitions, 1500-1700*. Houndmills: Palgrave.

Davis, N. Z. 1995. *Women on the Margins: Three Seventeenth-century Lives*. Cambridge, MA: Harvard University Press.

Demeter, T. 2012. 'Liberty, Necessity and the Foundation of Hume's "Science of Man"'. *History of the Human Sciences* 25(1): 15–31.

Fausto, C. 2012. 'Too Many Owners: Mastery and Ownership in Amazonia'. In *Animism in Rainforest and Tundra: Personhood, Animals, Plants and Things in Contemporary Amazonia and Siberia*, M. Brightman, V. Grotti and O. Ulturgasheva (eds). Oxford: Berghahn Books, pp. 29–47.

Firth, R. [1951] 1961. *Elements of Social Organization*. London: Watts & Co.

Fortes, M. 1969. *Kinship and the Social Order: The Legacy of Lewis Henry Morgan*. Chicago: Aldine Publishing Co.

Gow, P. 2009. 'Answering Daimã's Question: The Ontogeny of an Anthropological Epistemology in Eighteenth-Century Scotland'. *Social Analysis* 53(2): 19–39.

Hume, D. [1739-40] 2000. *A Treatise of Human Nature*, D. F. Norton and M. J. Norton (eds). Oxford: Oxford University Press.

Hume, D. [1748] n.d. 'An Inquiry Concerning Human Understanding'. In *Essays, Literary, Moral, and Political*. London: Ward, Lock, & Co.

Huxley, R. 2003. 'Natural History Collectors and Their Collections: "Simpling Macaronis" and Instruments of Empire'. In *Enlightenment: Discovering the World in the Eighteenth Century*, K. Sloan, with A. Burnett (eds). London: British Museum Press, pp. 80–91.

Ingold, T. 2013. 'Dreaming of Dragons: On the Imagination of Real Life'. *Journal of the Royal Anthropological Institute*, new ser., 19(4): 734–52.

Jacob, M.-A. 2012. *Matching Organs with Donors: Legality and Kinship in Transplants.* Philadelphia: University of Pennsylvania Press.

Locke, John. [1690] 1975. An Essay Concerning Human Understanding, P. Nidditch (ed). Oxford: Clarendon Press.

Porter, R. 2000. *Enlightenment: Britain and the Creation of the Modern World.* London: Allen Lane.

Pratt, M. L. 1992. *Imperial Eyes: Travel Writing and Transculturation.* London: Routledge.

Raffles, H. 2010. *Insectopedia.* New York: Pantheon Books.

Rapport, N. 1997. *Transcendent Individual: Towards a Literary and Liberal Anthropology.* London: Routledge.

Sabean, D. and Teuscher, S. 2007. 'Kinship in Europe: A New Approach to Long-Term Development'. In *Kinship in Europe: Approaches to Long-Term Development (1300–1900)*, D. Sabean, S. Teuscher and J. Mathieu (eds). Oxford: Berghahn Books.

Shapin, S. 1994. *A Social History of Truth: Civility and Science in Seventeenth-century England.* Chicago: Chicago University Press.

Sloan, K. 2003. '"Aimed at Universality and Belonging to the Nation": The Enlightenment and the British Museum'. In *Enlightenment: Discovering the World in the Eighteenth Century*, K. Sloan, with A. Burnett (eds). London: British Museum Press, pp. 12–25.

Strathern, M. 2014. 'Reading Relations Backwards'. *Journal of the Royal Anthropological Institute* 20(1) 3–19.

Tadmor, N. 2001. *Family and Friends in Eighteenth-century England: Household, Kinship, and Patronage.* Cambridge: Cambridge University Press.

Taylor, C. 1989. *Sources of the Self: The Making of Modern Identity.* Cambridge, MA: Harvard University Press.

Toren, C. 2009. 'Intersubjectivity as Epistemology'. *Social Analysis* 53(2): 130–46.

Zengotita, T. de. 1984. 'The Functional Reduction of Kinship in the Social Thought of John Locke'. In *Functionalism Historicized: Essays on British Social Anthropology*, G. W. Stocking (ed.). Madison: University of Wisconsin Press, pp. 10–30.

Index